Finally a book that offers a multi-pronged approach to EFL, through a detailed critical discourse analysis of language in education policies, textbooks and interviews with language learners. A must read for everyone interested in the global/local dynamics of English, particularly with a view to imagining a future of hope in a context of conflict.

Tommaso M. Milani, Professor of Multilingualism, University of Gothenburg

Teaching and learning English as a Foreign Language (EFL) may be compromised by becoming a cultural discourse reproducing difference and inequality. Though this claim seems controversial, the author presents a comprehensive and critical summary of her experience with EFL in Israel, and proposes an alternative reconstruction, moving EFL towards a critical pedagogy, a transformative cultural discourse of harmony, social justice and peace. Making EFL a central component in the struggle for global citizenship education in the global system, the rigorous critique and reconstruction, makes this book by Muzna Awayed-Bishara a must read in studies of cultural discourses and teaching English as a foreign language.

Carlos Alberto Torres, Distinguished Professor of Education, UNESCO UCLA Chair on Global Learning and Global Citizenship Education

EFL PEDAGOGY AS CULTURAL DISCOURSE

This book offers unique insight into the role that English as a Foreign Language (EFL) discourse plays in shaping the ideological terrain of contemporary Israel/Palestine through constructing the subjectivities of those who plan, teach, and learn it.

While the EFL curriculum is uniform across both Hebrew- and Arabic-speaking educational contexts, this book traces how its cultural content reproduces dominant hegemonic ideologies, and perpetuates the social misrepresentations of the Other that underlie inequality. The language of English teaching textbooks, the way that students understand their content, and the official policy documents that guide both EFL materials and teaching practices, are all thoroughly examined from the perspective of Critical Discourse Analysis. The theoretical and methodological foundation for further cross-cultural studies of Anglo-centric and other forms of hegemonic EFL discourses within local/global contexts, and for contesting their ideological effects, is also laid down.

Through promoting a transformative EFL cultural discourse which hopes to position EFL teaching as a possible arena for effecting social change, *EFL Pedagogy as Cultural Discourse* offers a unique context for students, scholars, and educators interested in linguistics, CDA, cultural discourse studies, English in local/global contexts, and EFL education.

Muzna Awayed-Bishara received her doctorate from the Department of English Language and Literature at the University of Haifa. She is currently a postdoctoral Fellow in the Center for the Study of Multiculturalism and Diversity at the Hebrew University of Jerusalem, and a tenured lecturer in the English Department at the Academic Arab College for Education in Haifa. Dr Awayed-Bishara is also currently a visiting scholar at the Paulo Freire Institute at the University of California in Los Angeles.

EFL PEDAGOGY AS CULTURAL DISCOURSE

Textbooks, Practice, and Policy for Arabs and Jews in Israel

Muzna Awayed-Bishara

First published 2020
by Routledge
2 Park Square, Milton Park, Abingdon, Oxon OX14 4RN

and by Routledge
52 Vanderbilt Avenue, New York, NY 10017

Routledge is an imprint of the Taylor & Francis Group, an informa business

© 2020 Muzna Awayed-Bishara

The right of Muzna Awayed-Bishara to be identified as author of this work has been asserted by her in accordance with sections 77 and 78 of the Copyright, Designs and Patents Act 1988.

All rights reserved. No part of this book may be reprinted or reproduced or utilised in any form or by any electronic, mechanical, or other means, now known or hereafter invented, including photocopying and recording, or in any information storage or retrieval system, without permission in writing from the publishers.

Trademark notice: Product or corporate names may be trademarks or registered trademarks, and are used only for identification and explanation without intent to infringe.

British Library Cataloguing in Publication Data
A catalogue record for this book is available from the British Library

Library of Congress Cataloging-in-Publication Data
Names: Awayed-Bishara, Muzna, author.
Title: EFL pedagogy as cultural discourse : textbooks, practice, and policy for Arabs and Jews in Israel / Muzna Awayed-Bishara.
Description: Abingdon, Oxon ; New York, NY : Routledge, 2020. | Includes bibliographical references and index.
Identifiers: LCCN 2019037599 (print) | LCCN 2019037600 (ebook) | ISBN 9781138308800 (hardback) | ISBN 9781138308817 (paperback) | ISBN 9781315143149 (ebook)
Subjects: LCSH: English language–Study and teaching–Israel. | English language–Study and teaching–Israel–Textbooks. | Palestinian Arabs–Education–Israel. | Language and culture–Israel.
Classification: LCC PE1068.I8 A93 2020 (print) | LCC PE1068.I8 (ebook) | DDC 306.442095694–dc23
LC record available at https://lccn.loc.gov/2019037599
LC ebook record available at https://lccn.loc.gov/2019037600

ISBN: 978-1-138-30880-0 (hbk)
ISBN: 978-1-138-30881-7 (pbk)
ISBN: 978-1-315-14314-9 (ebk)

Typeset in Bembo
by Taylor & Francis Books

Printed in the United Kingdom
by Henry Ling Limited

To my children, Majd and Munia: I hope this book might help make your future more promising. To my husband, Shadi: I hope this book translates what I learned from our partnership.

CONTENTS

List of tables   *x*
Preface   *xi*
Acknowledgments   *xiii*

1   Introduction: Why English?   1

2   EFL Discourse: Beyond Language Education   26

3   EFL Textbooks as Ideological Vehicles   57

4   Storied Selves: Analysis of EFL Learners' Cultural Representations   84

5   EFL Policy Discourse: Global and Local Perspectives   110

6   EFL as a Cultural Discourse: Toward a Transformative EFL Pedagogy   132

7   Conclusion: EFL as a Cultural Discourse of Action   155

Index   *174*

TABLES

3.1	Textbook sampling	65
4.1	Distribution of interviewees based on age, gender, ethnic, and religious affiliation	89
4.2	Examples of national identity discourse construction among speakers of Arabic	94
4.3	Examples of responses showing superiority/resentment	99
4.4	Examples of responses critiquing writing practices in EFL textbooks by speakers of Arabic	103
4.5	Examples of responses critiquing writing practices in EFL textbooks by speakers of Hebrew	105

PREFACE

Because my approach to English as a Foreign Language (EFL) pedagogy as a cultural discourse is deeply informed by my own social location, it is appropriate to begin this book with a brief autobiographical comment. I was born in Nazareth to a middle-class Palestinian family. Both my parents were born prior to the establishment of Israel in 1948, my father in Nazareth, and my mother in Haifa. In our Arabic-speaking home, I grew up hearing stories of the 1948 events which had brought upon us what we call the Palestinian catastrophe, or *al-Nakba*. Despite the hardships, I don't recall a moment where my parents expressed any feeling of hatred toward anyone. In due course, the Israeli government granted Palestinians Israeli citizenship, transforming them into citizens, but citizens who were also the "Other." For my law-abiding parents, this fact meant that they needed to find a way to put – or at least to pretend to put – the agonies of the past behind them, and to look ahead to the future. Conflicted as they might have been, they knew that they had no choice but to co-exist in their new Jewish-majority-controlled reality. In order not to lose their identity, I suppose, they made sure that all their children learned about their Palestinian roots as Israeli citizens. For my siblings and me, this meant reading Palestinian literature, and hearing the community's stories being told; listening to Palestinian and Eastern Arabic music; eating Palestinian food; keeping abreast of Arabic-speaking media and news; and, mainly, speaking Palestinian Arabic. In addition to these symbolic practices that form most of our everyday cultural life as Palestinians in Israel, something about my home education made me acknowledge the significance of learning about and learning *from* the other people in the world, people who were *different* from me. The only available way to learn about other people and their cultures during my childhood in the 1980s was through reading literature and novels written in languages other than Arabic.

Fascinated with how my American cousins used to read 'fat' novels during their regular summer visits, I decided to follow suit, perhaps out of childish jealousy. It was in the fourth grade that I read my first novel in English: a simplified version of Mark Twain's *The Adventures of Huckleberry Finn*. In many ways, Twain's classic novel shaped my relationship with English. In it, I learned about racial stereotypes, minorities, discrimination, racism, and social injustice. The older I grew, the more I realized how my reality as a member of a minority was not as remote as I thought from the reality of the Other in Twain's book. Reading in English also introduced me to different and remote places, people, music, customs, inventions, art, folklore, and other exciting manifestations of culture. I admit to being whirled away by my imaginings of how different my life would have been had I been a member of this fascinating Western world. I dreamt of traveling to the United States, or England, and visiting the Statue of Liberty, or London's Tower Bridge. I was passionate about Western pop singers and music, and I memorized the words of the number one hits on the British and American charts. By the time I graduated from school, becoming an English major was a straightforward choice for me to make.

My admiration for English, and all that English was related to and represented, was changed after I graduated, when I started to teach English as a Foreign Language to speakers of Arabic. As an English teacher, I was required to use textbooks and literature authorized by Israel's Ministry of Education. It was through these set texts that I discovered a different aspect to English, altogether less admirable and less fascinating. My hardest lesson was that, despite my enthusiastic attitude to English, I simply did not exist in these English textbooks. It was, as Adrienne Rich so perfectly expresses it, "a moment of psychic disequilibrium" – as if I was looking "into a mirror and saw nothing" (Rich, 1986, p. 199). In this book, then, I offer my own critical perspective on the complexity of teaching English to speakers of other less influential or less "admired" languages. So while I remain conscious of the biases I might have as a non-Western scholar academically studying the ideological role of English discourses, I also recognize that it may be an impossible task to completely hold my national and cultural inclinations from surfacing between the lines of this book.

ACKNOWLEDGMENTS

This book has grown out of several years of work, in different contexts, with different people, and I would like to acknowledge them all. First, I initially developed some of the arguments presented here in my doctoral thesis at the University of Haifa, and for that stage I owe my sincere gratitude to my supervisor, Ron Kuzar, who was the first person to kindly, patiently, and professionally guide me into becoming a real academic.

Second, I must acknowledge Tommaso Milani, whom I met while still a doctoral student, at my first international conference at Georgetown University. Meeting Tommaso marked a turning point in my academic and personal life, as he embodies the true meaning of what human and academic collaboration means. I sincerely acknowledge his comments, encouragement, insights, and valuable suggestions that have contributed immensely to enhancing the arguments I make in this book.

The third stage I want to acknowledge is the opportunity to do research that arose when I was granted a postdoctoral fellowship at the Center for the Study of Multiculturalism and Diversity, at the Hebrew University of Jerusalem. For this, I owe a sincere debt of gratitude to Michael Karayanni, the Aacademic Director of the Center, and to Michal Barak, the Executive Director. The completion of this book would not have been possible without the fellowship.

I am also very grateful to the editor of the Cultural Discourse Studies Series, Shi-xu, whose scholarly devotion to advancing discourses of human cultural coexistence, harmony, and prosperity inspired the core arguments of this book. Writing this book from a non-Western, subaltern position is a great privilege, and it was built on Shi-xu's discursive approach to reconstructing cultural discourses in the service of social justice, human collaboration, and harmony.

Writing the last two chapters of this book also marks another important stage of my academic life which I owe to Carlos Alberto Torres, the UNESCO Chair in Global Learning and Global Citizenship Education, and the Director of the Paulo

Freire Institute at UCLA. My acquaintance with Carlos has made me see the importance of thinking beyond the local reality of oppression, and has led me to believe that our ultimate goal as educators is to help our students see that they have an agentive role in forging more just, peaceful, and tolerant societies.

I am very grateful to Zohar Kampf from the Hebrew University of Jerusalem, and to Camilia Suleiman from Michigan State University, for reading chapters in various stages of readiness. Their insights were both helpful and inspiring.

Other than being a devoted, loving, and supportive brother-in-law, I am immensely grateful to attorney Mazen Qupty, for reading some chapters of this book and for offering his professional legal insights. I warmly thank Mazen for standing next to me and supporting me throughout all of my academic endeavors.

I would also like to acknowledge SAGE Publications for allowing me to reprint here parts of an article I published in *Discourse & Society* in 2015, and to Routledge's *Journal of Multicultural Discourses* for allowing me to reuse a short part of an article I published in 2018.

I am also very grateful to my copy-editor, Scott Burnett, who provided some excellent suggestions and helped me complete the tortuous mission of writing about the hegemony of 'native speakerist' English in a non-native voice. I could not have done this without his brilliant and sharp insights.

Who I am today, I owe to my parents, Hanan and Ezzat Awayed, who brought me up to believe that dialogue, tolerance, hard work, and love are our best resources as human beings. And, finally, I want to thank my children, Majd and Munia, for putting up with the long hours of work it took to write this book, and for growing up to be the inspiring, responsible, critical, and intelligent young people they are today. And Shadi Bishara, my husband, for his unconditional support, love, help, partnership, and for always believing in me.

Muzna Awayed-Bishara
May 2019

1
INTRODUCTION
Why English?

The question of who owns English in this era of ever-intensifying globalization draws attention to what exactly this "ownership" entails, and to the cultural dimensions of the increasing numbers of people teaching and learning English as a foreign or international language. As the world opens up its channels of communication in unprecedented ways, people with different linguistic and cultural profiles are inescapably compelled to use English to achieve academic, economic, or personal mobility. Still, there is not yet a full understanding of the forces of globalization and internationalization, or a clear evaluation of English as a world language (Graddol, 2006). In the language teaching profession, the complexity of teaching English to speakers of other languages in a culturally globalized and globalizing world has yet to be clearly resolved. Scholarship in language and culture pedagogies in the last two decades suggests that foreign language education in general, and English as a foreign language in particular, play an important role in globalization and internationalization (Byram, 2008; 2011; Kumaravadivelu, 2008; Risager, 2007). Indeed, the emphasis in the goals of twenty-first-century foreign language education has shifted from simply focusing on "linguistic" competence, to developing a broader "intercultural" competence. Situated mainly in Europe and the United States, such scholarship does not, however, offer answers to the question of how foreign language pedagogies – particularly in English in educational settings outside of Europe or North America – might become transformative. There is a need not only to critically study how foreign language pedagogies might serve transformative goals in non-Western educational settings, but also to study this phenomenon from a non-Western point of view.

In many cases, English language education discourses still play a leading role in the construction of ideologies that perpetuate Anglo-centric hegemonies, as well as reproducing essentialist binaries such as Self/Other, Native/Non-Native, Western/Non-Western, and Dominant/Subordinate. The globalization of English, the increasing number of its non-native speakers, and the role cultural representations play in shaping ideologies of Self and Other among speakers of different languages constitute the basis of my inquiries in this book. Against this backdrop, my central aim is to examine how English as a Foreign Language (EFL) is discursively pedagogized under conditions characterized by unequal power relations. Are EFL pedagogies approached from globally oriented perspectives, or is what is claimed as "global" actually a reproduction of hegemonic West-/Anglo-/American-centrism? Are EFL discourses constituted in a way that enables the growth of globally aware learners capable of critically examining inter-/intra-cultural practices and dilemmas? And, ultimately, is EFL pedagogy a cultural discourse?

In this volume, I explore these questions in the Israeli EFL context through the lens of two central theoretical frameworks that uninterruptedly enable two central tasks: (1) an evaluation of EFL discourse as cultural practice in reproducing hegemonic ideologies of West-/Anglo-centrism; and (2) a reconstruction of EFL discourse with the aim of coining a culturally transformative EFL pedagogy. The relevant frameworks are Critical Discourse Analysis (CDA), which I use as a diagnostic tool for scrutinizing West-centric and hegemonic ideologies in EFL discourse, and Cultural Discourse Studies (CDS), which I implement as the remedial tool for reconstructing the role of EFL discourse as cultural practice in effecting social change at both the local and the global scales. The idea is that "cultural realities should not only be interpreted/ analyzed but also transformed" (Guilherme, 2002, p. 123). Together, they make for a pragmatically motivated, interventionalist project "beyond mere description, explanation, interpretation or 'analysis' of just any text or talk" (Shi-xu, 2005, p. 68).

Investigating the cultural and ideological aspects of EFL discourse in a place as filled with conflict as Israel must, furthermore, be contemplated in light of a number of critical observations. The first of these is that the National English Curriculum in Israel is uniform throughout all levels of schooling for all citizens, including the Jewish population, who constitute the majority, and the Palestinian Arab population, who constitute the largest minority. The learning populations use the same EFL materials and equally comply with the state's general EFL policy. CDA studies of these materials indicate that EFL discourse *interpellates* (Althusser, [1971] 2000) students into subject positions that reproduce and perpetuate Anglo-centric and Jewish/Zionist hegemonic ideas, thereby marginalizing Palestinian Arab cultural and communal practices (Awayed-Bishara, 2015; 2018). Despite the ways in which these materials may serve as a dividing device, I will argue in this volume that reconstructing EFL discourse as cultural practice might be alternatively directed at effecting social change, insofar as the English curriculum is uniform to all EFL learners in Israel.

The second critical observation is that Israel's National English Ccurriculum adopts a global rather than an Anglo-centric approach that takes into account how English is no longer considered the sole asset of English-speaking countries, such as the United States or the United Kingdom. The fact that the numbers of non-native speakers of English are higher than the numbers of its native speakers must, according to the curriculum, form the basis for designing culturally adequate materials and teaching methods that would enable learners to cope with the dramatic transformations English is undergoing as the world's global or international language. To what extent and in what way this approach is translated into actual practice form another focal point for this book.

As I argue at length in Chapter 2, examining the cultural representations, practices, and policies of EFL entails a socially constitutive approach that perceives language as *discourse*. In this sense, discourse constitutes situations, objects of knowledge, and the social identities of, and relationships between, people and groups of people. Pivotal to the aims of this volume, discourse is epistemologically perceived as "constitutive in the sense that it helps to sustain and reproduce the social status quo, and in the sense that it contributes to transforming it" (Fairclough, Mulderrig, & Wodak, 2011, p. 358). Discourse is also seen as constitutive in more culturally oriented approaches in the sense that it cannot be separable from the world, or "reality" (Shi-xu, 2005). On that basis, I will argue that using the tools of CDA requires an additional level of theorization so as to explain the constitutive relationship between the three angles through which EFL discourse is culturally investigated in this volume: textbooks, practice, and policy. CDS tools augment my critical analysis of EFL discourse as they are used to reconstruct the role of "non-native," "non-Anglo," "non-hegemonic," and "non-Western" discourses in developing critical EFL pedagogies.

I will suggest various discursive trajectories for planning EFL teaching that focus on the cultural particularities of non-Western learners – in our case, Palestinian Arabs – who must acquire English in order to make their voices heard in the world. Within this critical discursive framework, narratives that represent Anglo-American and Western cultures as "superior" to others, as being more rationalistic and more modern, and that therefore marginalize the Other, are replaced by narratives that highlight authentic and balanced multicultural and egalitarian representations of the non-Western Other. In contrast to critical approaches to "multiculturalism" that signal its failings as a political project, I will deploy the term "multicultural" throughout this volume to denote presenting the positive values and norms of Eastern cultures as equal and not inferior to those presented in Western discourses, whether educational or otherwise. In line with CDS, I will argue that re-establishing local cultural discourses in EFL textbook writing and policies in Israel might aid Palestinian Arab students in learning English as an international language, helping them "become more successful in their own cultural milieu on the one side and on the other side help the international communities" (Shi-xu, 2005, p. 32) to better understand their non-Western cultural discourse, whose uniqueness is often marginalized in Israeli dominant educational discourses (Awayed-Bishara, 2015). My idea for reconstructing EFL discourse is meant to grant Palestinian Arab learners a place where they can feel they belong. If they do not belong to the national discourse of Israel's education system, then they must somehow belong to the entire world. Despite the inevitable risk of shoring up West-East dichotomies with such an approach, introducing Eastern cultural discourses into EFL pedagogies "will enrich and re-invigorate existing Western traditions" (Shi-xu, 2005, p. 32) and, within the Israeli-Palestinian context, might help bring both sides closer through EFL education. It certainly bears repeating that the globalization of English necessitates a re-examination of how learners from different linguistic and cultural backgrounds should learn English so that they may fairly and on equal terms access local and global opportunities.

Background and Rationale

Palestinian Arabs constitute some 20 percent of Israel's population. They are the largest indigenous minority, but used to constitute the majority in Palestine before 1948 (Al-Haj, 2002, p. 72) after which Israeli citizenship was imposed on them. Many Arab citizens of Israel whose historical majority partly constructs their identities as "Palestinians" see themselves as the legitimate owners of the land, and the pursuers of a historical legacy of the Palestinian struggle against Israel's military, land-confiscating, oppressive, and Zionist neo-colonialist incursions inside and outside of the green line. The fact that Arab citizens also speak Arabic as their native language comprises the other component of "Palestinian Arab" as the term of reference that I use in this volume. By using this term, I do not intend any essentialist or homogenizing association of a certain language with a particular group of people. Rather, I use "Palestinian Arab" so as to underscore the complexity of *both* the national and linguistic aspects of being a *Palestinian* and a *speaker of Arabic* in Israel. These aspects fundamentally form my claims regarding the cultural suitability of EFL discourses to the cultural milieu of the Palestinian Arab learning community. At the national level, Palestinian citizens of the state do not share the Zionist aspirations most Jewish citizens have. In other words, most Palestinian Arabs do not pay tribute to Jewish or Zionist symbols, such as the Israeli flag, the national anthem, the army, or the idea that Israel is a Jewish state built on the land of Zion. At the linguistic level, the fact that Palestinian citizens are native speakers of Arabic also marks their identity as an Other that is linguistically differentiated from the Hebrew-speaking majority. On that basis, I will interchangeably use "Palestinian Arabs" and "speakers of Arabic" throughout this volume. At the external level, the ongoing Israeli-Palestinian conflict has separated the Palestinian Arab minority in Israel from Palestinians in the West Bank and Gaza, as well as from other Arabs – with whom they share a culture and a language. Palestinian Arabs are thus "largely disconnected from the other Arab countries, with minimal acceptance, communication, and freedom of movement" (Abu-Saad, 2006, p. 2). As Israeli citizens, they are discriminated against at the social, educational, economic, and political levels. Dwairy (2004) summarizes how Israel has treated its Palestinian Arab citizens since its inception, as "foster citizens" whose national identity and cultural heritage are rejected by the Jewish majority. In July 2018, Israel passed a Nation State Law that defines Israel as the homeland of the Jewish people alone, reinforcing, thus, the second-class status of its non-Jewish citizens. On the linguistic level, the Nation State Law transformed the status of Arabic as an official language into a language with a *special* status. The implications of this law and the way it shapes the national, educational, and linguistic realities of the Palestinian minority will be further discussed throughout this volume.

The teaching of English as a foreign language to Palestinian Arab learners offers a distinctive educational experience where curricula, textbook design, policy, and schooling practices are intertwined with socio-political and ideological agendas. Since its establishment, Israel has maintained two separate schooling systems at both the public and private levels. One system is for the Jewish majority (subdivided into secular and religious) where Hebrew is the language of instruction. The other system is for the Palestinian Arab minority, and Arabic serves as the main language of instruction (a fact that has not been affected by the Nation State Law). This is also the case in mixed cities (such as Haifa, Jaffa, and Acre) where Jews and Palestinian Arabs live, but have separate schools. Considering Israel's ethnic diversity, the subdivisions in the educational system might falsely appear to accommodate cultural differences and educational pluralism. However, they mainly serve the interests of the dominant ethnic group, while maintaining the marginalization of the indigenous Palestinian Arab community (Abu-Saad, 2004, 2006; Al-Haj, 1995, 2002; Human Rights Watch, 2001; Mar'i, 1978; Peres, Ehrlich, & Yuval-Davis, 1970; Swirski, 1999). Whereas Hebrew is a compulsory subject taught from an early age until graduation in Arabic-medium schools, Arabic in Hebrew-medium schools is compulsory for three years only, and even then this is a directive that many schools are either exempted from, or simply disregard (Or & Shohamy, 2015). Despite the fact that Arabic used to be an official language until July 2018, and is the mother tongue of the largest minority in Israel, less than 4 percent of Jewish youth voluntarily take a matriculation test in Arabic (Lev-Ari, 2003). Disregard for Arabic is often augmented in governmental discourses that tend to foster Jewish learners' negative attitudes and lack of desire to learn Arabic. A former Education Ministry Director-general, Ronit Tirosh, describes the way Jewish students feel toward the Arabic language as antagonistic, and states:

> [Arabic] is a language that is identified with a population that makes your life difficult and endangers your security. Even so, students understand that knowing Arabic helps them to view life in Israel through the eyes of the Arabs ... We thought about making Arabic compulsory for matriculation, but concluded that if less than 10% of students learn it voluntarily, it would be impossible to force it on the rest.
>
> *(cited in Lev-Ari, 2003)*

Considering the small number of people who study Arabic in Israel, we may conclude that Arabic cannot possibly play a bridging role in facilitating the way Jewish learners view "life in Israel through the eyes of the Arabs." Insofar as Israel has two main spoken languages, Hebrew and Arabic, Tirosh's statement – which is an official policy statement – implies that promoting multilingualism among Israeli citizens is not a major political concern.

This may be compared to the case of multilingual Europe, where Byram (2008) analyzes policy documents from the Council of Europe and the European Union to examine the role language education might have in shaping experiences of otherness. The Council of Europe calls for the development of a plurilingual competence, which is "a dynamic and changing repertoire of languages and language varieties one might acquire over a lifetime of interaction in a multilingual area such as Europe" (p. 125). Such attempts are, according to Byram, initiated to sustain interest in the moral development of a social and international identity among Europeans. This is significant in comparison to Israeli multilingualism, specifically at the level of citizenship. In promoting multilingualism, the Council of Europe emphasizes the need to construct a *European* citizenship as opposed to more narrowly nationalistic identity constructions (e.g. French, Italian, etc.). Other than underscoring the need to know languages in order to be able to live in other countries, there is another dimension to the European case for multilingualism, which is "the importance of helping others live in one's own society, the reference to communicating feelings, [and] the inclusion of reference to other communities within one's own country" (p. 128). Considering Tirosh's stated position on the teaching of Arabic as a main language in multilingual Israel, we may fairly conclude that the marginalization of Arabic is state policy directed at the *exclusion* of reference to the Palestinian community within Israel – an exclusion now reinforced through the demise of the official status of Arabic.

While this policy is not without its problems, it is not my purpose here to critique those dimensions of the European experience. I will restrict myself to the insights gained from the official statements regarding the role of foreign language education in multilingual settings. The European experience, according to Byram, shows that

> [L]anguage learning and experience of otherness can have influence on one's sense of identity and on the evolution of identities that do not neatly fit into the traditions of national identity. This is done in the context of an analysis of policy documents that shows there is an aspiration at European level to create a European identity. There is theoretical evidence to suggest that this is possible, but the question is a matter of values and purposes in education. This has implications for teachers who need to decide if and how they want to play a role in this process. Language teaching is no more value-free than any other kind of teaching.
>
> *(p. 143)*

Language teaching in Israel is similarly entangled in ideology. Both schooling systems operate under the supervision of Israel's Ministry of Education, which determines and governs the policy and planning of curricular programs, staffing criteria, and textbook authorization. In such complex educational dynamics, Arab educators and administrators in the state-controlled Arab school system have no power to make decisions, and are forced to impose hegemonic Jewish-Israeli values on their learners by implementing curricular agendas (Adalah, 2003; Shohamy, 2003; Swirski, 1999). Despite the fact that the Arab school system uses its own curriculum, it is completely designed and supervised by the Ministry of Education. This fact, however, stands in sharp contrast to the state's Jewish religious school system, which is physically and administratively separate from the state's secular Jewish school system, and enjoys complete autonomy and control of its curricula (Adalah, 2003; Swirski, 1999). I will discuss this system in more depth with regard to EFL policy and planning in Chapter 5. Other than using different languages of instruction, the school systems use different curricula, particularly in the humanities and social sciences (Abu-Saad, 2006). One exception is the English curriculum, which is uniform across Arabic and Jewish schools. As I have stated, this fact is pivotal to the cultural implications of EFL teaching.

Curricular agendas in Israel reflect the dominant Jewish and Zionist ideologies, which include the construction of a unified national identity and collective memory based on a narrow perspective of the history of the Jews in Israel. In her analysis of the image of Palestine and the Palestinians reflected in contemporary Israeli schoolbooks, Nurit Peled-Elhanan (2012) argues that the use of an implicit "grand Zionist narrative" constitutes a defining feature of textual and paratextual elements in educational discourses. In the same context, while studying how the suppression of the history of indigenous minorities is a central principle in designing history textbooks, Abu-Saad (2006) confirms that this practice "has survived through numerous textbook reforms because its repression is of key importance in teaching history to mainstream students to foster and maintain their support for the ideologies/actions of settler states" (p. 6). Central to the discussion of Israeli educational discourses is, then, the construction of dichotomous Self-Other or We-They frameworks. While the *Self/We* category usually includes "Jews," the *Other/They* category includes "non-Jews," who are the target of continuous marginalization. Thereby, the construction of a Palestinian Arab identity is rarely recognized in the state-controlled educational system, and often is totally ignored (Abu-Saad, 2004; Al-Haj, 1995; Awayed-Bishara, 2015; Peled-Elhanan, 2012). Even though Palestinian Arabs are taught the Jewish narrative, neither Arabs nor Jews study the Palestinian one. Unlike Jewish students who read the literature and poetry of the Zionist movement celebrating the establishment of Israel in 1948, curricular materials in the Arabic-medium schools do not include the Palestinian Arab literary classics taught throughout the Arab world (Adalah, 2003). In contrast, Palestinian Arabs are required to learn about Jewish values and culture (Adalah, 2003; Al-Haj, 2002; Mar'i, 1978; Peres et al., 1970). The result is that Palestinian students spend many more class hours on the study of Hebrew, Jewish history, and Jewish culture than they do on Arabic literature and history (Abu-Saad, 2006). Perhaps the best example to illustrate how such practices are discursively and practically legitimized in Israeli discourse is the recurrence of right-wing attempts by the government to defame Palestine's poet laureate, Mahmoud Darwish, and to ban the teaching of his work in both schooling systems. In this context, former Israel's Defense Minister, Avigdor Liberman, called Darwish's poems "fuel for terror attacks" (Skop, 2016). In another incident, Culture Minister Miri Regev walked out of the Association of Composers, Authors, and Publishers awards' ceremony held in the Habima Theatre in Tel Aviv in June 2017, due to the group's decision to allow an artist to pay tribute to a poem written by Darwish (*Times of Israel* Staff, 2017). So, not only are Palestinian Arabs not taught their own national literature and history, they also often have to cope with serious conflicts within themselves when the history and national values taught at school basically invalidate and contradict their own historical, national, and even *existential* dispositions.

In the majority-controlled schooling system, schoolbooks are perceived as a major channel for transmitting ideas and ideologies in a way that may shape learners' identities and construct a desired collective memory. Nasser and Nasser (2008) identify the significant role schoolbooks play in modern states and explain that "through education, a state's elite can grant or deny certain individuals or groups membership in a nation, and have the power to produce knowledge that reconstructs their past and collective memory" (p. 629). Wertsch (2002) notes that "it is hard to think of a more extended and massive effort to create and control collective memory than that mounted by modern states, especially through their education system" (p. 172). More specifically, Wertsch argues that the main task of schoolbooks is to construct a continuous national narrative or collective memory in order to construe and consolidate the national identity for all citizens, or at least of those who constitute the dominant group. As stated earlier, the choice of curricular materials in both the Jewish and Arab subdivisions in Israel is administered and determined by educators and government officials with mainstream Jewish-Zionist views. This form of majority-controlled educational policy creates inequality and segregation between the two sectors since "[the] ethnocratic public space is formulated around a set of cultural and religious symbols, representations, traditions and practices which tend to reinforce the narratives of the dominant ethno-national group while silencing, degrading or ridiculing contesting cultures or perspectives" (Yiftachel, 2006, p. 37). Yiftachel's observations underscore the call I make in this volume for a transformative EFL cultural pedagogy. As such, a state policy "may influence not only the historical collective memory and identity of each student but, more significantly, may shape inter-group relations as well as the roles Palestinian and Jewish students will occupy as adult citizens" (Nasser & Nasser, 2008, p. 629).

Studying the ideological role Israeli textbooks play in shaping learners' identities and political dispositions has been a concern for many textbook researchers, especially regarding subjects such as history, civil sciences, and geography. For instance, Podeh (2002), who studied Israeli schoolbooks published between 1948 and 2000, claims that they are "agents of memory whose aim is to ensure the transmission of certain 'approved knowledge' to the younger generation" (p. 5). Podeh argues elsewhere that "since the state controls the educational apparatus, it can shape the nation's collective memory by determining what is to be included and what excluded from the curricula and from textbooks" (2000, p. 1). Furthermore, other studies show that Israeli schoolbooks aim at inculcating the collective memory created by Zionism which constitutes "an entirely novel Jewish collective memory" (Zerubavel, 2002) and "national narratives [that] involve a peculiar mix of inspirational heroes and the flat facts the young citizens are supposed to believe in" (Tyack, 2003). Regarding the representation of Palestinian Arabs in Israeli textbooks, Peled-Elhanan (2012, p. 49) concludes:

> None of the textbooks studied … includes, whether verbally or visually, any positive cultural or social aspect of Palestinian life-world: neither literature nor poetry, neither history nor agriculture, neither art nor architecture, neither customs nor traditions are ever mentioned. None of the books contain photographs of Palestinian human beings and all represent them in racist icons or

demeaning classificatory images such as terrorists, refugees and primitive farmers – the three 'problems' they constitute for Israel.

These findings only underscore the role of ideology in pedagogical representation, and show how the "transformation of knowledge into pedagogic communication is made by the pedagogic device, which like the language device, has rules which are not ideologically free" (Bernstein, 1996, pp. 39–41). Such pedagogic communication acts selectively on the meaning potential, namely, on the potential discourse that is available to be pedagogized.

That being said, I argue that a socially situated orientation to pedagogy in which learning is perceived as a value-free or egalitarian process is hard to achieve. Contrary to what the National English Curriculum states in its rationale, EFL education policy in Israel is directed by hegemonic local and national agendas (rather than global or international). As I will show in detail in Chapter 3, Chapter 4 and Chapter 5, school textbooks, curricula, and language policies tend to reflect the dominant ideology of mainstream groups in Israel, whose main objective is to reproduce and perpetuate these ideologies, while presupposing that subjects are passive, lacking agency to contain and maintain linguistic and ideological controversies. Thus, the reproductive orientation of school textbooks and educational discourses seems to allow certain discourses of inequality and discrimination to prevail. Conversely, I argue (mainly in Chapter 6 and Chapter 7) that students should be given textual exposure that might enable them to act as motivated agents who are able to question and subversively resist discourses of inequality. It stands to reason then that there is a need to maintain a critical perspective on ideological orientation of language, and its effect on the individual subject.

Of special interest to this volume is the role that EFL discourse – as a state-controlled apparatus – plays in complicating the way Palestinian Arabs formulate their national and cultural identity as citizens of Israel. To illustrate what prompts this investigation, let me first present a general overview of the status of English in Israel, with particular emphasis on the Arabic-speaking population.

The Status of English in Israel

English does not have an official status in Israel, but, as in many other countries, emphasis is placed on its pragmatic and functional importance as a conduit to global communication and academic, as well as professional, advancement. In Israel, English is frequently employed in business, academic, and communicative settings at the expense of Hebrew (Israel's main official language), not to mention Arabic. Spolsky and Shohamy (1999) assert that despite Israeli academic life being mainly conducted in Hebrew, "English in fact serves as the normal *lingua franca*" (p. 171). Yet the role that English plays in Israel is not uniform, due to the diversity of the groups constituting Israel's population. Among these groups, for many of whom EFL is also important, there are other less privileged groups, such as immigrants whose first language is neither Hebrew nor Arabic. However, I will argue in this volume that the latter are not targeted for social exclusion in the same way that Palestinian Arabs are. Discussing the role of English with regard to these groups is therefore beyond the scope of this volume. I focus on the Palestinian Arab minority, for whom Arabic is the first language, and whose national identity is contested while studying EFL. Whether the findings of this study may be similarly applied to other groups is a question for future research.

For Palestinian Arabs living in Israel, English constitutes a third language after Arabic and Hebrew. In fact, it might be considered a fourth spoken language, taking into account the diglossic context of Arabic (Ferguson, 1959), where native speakers of Arabic use a colloquial variety for everyday speech, but learn to read and write in a linguistically distant variety – Modern Standard Arabic (Saiegh-Haddad & Henkin-Roitfarb, 2014). The linguistic distance between spoken and standard Arabic has been shown to negatively impact the development of basic reading skills in Modern Standard Arabic (Saiegh-Haddad, 2003; 2004; 2007; 2011; Saiegh-Haddad, Levin, Hende, & Ziv, 2011). Having said that, the fact that young Arabic-speaking children are forced to develop reading skills simultaneously in typologically different languages (Semitic and Indo-European) and in three different alphabets (Koda, 2008) clearly also makes the linguistic and academic development of young Arabic speakers a formidable task.

Unlike their Hebrew-speaking compatriots, Palestinian Arabs' first priority (before English) is to master Hebrew (the dominant language of academic instruction), since Hebrew is the lingua franca within Israel (Shohamy, 2014). A study by Shohamy and Donitsa-Schmidt (1997) asked Jewish Israeli adults, Russian Jews, and Arabs to rank the languages (including their own) that they considered most important as a spoken language. Whereas three-quarters of the Israeli Jews placed English as their first priority, both Russian immigrants and Arabs ranked Hebrew as more important for them than English. Although Arabic had a *de jure* official status until July 2018, it has been marginalized in everyday life in the media, academia, public services, linguistic landscape, and political discourse. It is not surprising then, that most Palestinian Arabs tend to undermine the importance of Arabic for upward mobility in Israel's social and professional scales. In their study of the attitudes of Palestinian Arab students at Haifa University toward Arabic, Shohamy and Abu Ghazaleh-Mahajneh (2012) indicate that these students expressed

> feelings of frustration and lack of respect given that their home language had no representation on campus, especially in the linguistic landscape; they therefore felt that they were forced to *surrender* to Hebrew and English ideologies and overlook their own language.
>
> (p. 13; emphasis in the original)

In addition to the complexity of learning Modern Standard Arabic and Hebrew, speakers of Arabic encounter even more difficulties when learning English since

> [they] are expected to reach identical levels of proficiency in English as Jews, and they are in fact being compared on the same English tests at the end of

High School; the scores on these tests are used as the main criteria for acceptance to all Israeli universities.

(Shohamy, 2014, p. 11)

Shohamy further argues that ignoring the less propitious conditions for learning English in the Arab community constitutes a major source of inequality:

> For Arab students, the lack of high proficiency in English poses a major obstacle, and it is detrimental to their participation in higher education. It is no surprise then that the scores of the Arab students on those final tests are substantially lower than those of Jewish students … The overlooking of [their] rich linguistic repertoire can be viewed as an act of marginalization, exclusion, and injustice.

The positive connotations of "multilingualism" seem not to apply to the rich multilingual repertoire of Arab citizens of Israel. Rather than internalizing the disregard Israelis display towards Arabic, Palestinian Arabs tend to associate both Hebrew and English with colonialism, occupation, oppression, and marginalization (Shohamy, 2007). Like Israeli citizenship, the Hebrew language was imposed on them following the establishment of Israel in 1948. By the same token, English has often been viewed "as a 'Jewish' *lingua franca*, especially given the large number of Jewish immigrants in Israel who come from English-speaking countries" (Shohamy, 2014, p. 11). English seems also to be identified with Western and chiefly American hegemonic forces that reinforce the Arabs' "otherness" (Shohamy, 2014). Jewish citizens for whom Hebrew is the first language rarely experience such a linguistic reality, because for *them* mastering English is a top priority. It goes without saying that, for Arabic speakers, mastering Hebrew and English will open more academic and professional doors than any other languages. "Arab" multilingualism therefore results in few positive outcomes in Israel, where language policies (LPs) and language educational policies (LEPs) appear to marginalize the Palestinian Arab minority, their language, and culture. Shohamy concludes that in Israel, "being multilingual for Arabs and immigrants not only does not provide any academic advantage but also penalizes them as they are not knowledgeable in the languages that the society values the most, overlooking their whole linguistic repertoire" (p. 12). In critiquing how language policy-makers often overlook the experience that plurilingual learners might undergo when learning a foreign language, Byram (2008) states that there is a mistaken assumption about the ability of learners to compartmentalize their languages while learning, and of teachers to compartmentalize their teaching. In this regard,

> the ability to learn languages, to become a plurilingual "language person" with a range of competences to different levels in different languages, needs to be

the focus of language teaching just as much as the ability in a particular language being taught at a particular time.

(p. 17)

This raises the question, a central concern of this study, of whether the National English Curriculum in Israel, which is uniform for Hebrew and Arabic speakers, considers the specific conditions under which Arabic speakers learn English, and whether equal opportunities are provided for all learners to achieve the high level of English required by academic institutions, the basic precondition for achieving academic and professional advancement.

The National English Curriculum: An Ideological State Apparatus

The National English Curriculum is one of the official determiners of English language policy and planning in Israel. The curriculum states in its rationale that an overall set of principles is presented as guidelines for EFL teachers, which aims at reaching the utmost level of proficiency in the target language. Nevertheless, the Curriculum Writing Committee emphasizes that English teaching in Israel should be viewed as autonomous and varied, in light of the diversity of Israel's learning population: "We have left to course book writers, schools and teachers as much freedom as possible in choosing the methodology; we confidently leave it to them to add the creative imagination that will bring the teaching of English alive" (Spolsky et al., 2015).

Although this statement of intent seems to promote local autonomy, the English language teaching educational system functions quite differently, as a centralized and top-down hierarchy. The Chief Inspectorate determines teaching or testing policies that are forwarded to the schools' English coordinators in the form of Director-General Circulars (termed in Hebrew: *hozrei mankal*). In accordance with these communiqués, coordinators plan curricular teaching programs that are obligatory for the school's English teaching staff. Although the curriculum explicitly states that teachers are granted the autonomy to choose their materials and teaching style, they are still shackled by instructions handed down to them by the English Inspectorate, and other inconsistent curricular requirements. An example of such inconsistency is evident elsewhere in the curriculum requiring that teaching materials need to include a course book that has been approved by the Ministry of Education (Ministry of Education, 2018). Course-book writers, schools, and teachers are "free" to choose their materials and methodologies as long as they align with what the Ministry of Education approves in its authorized textbooks. It stands to reason then that if teachers find the materials offered in authorized textbooks unsuitable for their students' cultural milieus, for example, they have to either disregard the ministry's curricular instruction, and use more relevant materials, or simply comply with it, in which case, a heavy price must be paid. Teachers employed by the Ministry of Education who disregard curricular policies are liable to face penalties, beginning with notifications explaining the severity of the matter, and concluding with investigations that might result in serious legal outcomes. If they simply comply, they do so while overlooking how issues of cultural suitability, representation, and cultural connectedness in EFL textbooks might negatively shape teaching and learning processes in their classroom. For instance, analysis of student responses to the cultural content of EFL texts indicates that such materials overlook the need to foster students who are able to effectively construct critical stances about other cultures on both local and global scales, as I will show in Chapter 4. Spolsky and Shohamy (1999) support this claim, and state that matriculation tests, for example, have often been used to promote what the English Inspectorate perceives to be desirable curricular innovations, even at the expense of other urgent matters. Such policies leave English teachers no choice but to limit their teaching materials to those offered by the Inspectorate, i.e. its authorized textbooks, or face the penalties. Incidentally, the English Inspectorate has often vehemently intervened in matters involving local language policy. Such was the case in 1993, for instance, when the Tel Aviv Municipality was the first to proceed with an experimental project whereby students began their English studies at age 8, rather than age 9, in five municipal schools. Empowering local stakeholders over centralized forces was not welcomed by the English Inspectorate (Inbar-Lourie, 2005). This raises the question of how the English Inspectorate would have dealt with similar local language changes among less influential and central localities in Israel, given their severe reaction in metropolitan Tel Aviv.

Just as with other subjects, the choice of EFL curricular materials is administered and determined by educators and government officials with mainstream Jewish-Zionist views. Shohamy (2003) relates the policy for teaching EFL in Israel to this general top-down imposition of LEP, where there is a "limited representation of broad sectors of the population in decisions and in implementation of LEP, even though they are strongly affected by it" (p. 282). Thus, current LEP in Israel serves the interests of dominant groups imposing their ideologies by means of the educational system. As such, the English curriculum seems to be halfway between repression and an "ideological state apparatus" (Althusser, [1971] 2000) acting both by direct policing and indirect ideology.

This volume questions whether curricular policies provide equal educational EFL opportunities to diverse learning populations, particularly to speakers of Arabic. Let me first present the elements that constitute a learner as "diverse" in the Israeli EFL discourse and consequently merit special attention to the way s/he should be taught English. For this purpose, I review the central role that "the native speaker" plays in constructing the notion of "learner diversity" regarding the way English should be taught in Israeli schools.

Constructing "Native-Speakerism" in EFL Discourse

Of particular relevance for EFL learning in Israel, and perhaps elsewhere, is the unequal involvement of native speakers of English in the practice of language teaching across a diverse learning population. Following the establishment of the State of Israel, a relatively large number of immigrants from North America and other English-speaking countries immigrated to Israel. According to a 1983 census, 60,000 people reported English as their first language, and another 40,000 have been added since then (Spolsky & Shohamy, 1999). Spolsky and Shohamy report that:

> English-speaking immigrants and their children have furnished an important reservoir of native speakers to fill teaching and other jobs requiring English … In Jewish schools, about 40% of the teachers of English are native speakers of English, a figure that would be hard to match anywhere, but in Arab schools all teachers are native speakers of Arabic.
>
> *(p. 165)*

This dominant group of native speakers profoundly shapes EFL discourse in Israel, largely defining the way in which English should be approached. The concept of the "native speaker" of a language is by no means uncontroversial (Byram, 2008; Davies, 2003; Kramsch, 1998). In broader international EFL frameworks, native speaker norms are still treated as international norms, contradicting the global circumstances of English being spoken by more non-native than native speakers (Davies, 2003; Jenkins, 2000; Seidlhofer, 2003). That is, many language teachers, either consciously or subconsciously, still use it as a goal against which they assess their students, hoping that students will move ever nearer native speaker competence. Considering the extreme, yet possible, difficulty of reaching a native speaker level, Davies (2003, p. 197) indicates the distinction teachers need to make between using this goal as an inspiration and the measurement used for attaining it:

> The native speaker is a fine myth: we need it as a model, a goal, almost an inspiration. But it is useless as a measure; it will not help us define our goals. So in spite of … my conviction that there is a continuum between native speakers and non-native speakers, nevertheless, I recognize that for language teaching purposes what is crucial is the description of adequate partial competences.

Aside from filling teaching and other major administrative EFL jobs, native speakers also corner the EFL textbook-writing market in Israel, as I will show in Chapter 5. When writing EFL textbooks, native speakers:

> consciously or unconsciously transmit their views, values, beliefs, attitudes, and feelings of their own English-speaking society – usually the United States or the United Kingdom. As such, when learners acquire a new set of English

discourse as part of their evolving systemic knowledge, they partake of the cultural system which the set entails.

(Alptekin, 1993, p. 138)

EFL discourse thus needs to be addressed from both local and global perspectives. The role that "native speakers" of English play as architects of EFL pedagogies should also be considered in the larger frameworks of international EFL or ELT (English Language Teaching). The whole notion of "native-speakerism" is associated with Adrian Holliday (2006), and is recognized as a *key term* that

> reflects a traditional orientation towards English language education rooted in dichotomous 'us' and 'them' dynamics in which 'native speakers' of English are considered the norm, the owners of the English language and its naturally endowed teaching experts, in contrast to 'non-native speakers' of English who are generally considered deficient, an ideology otherwise termed cultural disbelief.
>
> *(Houghton & Rivers, 2013, p. 1)*

According to Holliday (2013, p. 21; emphasis in original), *cultural disbelief* "imagines that while 'other cultures' have the right to be themselves, they present a 'problem' by not being good at taking part in activities which require an *imagined* Western world view." Holliday's view of cultural reduction, or culturism, falls within the broader chauvinistic narrative of Orientalism (Said, 1978) where the behavior of "non-native speakers" is corrected by "native speakers" through English language education. This is done due to what Holliday calls their "moral mission" to introduce a "superior" culture of teaching and learning to teachers and learners who are presumably incapable of succeeding on their own terms (Holliday, 2006, p. 386). Prioritizing native speaker teachers may also have serious implications regarding some false assumptions about how English teaching professionalism is assessed. In this regard, Holliday postulates:

> There is therefore something deep within the profession *everywhere* which makes it possible for 'native speaker' and 'non-native speaker' to continue as a basic currency not only for labeling teachers but also for judging them through forms of chauvinism of which we are largely unaware and easily put aside.
>
> *(2013, p. 18; emphasis added)*

From a Critical Discourse Analysis (CDA) perspective, I take the notion of native-speakerism one step further, studying it as a hegemonic discourse shaping the planning of EFL policies in Israel, with similar implications for other countries. Through the use of native-speakerist discourse – which I will claim in this volume is overt and explicit – the Ministry of Education and the English Inspectorate maintain a policy that takes into account the special needs of EFL learners/teachers who are "native speakers" of English, while disregarding the special needs of EFL learners/teachers who are "speakers of Arabic" and whose diverse linguistic repertoire requires special attention. In order to understand the relationship between native-speakerism and ideology in EFL policy and planning in Israel, it is also important to study this issue from a postmodern social-constructivist point of view that sees reality as it is constructed through discourse. Taking such a postmodernist view of LEPs might enable a shift from "a practical, modernist preoccupation with what is the most efficient way to teach a language, [to] ... an understanding that what may appear most efficient is itself always ideologically driven" (p. 19). Holliday further states that

> [Although] the modernist paradigm will claim that national cultural descriptions are neutral and indeed celebratory of cultural difference, as long as they are carefully researched, the postmodern view is that the boundaries between cultural realities are blurred and negotiable and that descriptions of cultures are ideological.
>
> *(p. 21)*

Discourse analysis of English textbooks in Israel has shown a strong tendency toward presenting Anglo-centric cultures as superior to non-Western cultures through constructing positive Self-narratives to describe Westerners as opposed to negative Other-narratives to describe non-Westerners (Awayed-Bishara, 2015). In Chapter 3 and Chapter 5, I will illustrate how Anglo-centric ideologies in Israel respectively dominate EFL textbooks, and policies. Moving away from native-speakerism and Anglo-centrism, current approaches to foreign language education offer different goals for adapting the teaching of English to global and international needs.

Culture in Twenty-first-century EFL Education

As a consequence of globalization and internationalization, foreign language education programs, including EFL, have shifted their focus from a framework of four skills (listening, reading, speaking, and writing) to a framework focusing on what can be accomplished through English (communication, intercultural connectedness between communities, etc.). The role of culture teaching in the foreign language classroom has long been discussed, and so has the view on why and how teachers need to integrate the teaching of culture in their classroom. There is still no real consensus about what culture really is. To the British cultural critic Stuart Hall (1997), the concept of culture is so intangible that there is not much point in trying to define it. Despite its elusive nature, many scholars agree that language and culture are two sides of the same coin, and are thus inseparable. One widely used definition was developed by the American anthropologist Clifford Geertz, for whom culture "denotes a historically transmitted pattern of meanings embodied in symbols, a system of inherited conceptions in symbolic forms by means of which people communicate, perpetuate and develop their knowledge about and attitudes towards life" ([1973] 2000, p. 89). It follows that culture, in its widest sense, stands for creative endeavors such as art, architecture, theatre, dance, music, and literature.

Such endeavors, according to Kumaravadivelu (2008, p. 10), "constitute the intellectual and aesthetic life of a community … which is generally referred to as Culture with a capital C." In its narrower sense, "culture with a small c stands for beliefs, morals, customs, norms, and values that govern the practice of everyday life."

The academic literature on culture teaching in the foreign language classroom arises from "multiple theoretical and philosophical positions" (Risager, 2011, p. 485). However, Weninger and Kiss (2013) identify three major periods that mark how perceptions about why and how culture needs to be taught in foreign language education have changed. The first period is from the 1950s to the early 1990s, when culture is viewed as an object of study. In other words, students were expected to learn factual information about national cultures for the mere goal of assimilating them into the target language society, so that they became members of that society. When taught outside the UK, the USA, or Australia – i.e. Kachru's (1990) "first circle" countries – "English was taught around the world as the language of native speakers living in [these countries] and their respective national cultures" (Kramsch, 2015, p. 404). Teaching native speakers' culture entailed the teaching of "the speech habits of native speakers in formal, written, or academic situations [which] were captured as the big C culture of literature and the arts" (p. 403). Critics soon started to problematize the notion of the native speaker as the model language user and the goal of instruction. In this regard, Street (1993) associates the problematicity of the first period with the use of *culture* as a noun which creates the false impression that it is an object or a thing. In "Culture Is a Verb," he argues that culture should be understood as a verb rather than a noun; an understanding that altogether requires a view on culture not in terms of what it *is* but what it *does* (Street, 1993; see also Hall, 1997).

In light of the problematic notion of culture teaching in the first period, the increasing impact of globalization in the second half of the 1990s brought with it changes in how learners' needs were viewed. The approach of the second period (Kramsch, 1993) introduced a broader view on cultural information that included more than facts about famous people, places, and historical events. The argument is that successful language acquisition entails cultural awareness, which is developed through acquainting language learners with the cultural *practices* of the speakers of the target language. As mentioned above, the cultural behavior, habits, and everyday practices of target language speakers are referred to as culture with a small c (see also Pulverness, 1995; Tomalin & Stempleski, 1993). Culture with a small c was thus incorporated into the language curriculum.

Emphasizing the interconnectedness between English and its role as a global language, Prodromou (1992) questions the validity of talking about a target language culture. In response to such interconnectedness, movements promoting inter-, cross-, and trans-cultural approaches as opposed to the single, national culture model started to gain prominence. At the end of the 1990s, Byram (1997) introduced a new perspective on the role of foreign language education in developing what he termed an *intercultural competence*. Byram defines intercultural competence as the ability to successfully communicate with people from different cultural and geographical contexts. Currently, however, scholars such as Kumaravadivelu (2008) and Byram himself (2008; 2011) argue that fostering intercultural competence is not even sufficient. Both scholars, thus, call for global cultural consciousness and intercultural citizenship as key outcomes of foreign language learning. They argue that language education, including EFL education, must have transformative goals whose achievement is duty-bound to foster learners' cultural reflection and understanding within a critically oriented pedagogy. Within this critical pedagogy, EFL materials and discourse need to promote the development of a reflexive and globally aware learner. Kumaravadivelu (2008, p. 189) notes:

> The task of promoting global cultural consciousness in the classroom can hardly be accomplished unless a concerted effort is made to use materials that will prompt learners to confront some of the taken-for-granted cultural beliefs about the Self and the Other.

In sum, the third period treats culture as an ever-intensifying, complex, and transnational phenomenon (Risager, 2007).

To summarize, EFL teaching in the first half of the twentieth century focused mainly on preparing for the study of high culture. In the other half, the focus shifted toward preparing students to converse with native speakers (Byram, 2011). Currently, scholarship on foreign language teaching calls for transformative EFL pedagogies that must also have, along with the other previous goals, moral and political educational objectives (Byram, 2008; 2011; Kumaravadivelu, 2008). Namely, students are not expected to abandon the idea of learning English in order to study the cultures it is associated with or communicate with native speakers. Rather, teachers and schools are expected to develop in their young students – i.e. the future citizens – what Byram (1997; 2011) now calls "critical cultural awareness." For Byram, critical cultural awareness is a central term in the definition of intercultural communicative competence (ICC), which he first coined in 1997 in a direct link to political education. That is, critical cultural awareness is defined as "an ability to evaluate, critically and on the basis of explicit criteria, perspectives, practices and products in one's *own* and other cultures and countries" (Byram, 1997, p. 53; my emphasis).

Hence, an emphasis on one's knowledge of one's own culture becomes the hallmark of foreign language teaching programs. A growing body of literature stemming from the analysis of learners' needs in a student-centered context emphasizes the significance of learners' own native cultures (Shin, Eslami, & Chen, 2011). In order to facilitate effective foreign language learning, the use of students' own experiences is encouraged (Alptekin, 2002). Shin et al. (2011) underscore how learners' cultures and experiences need to be validated in teaching English as a foreign language, so as to help learners utilize their own life experiences in order to facilitate their identification with different varieties of English and their associated cultures. The process of educating students towards critical cultural awareness entails, according to Byram (2011, p. 163), the ability to do the following:

1. Identify and interpret explicit or implicit values in documents and events in one's own and other cultures.
2. Make an evaluative analysis of the documents and events which refers to an explicit perspective and criteria.
3. Interact and mediate in intercultural exchanges by drawing upon one's knowledge, skills and attitudes.

Together with "critical cultural awareness," Byram (2011) also provides other crucial elements that define the aims of foreign language teaching. These elements constitute students' intercultural competence and are listed under attitudes, knowledge, and skills:

- *attitudes*: curiosity and openness, readiness to suspend disbelief about other cultures and belief about one's own;
- *knowledge*: of social groups and their products and practices in one's own and in one's interlocutor's country, and of the general processes of societal and individual interaction;
- *skills of interpreting and relating*: ability to interpret a document or event from another culture, to explain it, and relate it to documents or events from one's own;
- *skills of discovery and interaction*: ability to acquire new knowledge of a culture and cultural practices and the ability to operate knowledge, attitudes, and skills under the constraints of real-time communication and interaction.

Because of the significance that English has between and within other countries, the definition of critical cultural awareness underscores the importance of learners being aware of their home ideology – i.e. political, religious, and linguistic knowledge – so they are able to evaluate and learn from other cultures. It follows that "language education cannot and should not avoid educational and political duties and responsibilities" (p. 149). In an education system directed at disparate groups within one country, critical cultural awareness is directly connected to the concept of "political awareness," which is defined as:

> Critical awareness, independent judgment and political *engagement*. The precondition for democratic *engagement* is that the citizen becomes aware of the relationship between individual destiny and social processes and structures. Political awareness is formed through the recognition of one's own interests and the experience of social conflicts and relationships of governance. The politically aware and informed person should not be a passive object of politics, but as a subject should participate in politics.
>
> *(Gagel, 2000, cited in Byram, 2008, p. 164)*

This volume aims to offer (in Chapter 6 and Chapter 7) a new discourse for coining a transformative EFL pedagogy that directs teachers in multi-ethnic countries (such as Israel) to understand the extent of their responsibility for the co-constructions of the cultural and political identity of their students as a result of their education. In this type of education, teachers discuss with their students issues that are different from the *preferred* Anglo-centric topics offered in the authorized textbook (Awayed-Bishara, 2015). Alternatively, "different" topics are generated from students' everyday experiences and their conception of themselves and others. In the context of EFL classes, especially in light of the current emphasis on spoken language skills, the reproductive orientation of Anglo-centric EFL materials stifles the voices of marginal populations. In particular, the National English Curriculum (Ministry of Education, 2018) ostensibly encourages teachers to dialogically discuss culturally related topics as part of promoting their students' linguistic and intercultural competence. Rather, an analysis of student responses to the cultural content of EFL texts indicates that such educational materials overlook the need to foster students who are able to effectively construct critical stances about other cultures on both local and the global scales (see Chapter 4). Against this non-dialogical backdrop, students act as passive receptacles. In analyzing Portuguese teachers' accounts of their practice, Guilherme (2002, p. 204) points out how "most participants do not include critical agency in their understanding of a critical pedagogy [as] they do not engage in a committed transformation of their social realities, nor do they expect their students to do so in the present." Rather than discussing unrepresentative cultural ideas with their students, teachers should encourage students to discuss their everyday encounters, knowledge about, and experiences with people from other cultures. Despite the inevitable risk of bringing up negative stereotypes and prejudices, the idea is to transform students' negative beliefs through engaging them in on-going reflective and critical practices about the Self and the Other. In other words, working as transformative pedagogues requires teachers to engage their students with practices of self-examination and self-empowerment so they form a deeper understanding of who the Other is. In studying the potential political action in the teaching of English to students from all different ethnic and language groups in Latvia, Kalnberzina (2000) encourages teachers in other countries "not to avoid topics that might seem dangerous at times but use them as a possibility to be made use of" (p. 125). These claims are based on experience with students in the English classroom, where they addressed topics that seemed painful in Latvian society, but turned out to be the most necessary of all.

What I similarly hope to achieve in this study is an understanding that the principles of EFL education in the era of globalization cannot ignore the great responsibility educators have to develop *locally* minded and *globally* aware students capable of critically responding to, and ultimately acting to change, cultural and political misrepresentations and inequalities. Transforming students from passive receptacles to creative agents might bring about social change in an era of ever-intensifying conflicts and world rifts.

The Structure of the Book

Apart from this introduction and the theoretical chapter (Chapter 2), the book is divided into two sections: Chapter 3, Chapter 4 and Chapter 5 deal with the reproductive and hegemonic nature of EFL discourse in Israel (as analyzed in textbooks, students' talk, and policy documents), and Chapter 6 and Chapter 7 deal with the way EFL discourse can be reconstructed to devise a transformative EFL pedagogy.

Chapter 2 presents the theoretical and methodological framework on which the analysis of EFL discourse is based. Chapter 3 presents an analysis of the cultural suitability of EFL textbooks and other authorized materials used in Israeli schools. Chapter 4 presents an analysis of EFL students' responses on the cultural content of EFL materials and issues of identity politics. Chapter 5 presents an analysis of EFL policy documents in Israel and interviews with textbook writers in Israel regarding the production processes of EFL materials. Chapter 6 moves toward a conclusion by summarizing the general nature of EFL discourse in Israel, showing how it necessitates the reconstruction of EFL pedagogical discourse. It will thus offer a transformative approach to EFL pedagogy as cultural discourse that can be integrated in the EFL classroom and other EFL education programs. Chapter 7, the final chapter, addresses the Palestinian-Arab community as a whole – i.e. teachers, students, parents, and other social actors – and suggests that stepping out of the trap of circles of rights discourses into more responsibility-oriented discourses is a necessary step toward effecting social change, and to achieve better educational opportunities.

References

Abu-Saad, I. (2004). Separate and unequal: The role of the state educational system in maintaining the subordination of Israel's Palestinian Arab citizens. *Social Identities*, 10(1), 101–127. doi.org/10.1080/1350463042000191010.

Abu-Saad, I. (2006). State-controlled education and identity formation among the Palestinian Arab minority in Israel. *American Behavioral Scientist*, 49(8), 1085–1100. doi.org/10.1177/0002764205284720.

Adalah. (2003). Education rights: Palestinian citizens of Israel (UN CESCR Information Sheet No. 2). Shafa'amr: Adalah, The Legal Center for Arab Minority Rights in Israel. Available at:/www.adalah.org/uploads/oldfiles/eng/intladvocacy/CESCR-education.pdf

Al-Haj, M. (1995). *Education, empowerment, and control: The case of the Arabs in Israel*. Albany, NY: State University of New York Press.

Al-Haj, M. (2002). Multiculturalism in deeply divided societies: The Israeli case. *International Journal of Intercultural Relations*, 26, 169–183. Available at: doi:10.1016/S0147-1767(01)00048–00047.

Alptekin, C. (1993). Target-language culture in EFL materials. *English Language Teaching Journal*, 47(2), 136–143. doi:10.1093/elt/47.2.136.

Alptekin, C. (2002). Towards intercultural communicative competence in ELT. *ELT Journal: English Language Teaching Journal*, 56(1), 57–64. doi:10.1093/elt/56.1.57.

Althusser, L. ([1971] 2000). Ideology interpellates individuals as subjects. In P. Du Gay, J. Evans, & P. Redman (Eds.), *Identity: A reader* (pp. 31–38). London: SAGE Publications.

Awayed-Bishara, M. (2015). Analyzing the cultural content of materials used for teaching English to high school speakers of Arabic in Israel. *Discourse & Society*, 26(5), 517–542. doi:26376399.

Awayed-Bishara, M. (2018). EFL discourse as cultural practice. *Journal of Multicultural Discourses*, 13(3), 243–258. doi:10.1080/17447143.2017.1379528.

Bernstein, B. (1996). *Pedagogy, symbolic control and identity: Theory, research, critique*. London: Taylor & Francis.

Byram, M. S. (1997). *Teaching and assessing intercultural communicative competence*. Clevedon: Multilingual Matters.

Byram, M. S. (2008). *From foreign language education to education for intercultural citizenship: Essays and reflections*. Clevedon: Multilingual Matters.

Byram, M. S. (2011). Intercultural citizenship from an international perspective. *Journal of the NUS Teaching Academy*, 1(1), 10–20.

Davies, A. (2003). *The native speaker: Myth and reality*. Clevedon: Multilingual Matters.

Dwairy, M. (2004). Culturally sensitive education: Adapting self-oriented assertiveness training to collective minorities. *Journal of Social Issues*, 60(2), 423–436. doi:10.1111/j.0022-4537.2004.00114.x.

Fairclough, N., Mulderrig, J., & Wodak, R. (2011). Critical discourse analysis. In T. A. van Dijk (Ed.), *Discourse studies: A multidisciplinary introduction* (2nd ed., pp. 357–378). London: SAGE Publications.

Ferguson, C. A. (1959). Diglossia. *WORD*, 15(2), 325–340. doi:10.1080/00437956.1959.11659702.

Geertz, C. ([1973] 2000). *The interpretation of cultures*. New York: Basic Books.

Graddol, D. (2006). English next: Why global English may mean the end of "English as a foreign language." London: British Council. Available at: http://englishagenda.britishcouncil.org/sites/default/files/attachments/books-english-next.pdf

Guilherme, M. (2002). *Critical citizens for an intercultural world: Foreign language education as cultural politics*. Clevedon: Multilingual Matters.

Hall, S. (1997). The spectacle of the "Other." In S. Hall (Ed.), *Representation: Cultural representations and signifying practices* (pp. 223–290). London: SAGE Publications.

Holliday, A. (2006). Native-speakerism. *English Language Teaching Journal*, 60(4), 385–387. doi:10.1093/elt/ccl030.

Holliday, A. (2013). "Native speaker" teachers and cultural belief. In S. A. Houghton & D. J. Rivers (Eds.), *Native-speakerism in Japan: Intergroup dynamics in foreign language education* (pp. 17–28). Bristol: Multilingual Matters.

Houghton, S., & Rivers, D. J. (2013). Introduction: Redefining native-speakerism. In S. A. Houghton & D. J. Rivers (Eds.), *Native-speakerism in Japan: Intergroup dynamics in foreign language education* (pp. 1–16). Bristol: Multilingual Matters.

Human Rights Watch. (2001). *Second class: Discrimination against Palestinian Arab children in Israel's schools*. New York: Human Rights Watch.

Inbar-Lourie, O. (2005). English language teaching in Israel: Challenging diversity. In G. Braine (Ed.), *Teaching English to the world: History, curriculum, and practice* (pp. 81–92). Mahwah, NJ: Lawrence Erlbaum Associates, Inc.

Jenkins, J. (2000). *The phonology of English as an international language: New models, new norms, new goals*. Oxford: Oxford University Press.

Kachru, B. B. (1990). *The alchemy of English: The spread, functions and models of non-native Englishes*. Chicago, IL: University of Illinois Press.

Kalnberzina, V. (2000). Latvian module: Understanding "social identity." In M. S. Byram & M. Tost Planet (Eds.), *Social identity and the European dimension: Intercultural competence through foreign language learning* (pp. 109–126). Strasbourg: Council of Europe.

Koda, K. (2008). Impacts of prior literacy experience on second language learning to read. In K. Koda & A. M. Zehler (Eds.), *Learning to read across languages: Cross-linguistic relationships in first- and second-language literacy development* (pp. 68–96). New York: Routledge.
Kramsch, C. (1993). *Context and culture in language teaching.* Oxford: Oxford University Press.
Kramsch, C. (1998). *Language and culture.* Oxford: Oxford University Press.
Kramsch, C. (2015). Language and culture in second language learning. In F. Sharifian (Ed.), *The Routledge handbook of language and culture* (pp. 403–416). New York: Routledge.
Kumaravadivelu, B. (2008). *Cultural globalization and language education.* New Haven, CT: Yale University Press.
Lev-Ari, S. (2003). Know thy neighbor: The study of Arabic, Arab culture and the Koran could improve life in Israel. *Ha'aretz*, February 26. Available at: www.haaretz.com/israel-news/culture/1.4889678
Mar'i, S. K. (1978). *Arab education in Israel.* Syracuse, NY: Syracuse University Press.
Ministry of Education. (2018). Revised English Curriculum including Band III Lexis: Principles and standards for learning English as an international language for all grades. Jerusalem: Ministry of Education, State of Israel. Available at: http://meyda.education.gov.il/files/Mazkirut_Pedagogit/English/Curriculum2018July.pdf
Nasser, R., & Nasser, I. (2008). Textbooks as a vehicle for segregation and domination: State efforts to shape Palestinian Israelis' identities as citizens. *Journal of Curriculum Studies*, 40(5), 627–650. doi:10.1080/00220270802072804.
Or, I. G., & Shohamy, E. (2015). Contrasting Arabic and Hebrew textbooks in Israel: A focus on culture. In X. L. Curdt-Christiansen & C. Weninger (Eds.), *Language, ideology and education: The politics of textbooks in language education* (pp. 109–126). New York: Routledge.
Peled-Elhanan, N. (2012). *Palestine in Israeli school books: Ideology and propaganda in education.* London: I.B. Tauris.
Peres, Y., Ehrlich, A., & Yuval-Davis, N. (1970). National education for Arab youth in Israel: A comparison of curricula. *Race*, 12(1), 26–36.
Podeh, E. (2000). History and memory in the Israeli educational system: The portrayal of the Arab-Israeli conflict in history textbooks (1948–2000) . *History and Memory*, 12(1), 65–100. doi:10.1353/ham.2000.0005.
Podeh, E. (2002). *The Arab-Israeli conflict in Israeli history textbooks, 1948–2000.* Westport, CT: Bergin and Garvey.
Prodromou, L. (1992). What culture? Which culture? Cross-cultural factors in language learning. *English Language Teaching Journal*, 46(1), 39–50. doi:10.1093/elt/46.1.39.
Pulverness, A. (1995). Cultural studies, British studies and EFL. *Modern English Teacher*, 4(2), 7–11.
Risager, K. (2007). *Language and culture pedagogy: From a national to a transnational paradigm.* Clevedon: Multilingual Matters.
Risager, K. (2011). The cultural dimensions of language teaching and learning. *Language Teaching*, 44(4), 485–499.
Said, E. W. (1978). *Orientalism.* New York: Vintage Books.
Saiegh-Haddad, E. (2003). Linguistic distance and initial reading acquisition: The case of Arabic diglossia. *Applied Psycholinguistics*, 24(3), 431–451.
Saiegh-Haddad, E. (2004). The impact of phonemic and lexical distance on the phonological analysis of words and pseudowords in a diglossic context. *Applied Psycholinguistics*, 25 (4), 495–512. doi:10.1017/S0142716404001249.
Saiegh-Haddad, E. (2007). Linguistic constraints on children's ability to isolate phonemes in Arabic. *Applied Psycholinguistics*, 28(4), 607–625. doi:10.1017/S0142716407070336.

Saiegh-Haddad, E. (2011). Phonological processing in diglossic Arabic: The role of linguistic distance. In E. Broselow & H. Ouali (Eds.), *Perspectives on Arabic linguistics: Papers from the annual symposia on Arabic linguistics* (vol. XXII–XXIII, pp. 269–280). Amsterdam: John Benjamins.

Saiegh-Haddad, E., & Henkin-Roitfarb, R. (2014). The structure of Arabic language and orthography. In E. Saiegh-Haddad & R. M. Joshi (Eds.), *Handbook of Arabic literacy: Insights and perspectives* (vol. 9, pp. 3–30). Dordrecht: Springer.

Saiegh-Haddad, E., Levin, I., Hende, N., & Ziv, M. (2011). The linguistic affiliation constraint and phoneme recognition in diglossic Arabic. *Journal of Child Language*, 38(2), 297–315.

Seidlhofer, B. (2003). *A concept of international English and related issues: From "real English" to "realistic English"?* Strasbourg: Language Policy Division, Council of Europe.

Shin, J., Eslami, Z. R., & Chen, W.-C. (2011). Presentation of local and international culture in current international English-language teaching textbooks. *Language, Culture and Curriculum*, 24(3), 253–268. doi:10.1080/07908318.2011.614694.

Shi-xu. (2005). *A cultural approach to discourse*. New York: Palgrave Macmillan.

Shohamy, E. (2003). Implications of language education policies for language study in schools and universities. *The Modern Language Journal*, 87(2), 278–286.

Shohamy, E. (2007). Reinterpreting globalization in multilingual contexts. *International Multilingual Research Journal*, 1(2), 127–133. doi:10.1080/19313150701495421.

Shohamy, E. (2014). The weight of English in global perspective: The role of English in Israel. *Review of Research in Education*, 38(1), 273–289. doi:10.3102/0091732X13509773.

Shohamy, E., & Abu Ghazaleh-Mahajneh, M. (2012). Linguistic landscape as a tool for interpreting language vitality: Arabic as a "minority" language in Israel. In D. Gorter, H. F. Marten, & L. Van Mensel (Eds.), *Minority languages in the linguistic landscape* (pp. 89–108). Basingstoke: Palgrave Macmillan.

Shohamy, E., & Donitsa-Schmidt, S. (1997). *Attitudes, stereotypes and priorities of Jews towards Arabic and Arabs toward Hebrew*. Tel Aviv: The Stainmintz Center for Peace in the Middle East, Tel Aviv University.

Skop, Y. (2016, July 20). While politicians rage over Mahmoud Darwish, his poems are quietly being taught in Israeli schools. *Ha'aretz*. Available at: www.haaretz.com/israel-news/israeli-schools-feature-works-of-palestinian-poet-dissed-by-lieberman-1.5413419

Spolsky, B., Ben Meir, D., Inbar, O., Orland, L., Steiner, J., & Vermel, J. (2015). English curriculum for all grades [Israeli Ministry of Education]. Available at: http://retro.education.gov.il/tochniyot_limudim/eng1.htm (accessed March 8, 2019).

Spolsky, B., & Shohamy, E. (1999). *The languages of Israel: Policy, ideology and practice*. Clevedon: Multilingual Matters.

Street, B. V. (1993). Culture is a verb: Anthropological aspects of language and cultural process. In D. Graddol, L. Thompson, & M. S. Byram (Eds.), *Language and culture: Papers from the annual meeting of the British Association of Applied Linguistics* (pp. 23–43). Clevedon: Multilingual Matters.

Swirski, S. (1999). *Politics and education in Israel: Comparisons with the United States*. New York: Falmer Press.

Times of Israel Staff. (2017). Minister storms out of ceremony to protest Palestinian poem. *The Times of Israel*, June 13. Available at: www.timesofisrael.com/minister-storms-out-of-ceremony-to-protest-palestinian-poem/

Tomalin, B., & Stempleski, S. (1993). *Cultural awareness*. Oxford: Oxford University Press.

Tyack, D. B. (2003). *Seeking common ground: Public schools in a diverse society*. Cambridge, MA: Harvard University Press.

Weninger, C., & Kiss, T. (2013). Culture in English as a Foreign Language (EFL) textbooks: A semiotic approach. *TESOL Quarterly*, 47(4), 694–716. doi:10.1002/tesq.87.

Wertsch, J. V. (2002). *Voices of collective remembering*. Cambridge: Cambridge University Press.
Yiftachel, O. (2006). *Ethnocracy: Land and identity politics in Israel/Palestine*. Philadelphia, PA: University of Pennsylvania Press.
Zerubavel, Y. (2002). The "Mythological Sabra" and Jewish past: Trauma, memory, and contested identities. *Israel Studies*, 7(2), 115–144.

2

EFL DISCOURSE

Beyond Language Education

This chapter provides the theoretical and methodological framework for this study. It first presents the principles for analyzing the language used for teaching, learning, and policing EFL as discourse. It then introduces the critical and text-oriented approaches to discourse analysis that are used to analyze the cultural representation of EFL discourse and its function either in perpetuating hegemonic ideologies, or effecting social change. It then provides an illustration of how the ideological dimensions of EFL discourse are examined in this volume through applying Althusser's notions of "interpellation" and "ideological state apparatuses," and Gramsci's notion of "hegemony." The connection between EFL discourse and culture is finally analyzed through identifying current perceptions of the role that culture plays in EFL pedagogical discourses, so as to illustrate how Cultural Discourse Studies (CDS) may complement the theoretical framework in understanding EFL discourse as a specifically *cultural* practice.

Introduction: A Theoretical and Methodological Framework

This volume sets out to investigate the semiotic resources used in the cultural representation of different groups, values, and ideologies in EFL discourse in Israel. An analysis of the ideology of those policing and those who are affected by EFL policy requires a nuanced theoretical framework that can critically capture the dynamics between ideologically driven educational policies, and the globalizing status of English. Studying the way cultural representations are discursively manifested in the Israeli EFL context might shed light on interventionalist educational paths for contesting discriminatory discourses and effecting social change. I will argue that establishing a transformative EFL pedagogy, applicable in the ever intensifying yet challenging pluralistic spirit of the twenty-first century, compels the construction of a new discourse that accentuates *how* the different cultural groups to whom English is pertinent can equally inform and learn from one another. That is, EFL discourses in multilingual contexts should be modified so as to bring the West and the Rest into dialogue with one another for the sake of reducing conflict, promoting human prosperity, and building critical global awareness.

In accordance with the principles that govern the active and professional role that discourse analysts can play in promoting progressive discourses of cultural coexistence, I use a holistic model for a transformative EFL pedagogy understood as a cultural discursive practice (Awayed-Bishara, 2018) that might enable a "dialogue with local cultural communities" (Shi-xu, 2005, p. 10). At this juncture, it is crucial to highlight that current critical approaches to analyzing discourse, which are mostly Western, might not be sufficient when it comes to bringing non-Western groups into dialogue with hegemonic, Anglo-centric ideologies that dominate EFL research in many contexts. As such, and more specifically, I intend to bring together Critical Discourse Analysis (CDA) and CDS in order to analyze EFL pedagogy as a cultural discourse. I begin by showing how these two scholarly traditions are harmonious, and yet different and end by foregrounding the reasons why they should be brought into dialogue to inform one another when it comes to EFL cultural discourses.

Constructing EFL as Discourse

I explore the interplay between language, culture, and ideology in my research on the premise that the language used for teaching English to speakers of other languages shapes, and is shaped by, ideologically determined agendas. This entails an examination of the cultural content of various forms of EFL discourse, and thus an analysis of the elements of English teaching and learning that may be culturally biased. The data under examination for this purpose in this book are texts and narratives from six English textbooks that mainly deal with culture-related issues (in Chapter 3), EFL learners' (both Israeli Jews and Palestinian Arabs) attitudes toward four EFL texts (in Chapter 4), and EFL policy documents in Israel and interviews with EFL textbook writers (in Chapter 5). These three corpora make up what I term for the purposes of this volume "EFL discourse." A critical analysis of EFL discourse requires the application of a systematically integrated analytical model that presupposes an ideologically and socially motivated relationship between form and meaning.

As I stated earlier, the core assumption of this volume is that the language currently used for teaching and learning English shapes and is shaped by ideology. Analyzing the language used for teaching English in Israel suggests the relevance of related insights regarding the constitutive role that language plays in constructing individual identities and attitudes. Language must clearly be analyzed as a *discourse* that is socially constituted and shaped. Accordingly, just as discourse contributes to the reproduction and perpetuation of hegemonic and dominant ideologies, it is also the medium of their transformation. Armed with these assumptions about the ideological and constitutive role of discourse, the three analytical chapters in this volume employ theories of power and ideology in order to study EFL educational discourse. More specifically, they examine EFL discourse in Israel as a major arena that reproduces and perpetuates social realities of inequality, marginalization, and misrepresentation of the Other. These findings potentially open up possibilities for effecting educational and social change.

In the next section, I present the general theoretical framework for critically analyzing EFL discourse. Specific methodological detail is offered at the start of each analytical chapter, so as to situate each stage of the analysis in its relevant context.

Theoretical Framework

New research methodologies for understanding the globalized and diversified nature of EFL discourses are called for against the backdrop of the dominant positivistic theories of the past decades. When optimistic solutions to social problems are on the wane (Rorty, 1998), a critical perspective needs to guide broad inquiries into the role that scholars, discourse analysts, and EFL pedagogues can play in effecting social change. The question is: how do we ask broad questions about the reproduction of power and domination in educational discourse, while studying particular and situated practices in which learning about the world and the Other occurs? The question that follows the analysis of dominant and hegemonic discourses in educational settings is: how do we go about the de- and re-construction of an EFL discourse that serves a cultural politics of global/local coexistence and prosperity?

To start with, examining how EFL discourse addresses (or fails to address) the issue of cultural diversity helps us to understand how underlying ideologies shape learners' perceptions regarding the Other. Clearly, when "culturally diversified forms of paradigms converse with, critique and learn from one another on an egalitarian and democratic basis, human intellectual and cultural horizons will be expanded and chances of genuine intellectual innovation and common cultural prosperity increased" (Shi-xu, 2009, p. 32). My contention is that offering an interventionist culturally critical approach to EFL pedagogy must follow the unveiling of the problem, and acknowledging the harms that some current EFL discourses that reinforce binary divisions of the social world (into West/East, dominant/subordinate, etc.) cause to marginalized and socially excluded groups of learners. In offering academic or political solutions to bring about a change in educational settings characterized by unbalanced power relations, we need to bear in mind Derrida's (1978) critique of the binary and logocentric tradition of Western thought that tends to dichotomize representations of, say, Self/Other, while overlooking how this positioning constructs an illusory equivalence. Rather, binary terms are always hierarchically ranked, and therefore need to be deconstructed and contested.

My overriding concern, then, is to assert that constructing a paradigm of diversity, peace, and coexistence in general discourse and in EFL pedagogies in particular must confront the erasures of the past, and accept the Other as an equal, not only to learn about but also to learn *from*. That is, to bring about an attainable social change through EFL education, learners must learn to accept the legitimacy of the Other's voice in expressing one's pains and losses, existential problems, wisdom, and cultural reality. It is only within a true grassroots dialogue that amplifies the voice of the Other in a way that reclaims the legitimacy of that Other's cultural discourse that new solutions can find their way into the social, cultural, and particularly the educational arenas. If we are to transcend our acculturation, according to Rorty (1991), we must work toward "a culture which prides itself on not being monolithic – [but] on its tolerance for a plurality of subcultures and its willingness to listen to neighboring cultures" (p. 14).

The question is: How could discourse shape the transformation of cultural realities from monolithic- to pluralist-oriented paradigms? I will try to answer this question through looking at the specific case of teaching English to speakers of other languages in an era of globalization.

Critical Discourse Analysis

The last three decades have seen an epistemological shift in the way scholars link language and ideology. The structuralist and positivistic view, which envisaged language as a mirroring device for depicting a pre-existing social world, has been surpassed (Blommaert, 1996; Fairclough, 1989; Watts, 2001). Milani (2008) explains that this shift urges scholars to

> carefully attend to two ideologically laden interrelated processes: (i) the ways in which language (or better, discourse) is itself a crucial component in shaping those social categories (e.g., ethnic or national identity) that had previously been taken as givens; and (ii) the ways in which the discursive construction of social reality is deeply embedded in the (re)production or contestation of power asymmetries and domination.
>
> *(p. 32)*

Critical Discourse Analysis (CDA) is one strand of research that stems from this shift in the beginning of the 1990s, and can be grouped with other critical social research on language. CDA uses social theory (such as the work of Foucault, Bourdieu, and Habermas) as a way to "deconstruct and make transparent relations of power that contribute to the (re)production of social inequalities between individuals in specific contexts" (Milani, 2008).

In tandem with critical social approaches to the study of language, CDA scholars set out to study the constitutive role of discourse in shaping relations of power, struggle, and conflict, and inequalities in various socio-political contexts. Generally speaking, critical discourse analysts are interested in answering questions that "presuppose a study of the relations between discourse, power, dominance, social inequality and the position of the discourse analyst in such social relationships" (van Dijk, 1993, p. 249). Because of the complexity of studying and critiquing social inequality, van Dijk advocates for a focused approach:

> The way we approach these questions and dimensions is by focusing on the role of discourse in the (re)production and challenge of dominance. Dominance is defined ... as the exercise of social power by elites, institutions or groups, that results in social inequality, including political, cultural, class, ethnic, racial and gender inequality.
>
> *(p. 250)*

CDA regards language as social practice (Fairclough & Wodak, 1997) and considers the context of language use to be essential (Wodak, 2000). At the same time, CDA scholars also consider how language as social practice is not equally accessible by all individuals. Thus, in doing CDA, van Dijk (1997) explains that discourse analysts assume a political stance:

> Beyond observation, systematic description and explanation, [they] decide to make one crucial further step, and see the discourse analytical enterprise also as a political and moral task of responsible scholars. They emphasize that it is not always possible, or desirable, to neatly distinguish between doing 'value-free' and technical political critique on the other. They will claim that one can no less study racist discourse without a moral position about racism than a medical researcher can study cancer or AIDS without taking a position about the devastating nature of such diseases, or a sociologist can study the uprising of exploited peasants without being aware of the nature of their oppression and the legitimacy of their resistance ... Critical scholars of discourse do not merely observe such linkages between discourse and societal structures, but aim to be agents of change, and do so in solidarity with those who need such change most.
>
> *(p. 23)*

In practice, CDA scholars will attempt to study various structures, strategies or other properties of text, talk, verbal interaction or communication events and their role in reproducing harmful social formations (van Dijk, 1993, p. 250). One important aspect of CDA is the way discourse is conceived "as a social phenomenon and seeks, consequently, to improve the social-theoretical foundations for practicing discourse analysis as well as for situating discourse in society" (Blommaert & Bulcaen, 2000, p. 451). In this respect, Ruth Wodak (1997) emphasizes how

> [CDA] studies real, and often extended, instances of social interaction which take (partially) linguistic form. The critical approach is distinctive in its view of (a) the relationship between language and society, and (b) the relationship between analysis and the practices analyzed.
>
> *(p. 173)*

As a critical discourse analyst, I regard the language used for teaching, learning, and policing English as a semiotic tool that could contribute to our understanding of the ideological role some educational discourses play in reproducing Western hegemony and the marginalization of the Other. Bearing in mind the active role of language in the mediation and creation of reality, linguistic communication is characterized by human ideological motivation and meaning-making (Grace, 1987; Kress, 1990). In particular, linguistic forms impose socio-cultural meanings on the things, people, or events they "represent" and often manipulate the way such meanings are perceived (Fowler, Hedge, Kress, & Trew, 1979). For Fairclough (1992), the combinations of certain signifiers (words) with certain signifieds (meanings) are ideologically motivated and may be linguistically manifested in vocabularies, phrase structures, or modalities, as in the contrasting combination "terrorist" and "freedom fighter" (p. 75). Ideological motivation is often also manifested in choosing to present a clause in the passive rather than the active voice as in "The boy was kicked out of school" as opposed to "The principal kicked the boy out of school." It is to such socio-political interpretations of linguistic forms in texts that I will now turn.

Text-Oriented Discourse Analysis

In an overview of how scholars from different disciplinary backgrounds have engaged in linguistic, semiotic, and discourse analysis, Ruth Wodak (1996a, 1996b) outlines a shared perspective in which the concepts of power, ideology, and history figure centrally. Wodak points to the reliance of discourse analysts on Hallidayan linguistics, and Bernsteinian sociolinguistics, and also on the work of literary critics and social philosophers (e.g. Foucault, Bakhtin, and Vološinov) to develop the field as a critical enterprise. The interdisciplinary nature of critical linguistic research, Wodak suggests, is necessitated by the complex and multifaceted relationships between language and society. Much of the existing literature on CDA – whether approached from a philosophical, sociological, or political perspective – has focused on both microlinguistic and macrolinguistic features, as well as discursive and contextual dimensions. However, most of the studies rely in some way on Hallidayan systemic functional grammar. In this respect, understanding Halliday's terms and approach to grammar and linguistic analysis is crucial for conducting CDA.

In this framework, the relationship between the grammatical system and the way language is required to serve social and personal needs is central. Halliday sees the form-meaning relationship as socially motivated in the sense that "language is as it is because of its function in social structure ... and that language that people have access to depends upon their position in the social system" (1973, p. 65). Regarding his views on grammar, a socially motivated approach is also offered, since he sees "the grammar of a language as systems of "options" amongst which speakers make "selections" according to social circumstances, assuming that formal options have contrasting meanings, and that choices of forms are always meaningful" (Fairclough, 1992, p. 26). Halliday identifies three different yet continuously intertwined meta-functions of language: (1) the ideational; (2) the interpersonal; and (3) the textual functions. The ideational function, through which language lends structure to experience, entails a dialectical relationship with the social structure, both influencing and shaping it. While the interpersonal function constitutes the way participants use language and the relationships between them; the textual function constitutes coherence and cohesion in texts. By combining functional systemic linguistics, argumentation theory, and rhetoric (Reisigl & Wodak, 2000; van Leeuwen & Wodak, 1999), critical discourse analysts have presented a contrastive – more constitutive – view to previous structuralist notions that are based on the premise that linguistic communication makes up reality. The notion that language makes up reality within the structuralist tradition originates with de Saussure (1959), for whom a sign is composed of an arbitrary combination of the signifier (sound/image) and the signified (meaning), and with Whorf (1956), for whom language itself is thought and culture. In social semiotics, however, meanings are created in signs or sign-complexes in distinct ways and in specific modes, which means that none is arbitrary (Kress, 1993). Furthermore, no sign should be treated as a pre-given, but as a product of the sign maker which is often motivated by individual interests, perspectives, values, and positions regarding the message conveyed, and the recipients of the message, precisely because signs are made to function in particular ways in communication (Kress, 1993). Discourse is thus an "ideological product" in the sense that

> Any ideological product is not only itself a part of a reality (natural or social), just as is any physical body, any instrument of production, or any product for consumption, it also, in contradistinction to these other phenomena, reflects and refracts another reality outside itself. Everything ideological possesses *meaning*: it represents, depicts, or stands for something lying outside itself. In other words, it is a *sign. Without a sign there is no ideology.*
> (Vološinov, [1973] 1986, p. 9; emphasis in original)

Suffice it to say here that conducting a systematic discourse analysis may be optimized by studying the use of various linguistic devices in EFL-related texts and their ideological roles in constructing learners' knowledge, shaping identities, and perpetuating/reproducing dominant ideologies. Advocating a critical approach to discourse analysis makes it clear that the choice of certain grammatical structures, lexical items, rhetorical techniques, types of discourse, and deictic words, among other discursive elements, constitutes levels of meaning-making that go beyond their semantic make-up, and consequently require examination.

The elements of EFL – the textbooks, the teaching/learning practices, and educational policy-making – therefore constitute EFL discourse. While my research embraces a myriad of methodological approaches to CDA, I will rely mainly on Fairclough's (1992) three-dimensional framework for conceiving of and analyzing discourse. His approach is drawn from Marxist-inspired linguistics (Bakhtin, 1981; Pêcheux, 1975), sociolinguistics (Labov, 1972), the ethnography of communication (Sinclair & Coulthard, 1975), systemic functional linguistics (Halliday, 1978), critical linguistics (Fowler et al., 1979; Kress & Hodge, 1979), and social theories of discourse (Foucault, 1972). As a textually oriented approach to discourse analysis, Blommaert and Bulcaen consider Fairclough's construct to be "the most elaborate and ambitious attempt toward theorizing the CDA program" (2000, p. 448). This approach brings together "linguistically-oriented discourse analysis and social and political thought relevant to discourse and language … specifically in the study of social change" (Fairclough, 1992, p. 62).

What is important to note is that my analysis of EFL discourse is not only linguistically focused, but also grounded in the context in which it arises, because context is always a cultural model or reference (van Dijk, 2008). In this respect, and in line with Fairclough's approach, I will also apply Gramsci's (1971) notion of "hegemony," and Althusser's ([1971] 2000) concepts of "ideological state apparatuses" and "interpellation" in order to identify processes of ideological reproductions, and how they are discursively achieved in modern educational discourses, specifically in EFL discourse. Subsequently, I illustrate how the use of these theories, and Fairclough's three-dimensional approach to discourse, establish the basis for identifying, disclosing, and criticizing the character of EFL discourse in Israel. I then show why this synergic model is not entirely sufficient on its own to reconstruct EFL pedagogy as a cultural discourse, and how a Cultural Discourse Studies approach might offer a complementary methodology for forging a transformative EFL discourse.

Fairclough's Three-Dimensional Approach

One of the central aims of CDA is to grasp, uncover, and identify ways of overcoming the abuse of power (Fairclough, Mulderrig, & Wodak, 2011; van Dijk, 2001). Drawing on the work of Foucault (1971; 1972; 2001), CDA scholars consider power relations to be discursive. In order to point out how the social abuse of power is discursively manifested, Fairclough privileges the text as the best place to start. In his version of CDA, the key point is to understand the text's nature, appreciate how it is embedded in discursive processes, and enable an analysis of discursive and social change on the basis of the text (Fairclough, 1992; 1995; 2001).

He regards the text from two perspectives. The first perspective enables us to view the text as the material produced by the language user, and not merely a constitution of distinct units of words and phrases. Concurrently, we may also understand the text as a product of a larger discursive process that is more extensive and involves wider social processes (Fairclough, 2001, p. 20). He and Ruth Wodak compare the text to the tip of an iceberg, as analysis requires understanding the discursive and structural processes that lie below this tip (Fairclough & Wodak, 1997). Within this theoretical framework, he analyzes communicative events while applying a trans-disciplinary, three-dimensional model that perceives discourse as text, discursive practice, and socio-cultural practice (Fairclough, 1992; 1995; 2001). I will discuss each of these elements in turn.

Discourse as Text

In analyzing texts, questions of form and meaning are central. According to the linguistic and semiotic terminology that was prevalent in the 1950s, words and texts are analyzed as "signs" in which the relationship between the "signified" (meaning) and the "signifier" (form) is arbitrary (see de Saussure, 1959). In contrast to the notion of the "arbitrary" nature of the sign, critical approaches to discourse analysis assert that signs are socially and ideologically motivated (Fairclough, 1992; 2003). In other words, producers of text are socially motivated to choose particular signifiers that pick out particular signifieds. Aside from a producer's ideological preference for using certain words over others, Fairclough also makes an important distinction between the meaning potential of a text, and its interpretation. He explains that

> texts are made up of forms which past discursive practice, condensed into conventions, and endowed with meaning potential. The meaning potential of a form is generally heterogeneous, a complex of diverse, overlapping and sometimes contradictory meanings, so that texts are usually highly ambivalent and open to multiple interpretations.
>
> *(Fairclough, 1992, p. 75)*

Bearing in mind this dependence of meaning on interpretation, Fairclough further suggests that we use *meaning* both to refer to the potentials of forms, and to the meanings endorsed in interpretation. He recommends dividing textual analysis into four main categories: (1) "vocabulary" (e.g., choice of lexical items); (2) "grammar" (e.g., transitivity, modality, etc.); (3) "cohesion" (e.g., conjunction, schemata); and (4) "text structure" (e.g., turn-taking system) (see pp. 73–78). Insofar as identifying different forms in a text is essential for doing discourse analysis, analysts often consider the clause or the simple sentence as an important grammatical component, since every clause has a certain function within the text and thus may carry a different meaning, or serve a different ideological purpose:

> Every clause is multifunctional, and so every clause is a combination of ideational, interpersonal (identity and relational), and textual meanings. People make choices about the design and structure of their clauses which amount to choices about how to signify (and construct) social identities, social relationships, and knowledge and belief.
>
> *(p. 76)*

Another factor that Fairclough (2003) recommends taking into consideration when analyzing texts is the ways in which a particular voice is situated in relation to others, and other discourses (or texts) in relation to other discourses (or texts), i.e. interdiscursivity, or intertextuality. He suggests that "orientation towards difference" is part of a power struggle within a text, and that "when the voice of another is incorporated into a text there are always choices about how to 'frame it', how to contextualize it, in terms of other parts of the text – about relations between report and authorial account" (p. 53). In this respect, texts may combine different orientations to difference, such as openness, acceptance, or recognition, and accentuate conflict, or a struggle over meaning, in various ways (see pp. 41–42, for a detailed discussion of orientation to difference). On the basis of these different orientations to difference, any designation of a particular orientation to a specific text is a matter of interpretation. Gulliver (2010) finds the orientation to difference in texts particularly interesting for studying how identities are constructed, and states that

> [a] low orientation to difference in texts works toward the construction of identities as stable, coherent, and knowable, whereas an openness to difference can foreground some of the heterogeneity of social positions and the competing and contesting possible identity claims that could be performed.
>
> *(pp. 729–730)*

Employing a systematic text-oriented approach to discourse analysis thus facilitates the examination of the ideological function of particular discursive devices in EFL texts. Specific textual choices may be identified by paying close attention to various linguistic practices, such as whether a clause is presented in the active or passive voice, or which lexical items, or deictic words, have been chosen. For example, analyzing the use of vocabulary in written or spoken texts in EFL textbooks, or learners' responses to the cultural content of EFL materials, can show whether learners construct positive narratives of Self, or negative Other-narratives. Texts might use vocabulary that indicates advancement, knowledge, progress, or initiatives to describe groups constituting the Self, as opposed to using vocabulary that indicates underdevelopment, traditionalism, limited knowledge, and passivity to describe groups constituting the Other. In this respect, it is important to examine how texts shape the construction of group identity based on the overarching principle of positively presenting the Self while negatively presenting the Other. In observing discourses on immigration and ethnic relations, for instance, van Dijk (2000) notes how these types of texts organize binary Us/Them pairs of in-groups and out-groups. This principle can be expanded into four possibilities that might form what he terms an "ideological square" (p. 44). Identifying the features of texts that emphasize or de-emphasize traits ascribed to particular social actors against this ideological square enables analysis of a number of strategies that can be observed in texts. The four sides of the ideological square work to do the following:

- Emphasize positive things about Us.
- Emphasize negative things about Them.
- De-emphasize negative things about Us.
- De-emphasize positive things about Them. *(p. 44)*

Applying the ideological square to EFL discourse, as I will show in Chapter 3 and Chapter 4, reveals how Self and Other narratives are constructed. The choice of constructing a phrase in the active or passive voice is also analyzed (mainly in analyzing cultural representations in EFL textbooks) regarding members belonging to the majority (Self) as opposed to members belonging to the minority (Other). If the active voice were selected to describe the former, this would frame them as active, independent, and initiating, whereas the passive voice as applied to the latter would characterize them as passive, dependent, and lacking in initiative (see Chapter 3 for examples).

In tandem with one of the main goals mentioned at the beginning of this book, i.e. to uncover West-centric and hegemonic dominance in EFL discourse, the discourse-as-text approach is essential if we are to understand how domination and social exclusion are (re)produced in state-controlled, mainstream educational texts. My contention is that students perceive educational texts as *resources* from which they learn how to construct and relate to the world as it is described in these texts. The overriding concern in conducting the first stage of my analysis is, then, to uncover how EFL discourse draws the map of the world with its pluralistic cultures for the community of EFL learners who perceive English as a global language. EFL texts thus function as discursive devices shaping the construction of different types of socio-cultural events, perpetuating but also possibly *changing* the content of knowledge concerning other people, or stances about other people, and, last but by no means least, contesting hegemonic discourses and effecting social, educational, and global/local change. To identify the social-constructivist role of such educational texts, let us examine EFL discourse as *discursive practice*.

Discourse as Discursive Practice

Analyzing discourse as discursive practice involves understanding discourse as something constructed, disseminated, and consumed in society. Fairclough (1992) emphasizes that "texts are produced in specific ways in specific social contexts ... and have variable outcomes of an extra-discursive as well as a discursive sort" (p. 79). Of special concern to this research is the power of texts to effect social realities, whether in perpetuating a certain status quo, or in changing people's attitudes, beliefs, and practices. Texts produced by government entities — such as the Israeli Ministry of Education, for example — are distributed across a range of communities irrespective of their ethnicity. Textbooks, particularly first and second/foreign language textbooks, expose students to discourses that align with national policies and in the contexts of globalization and Westernization. Van Dijk (2004) considers that textbooks present influential discourses, including racist and prejudiced discourses, which are shaped by and take part in the reproduction of dominant ideologies. In a similar vein, Suaysuwan and Kapitzke (2005) state that "students learn not only subject matter from textbooks, they also acquire values, interests, and knowledge that form desires, habits, and identities" (p. 79). Ndura (2004) also postulates that in classrooms for teaching English to speakers of other languages "instructional materials play the role of cultural mediators as they transmit overt and covert social values, assumptions, and images" (p. 143). It is thus "very important to examine the content, activities, and ideologies represented in textbooks" (Duff & Uchida, 1997, pp. 470–471) and their role in the reproduction of dominant ideologies (van Dijk, 2004).

In the context of EFL, textbooks often reproduce hegemonic discourses that reinforce nationalizing or globalizing agendas. English textbooks in Japan, for example, are entangled in the demand for schools to disseminate nationalizing and internationalizing discourses, and present national cultures as objective facts, often misrepresenting them, "reinforcing stereotypes and an us-and-them mentality" (Schneer, Ramanathan, & Morgan, 2007, p. 605). Canagarajah (1993) finds that an American-produced English textbook used in a Sri Lankan university assumed "an urbanized, technocratic, Western culture that is alien to the students" (p. 609) and promoted Western notions of consumerism, industry, and upward social mobility. This is done in subtly racist ways, as Canagarajah notes, despite being presented as value-neutral. Other scholars who studied EFL textbooks have identified authoritative discourses (Bakhtin 1981) (such as religious texts, authorized textbooks, etc.) relevant to the fields of education, economics, the environment, tourism, religion, social control, consumption, nationalism, gender roles, and everyday lifestyles (Awayed-Bishara, 2015; J. J. Chen, 2005; Lee, 2005; Liu, 2005; Ndura, 2004; Suaysuwan & Kapitzke, 2005).

In Chapter 1, I showed how schoolbooks in Israel may be perceived as a major channel for the transmission and reproduction of dominant ideologies. Approaching discourse as discursive practice must therefore entail paying attention to coherence and intertextuality while analyzing vocabulary, grammar, cohesion, and text structure as per the discourse-as-text approach. Fairclough's suggested three aspects (i.e. discourse as text, discursive practice, and socio-cultural practice) link the EFL texts used in English education in Israel to their social, political, cultural, and national contexts.

Discourse as Socio-cultural Practice

This analysis of EFL discourse entails an examination of the ideological effects and hegemonic processes of disseminating dominant ideas and values, and their role in reproducing and perpetuating West/Anglo-centric narratives, while disregarding others. Fairclough's later work suggests that "social practices can be thought of as ways of controlling the selection of certain structural possibilities and the exclusion of others" (2003, p. 23). Understanding discourse as a socio-political practice focuses on meaning-making as the site of a power struggle for contesting hegemonic practices. That is, discursive practices utilize conventions that naturalize certain power relations and ideologies, and the ways in which these conventions are articulated are themselves a focus of struggle (Fairclough, 1992).

This third dimension constitutes the basic point from which Fairclough constructs his approach to social change in the sense that discursive change indicates a struggle for hegemony. Discursive change is viewed from the angle of intertextuality. That is, "the way in which discourse is being represented, respoken, or rewritten sheds light on the emergence of new orders of discourse, struggles over normativity, attempts at control, and resistance against regimes of power" (Blommaert & Bulcaen, 2000, p. 449). Within this dimension of text-oriented analysis, hegemony is seen as concerning itself with "power that is achieved through constructing alliances and integrating classes and groups through consent" (Blommaert & Bulcaen, 2000), so that "the articulation and rearticulation of orders of discourse [are] correspondingly one stake in hegemonic struggle" (Fairclough, 1992, p. 93). In this respect, analysis of the way high school students respond to the cultural content of EFL texts (in Chapter 4) indicates how some students use recontextualization to reproduce dominant narratives of Self-superiority and Other-inferiority, on the one hand, while others use it to contest narratives of inequality and discrimination. I will discuss the use of discourse as socio-cultural practice more thoroughly when I analyze students' responses in Chapter 4.

It is my intention to examine whether school textbooks and language policy documents in Israel reflect the dominant ideology of mainstream groups. The discursive orientation of school textbooks potentially allows particular discourses of inequality and discrimination to prevail. As an alternative, I will argue that students should be given textual exposure that interpellates them as motivated agents who are able to question and eventually contest discourses of inequality and Anglo/West-centrism. Shi-xu (2005) notes that

> discourses of power are often in disguise and ... therefore they need special critical attention. That is, dominant speakers or writers may conceal or make natural power relations and power practices by, for example, appealing to objectivity, neutrality or authority ... That is, ideological discourses are those ways of speaking that render unequal power relations and practices as if they were non-existent, natural or to be taken for granted.
>
> *(p. 28)*

It is therefore necessary to maintain a critical perspective toward the ideological orientation of discourse, and its effects on the individual subject. Among the many ways in which knowledge, power, and discourse are intertwined (Foucault, 1980), I pinpoint the role that EFL discourse plays in *creating* EFL agents capable of effecting social change. The next section discusses how the language used to teach/learn English in Israel functions as an "ideological state apparatus" (Althusser, [1971] 2000), thereby contributing to the reproduction of hegemony (Gramsci, 1971).

EFL Discourse and the Interpellation of Subjects

In terms of my interest in opening up possible ways of interpreting modes of reproduction in EFL discourse and reconstructing discursive ways to contest its Anglo-centric hegemony, questions about how we do things with words and how words do things to us are essential. In post-structuralist inquiries about how we do things with words, discourse constitutes the "site where our subjectivities are formed and reality is produced" (Pennycook, 2004, p. 10). Note that the subject itself is produced in discourse. In his critique of the structures imposed by the disciplinary constraints of (applied) linguistics, Pennycook (2004) observes that *performativity theory* links language use to identity in a way that avoids essentialist categories, affirming that identities are not given, but rather constructed in their linguistic performance. Performativity is furthermore not merely a productive theoretical approach for studying the constitutive link between language and ethnicity/gender/race/etc.; "it can also be employed as a discourse analytical framework" (Milani, 2007, pp. 102–103). From a social constructionist point of view, the discursive constitution of the subject enables us to conceptualize the relationship between language and the social on the premise that this relationship is dynamic and non-static. In this respect, Judith Butler (1997) argues that language should not be viewed as "a static and closed system whose utterances are functionally secured in advance by the "social positions" to which they are mimetically related" (p. 145). Rather, Butler suggests asking what forms of performatives can be enacted by social actors who are differently positioned on the map of social power. More specifically, in asking how social transformation operates through linguistic use, we need to consider the possibility of subversive agency emerging not only from the powerful (see Bourdieu, 1989) but also from the marginal. The performative, then, as Butler concludes, is "not merely an act used by a pregiven subject, but is one of the powerful and insidious ways in which subjects are called into social being, inaugurated into sociality by a variety of diffuse and powerful interpellations" (1999, p. 125). This perspective considers discourse as fundamentally performative, while other theories (Austin, 1962; Searle, 1969) deal with sentences as decontextualized "speech acts." In other words, unlike some common notions that identity is something we have and is the *cause* or *origin* of our actions, performativity postulates that identity is something we do; it is the *effect* of specific semiotic (i.e. meaning-making) choices within particular constraints (Milani, in press). Performativity structures the discursive forms of our actions and communication with others; "it simultaneously enables and constrains us" (Milani, in press).

The question that henceforth stands at the core of this study is: How do the dominant ideologies prevalent in EFL discourse interpellate learners? More particularly: How does the EFL discourse shape the construction of its subjects' ideological stances when exposed to cultural contents? What modifications in EFL discourse are needed to enable its recipients to act as motivated agents to contest and overturn negative hegemonic ideologies?

The way to examine how EFL discourse in Israel functions as a means of reproduction of existing power inequalities, or as a spur to social change, is to some extent related to perceiving the acting person as an *individual*, a *subject*, or an *agent*. Understanding the differences among these ways of viewing human beings is important for the analysis of how textbooks, students' interpretations of EFL texts, and language policy documents reproduce mainstream ideologies and shape learners' ideological viewpoints. The notion of the *individual* has traditionally invoked an enlightened, modern Western person, who is viewed as free and rational. The Western individual is cohesive, having no inner contradictions, and is

> able to act upon his decisions, and take responsibility for these actions. He may listen to different suggestions, then apply his own scientific logic, and draw conclusions. In doing so, he makes contribution to the benefit of the human race.
> *(Kuzar, 2011, p. 224)*

It is mainly to this notion of the Western individual that I respond in Chapter 3. I problematize it, showing that through being subconsciously subjugated by the hegemonic ideologies of EFL textbooks, Jewish Israeli learners are exposed to ideological narratives that *contradict* the attempts to construct them as Western individuals. Rather, learners are summoned to subject positions of reproducing Anglo-centric and Zionist ideologies. As opposed to the free and rational individual, then, the subject – in psychological Freudian terms – "often acts in an irrational manner, driven by factors he [*sic*] has no control over. The subject may develop some self-awareness, but this ability is limited" (p. 226).

Being aware of the subconscious aspect of the subject, Althusser ([1971] 2000) postulates that ideology acts upon the subject similarly, namely, the subject is unaware of being activated ("interpellated") by ideology. In this Althusserian view of the subject, "the representation of a person as an individual in possession of free will and free choice is itself an effect of ideological interpellation" (Kuzar, 2011, p. 226). The interpellation of subjects is, therefore, the process that constitutes the person as an ideological subject and in which he/she is *summoned* by an authoritative ideology. Althusser terms these authoritative ideologies (such as the media, educational texts, textbooks, or religion) "ideological state apparatuses" that usually operate in harmony under a common ideology. Furthermore, subjects act in conformity with ideological state apparatuses without being aware that they are doing so. It is important to understand how these ideologies manage to interpellate subjects in modern Western states, where values of free will and choice produce notions of the individual as the source of reason and truth, and furthermore where centralized State control of the apparatuses is not assumed. Of specific concern to this volume is understanding how the ideological interpellation of modern Jewish Israelis operates. Kuzar suggests that in the modern Jewish nation,

> [the] common ... denominator includes the self-image of the Jewish collective as a modern nation getting built in the land of Israel, i.e. Zionism. If the dominant ideology is successful, and the messages Jewish Israelis receive are harmonious, they develop an ideological mixture based on what they share with the western world on one hand, and on their specific membership in the Zionist collective on the other.
> *(p. 226)*

Consumers of textbooks and curricula may be interpellated into subject positions aligned with specific ideologies, and participate in the process of reproducing dominant mainstream ideological discourses. In such a discourse, an "inner voice" in the text addresses readers/learners, continuously informing them what type of intergroup relations to formulate (i.e. with the "in" or "out" group), what knowledge to construct, and what values or images about the Self/Other to accept or perpetuate. This could be done, for example, through presenting "Us" in a positive and progressive manner (for example, the right of Westerners to choose whom to marry) and "Them" in a negative and less-progressive manner (for example, arranged marriages in traditional groups, such as Bedouin society). The choice of clause type may also convey to the learner what ideas about people to form, for example, by using the active voice to positively represent an assertive, initiating character and the passive voice to represent a less positive, dependent one. It follows that if students repeatedly read a narrative about the essential role of army service in achieving success in one's future, they will internalize an underlying value that favors those who serve in the army, as opposed to those who do not (see Chapter 3 and Chapter 4 for examples). Through this ideological process of interpellation, students may carry these values with them into their everyday encounters outside the classroom, thus contributing to the reproduction of these values and others propounded in textbooks. In fact, while interviewing Jewish EFL learners (see Chapter 4), not only does one respondent display an unfavorable attitude toward citizens who do not serve in the Israeli army, but he also states that he considers this to be "retarded" behavior. The emergence of such ideological stances forms an important critical aspect of EFL discourse analysis in which discourse as a whole is seen as a regulating body that forms consciousness (Jäger, 2001). Jäger notes that "by functioning as the 'flow of "knowledge" – and/or the whole of stored societal knowledge – through all time' discourse creates the conditions for the formation of subjects and the structuring and shaping of societies" (p. 36).

These perspectives of interviewees cannot, however, always illuminate situations in which the interpellated subject encounters ideologically conflicted or controversial texts. Such exposure may awaken in them an inner voice of logic urging action against textual ideologies of inequality, discrimination, or a denial of the Other. From this it follows that this inner voice of logic is an active facet of the individual, as Jäger explains:

> The acting individual is absolutely involved when we talk about the realization of power relations (practice). It thinks, plans, constructs, interacts and fabricates. As such it also faces the problem of having to prevail, i.e. to get its own way, to find its place in society. However, it does this in the frame of the rampant growth of the network of discursive relations and arguments, in the context of 'living discourses' as long as it brings them to life, lives 'knitted into' them and contributes to their change.
>
> *(p. 39)*

While interviewing EFL learners, some Hebrew and Arabic speakers did – in fact – display their discontent with and rejection of some of the material that is found in the English texts they read. For example, some Hebrew and Arabic speakers criticized a text that specified that a teenage dropout from Britain was "black," but did not indicate that a white teenage dropout in a juxtaposed text was "white." Against this backdrop, I contemplate that a transformative EFL pedagogy must offer discursive strategies that teachers should utilize to promote their learners' criticality, and increase their sense of social justice while reading narratives about other people and other cultures.

It stands to reason, then, that viewing the person as a completely determined subject is problematic, as this view might undermine and overlook the constitutive and diverse potential of some individuals to take a subversive stance against dominant ideology. It also "understates the capacity of subjects to act individually or collectively as agents, including engagement in critique of, and opposition to, ideological practices" (Fairclough, 1992, p. 91). Van Dijk (2006) describes this tendency in theorizing subjectivity as a form of discursive manipulation, explaining that "manipulation will generally focus on social cognition, and hence on groups of people, rather than on individuals and their unique personal models" (p. 360). For him,

> manipulation not only involves power, but specifically *abuse of power*, that is, *domination*. That is, manipulation implies the exercise of a form of *illegitimate* influence by means of discourse: manipulators make others believe or do things that are in the interest of the manipulator, and against the best interests of the manipulated.
>
> *(Van Dijk, 2006; emphasis in original)*

By negatively presenting the way that groups of people think, speak, or behave, texts affect the perceived value of particular cultures, which opens up the possibility, as Shi-xu (2005) cautions, of perpetuating imperialist ideological discourses. These discourses can be conceptualized "as the ways of speaking and thinking that demean, dominate and discriminate against other groups and communities on the basis of 'race', color, ethnicity, nation and tradition, and yet render those repressive practices imperceptible through common sense" (p. 95). In other words, stereotypical representations are linguistically constructed in texts in a way that feels natural and harmless. For instance, the description of the constant desire of Westerners to visit Third World countries and offer health and educational services is often produced in EFL textbooks in an Orientalist (Said, 1978) manner where "we" (i.e. Westerners) are the good-hearted, always ready to jump to the rescue of "them" (i.e. non-westerners) who are underdeveloped, poor, and dependent (Awayed-Bishara, 2018). By critiquing the ideological line these types of narratives pursue, I do not mean to devalue the sincere endeavors of some Westerners, nor their contribution to advancing the situation of some Third World countries. Rather, my critique is of the way these narratives dominate the cultural representation of the Other in EFL textbooks in a way that denies learners the opportunities to learn about the *unique* and *inviolable value* of people from different cultures so they are also enabled to learn from other people's wisdom, cultural practices, and lifestyles. Presenting Western and non-Western cultures in an "Us-Them" binary where "We" are always one or more steps ahead of "Them" constitutes an ideological imperialist EFL discourse. This must be contested, bearing in mind how

> [cultural] imperialist discourse may conceal its hegemonic intent through indirect speech acts, for example. It may manipulate perception by keeping silence about certain topics or silencing alternative versions. It may perpetuate the same negative story about other cultures through repetition, fantasy, cliché or 'They are all always like that'. It may hierarchize and totalize knowledge by rhetorical ploys of 'integration', 'systematization' and universalization of cultural knowledge on the one hand and of exclusion of alternative forms of knowledge on the other hand, creating consequently an asymmetrical relation between this dominant discourse and other marginalized or silenced discourses.
>
> (Shi-xu, 2005, p. 95)

To offer ways of contesting such ideological discourses, we need to consider the individual subject as a whole. That is, the active counterpart of the interpellated subject is an agent, who is "endowed with a logic that is not fully predictable and can be creative, in which case it may be subversive" (Kuzar, 2011, p. 228). The subject and the agent are not independent sides of a person, but rather form a complementary whole. In order to activate the agentive aspect of the interpellated subject, we need to offer them ideological challenges that may cause subversive thinking, sometimes directly opposed to mainstream thought. With regard to the wide-ranging possibilities of achieving agency, Kuzar asserts that "what is fascinating about the logical mechanisms is the fact that they are generative and creative, and might therefore yield surprising and unexpected conclusions, even when fed with old input, let alone if the input is new." An ideological challenge inspiring creativity could present itself in school textbooks which offered an alternative narrative (as opposed to the previously described one) that focuses on individual resourcefulness rather than on political distinctions (such as army service). Through reading such alternative texts, individuals would be able to acknowledge and implement principles that should govern human relations (i.e. judging people on individual merit) and as a result might change their ideas and attitudes regarding others.

While trying to offer an alternative culturally minded discursive path for coining a transformative EFL pedagogy, which I will elaborate on in Chapter 6, I hold the view that people are affected by discursive practices against which they struggle in order to transform social conventions. This view is related to Vološinov's ([1973] 1986) notion of the linguistic sign as being an arena for social struggle, which becomes a struggle over meaning. To struggle over controversial meanings offered in school textbooks and policy documents implies that individuals ought to be subversive and to critically examine the linguistic signs they encounter in such texts. In order to activate this agentive facet of the subject, textbook designers and

EFL teachers should choose their materials with a more critical eye; bearing in mind that "the more creative the agent becomes in applying his logic, the better the chance for him to become subversive, hence doubting and challenging the premises of his native ideology" (Kuzar, 2011, p. 228). My position is also inspired by de Certeau's (1984) postulation that language can be used both to reproduce and preserve social conventions, but that it can also effect social change. As a tool, language might serve to set in motion particular types of social processes that should be examined within a community of practice and discourse. For, as Barker and Galasiński (2001, p. 47) have argued:

> [Change] is possible because we are unique inter-discursive individuals about whom it is possible to say that we can 're-articulate' ourselves, recreate ourselves anew in unique ways by making new languages … In so far as this applies to individuals, so it applies also to social formations. Social change becomes possible through rethinking the articulation of the elements of 'societies,' of redescribing the social order and possibilities for the future.

I argue that those involved in English education in Israel (and elsewhere) must take serious steps to change the status quo in which ethnolinguistic minorities (such as Palestinians in Israel) are denied equal educational and multilingual opportunities. Following the recent passing of the Jewish Nation State Law that defines Israel as the homeland for the Jewish people only, I am well aware of the skeptical voices regarding any idea of change that might be initiated for the benefit of the Palestinians in Israel. Having myself been conflicted with such an inner voice that keeps echoing in my head since then, I realize that for the stakeholders in the settler colonial Jewish state, granting equal educational and linguistic opportunities to the Palestinian minority is not a priority.

In this sense, I do not see any room for hope that the current state officials might initiate a change of discriminatory realities as a top-down practice. Against this backdrop, when I address "those involved in EFL education," I mainly address teachers, learners, parents, social and human rights activists, and all those who are sincerely concerned with combating deliberate policies of colonization, domination, discrimination, and denying equality. Together, those I have just mentioned could form a grassroots, bottom-up foundation for contesting discriminatory and racist discourses, particularly educational and EFL discourses, such that they may eventually effect social change and justice. If all of us are creative and determined enough, we might even offer viable alternatives to current materials, textbooks, and cultural contexts in order to refuse to let go of ourselves as human beings, despite this being incommensurable with the settler colonialist forces directly and overtly working against us. For that, people involved in the teaching of English to speakers of other languages must, now more than ever, be aware of how the Self and the Other are constructed in their discourse. Accepting that English might be the most commonly spoken language in the globe should render the speaking of English an arena for all people to use it on equal grounds, so as to make their voices heard and appreciated. Bringing about social transformation through the reconstruction of EFL pedagogies thus entails a greater emphasis on ethics and human agency (Foucault, 1986; 1987). In this way, similar to how "habitus" has a "transformative capacity" (Bourdieu & Wacquant, 1992; May, 1996), discourse is also "equipped with the intrinsic capacity or spirit to free itself from its past towards a 'better' future" (Shi-xu, 2005, p. 33).

This brings me to the last, but by no means the least, essential component of the theoretical framework. Having explored the useful tools of CDA for uncovering Anglo-centrism and inequalities in EFL discourse, I now present a culturally oriented approach to discourse that both complements CDA, and provides additional tools for reconstructing EFL discourse as a cultural practice in the service of promoting a cultural politics of human prosperity, critical global awareness, and social justice.

Cultural Discourse Studies: A Cultural Approach to EFL Discourse

CDA studies conventionally use three indispensable concepts: power, history, and ideology. Despite its concerns with relations of power and inequality in language, CDA has often neglected the concept of culture. Gavriely-Nuri (2016) suggests that CDA frameworks have mainly focused on exposing manipulative and repressive discursive strategies that perpetuate abuse of power and domination, while overlooking the importance of constructing theoretical and methodological frameworks "which can aid in the identification and defense of honest and positive types of discourse" (p. 16). In her view, the complexity surrounding the term "culture" and the fact that most CDA practitioners are linguists might weaken the link between "discourse" and "culture" and thus generate the necessity for a cultural approach in complementing the CDA program. In this regard, a cultural approach to critical discourse analysis,

> offers a way to enrich the on-going conversation on the encounter between culture/discourse in general and the triangle discourse/culture/critical analysis in particular, not only by focusing on a specific national culture but, first and foremost, by referring to culture as a discursive mechanism.
>
> *(p. 31)*

In this respect, a growing culturally critical and constructive scholarship is directed at challenging West/White-centric, colonialist discourse, on the one hand, and, on the other, at promoting the principles of pluralistic research of the particularities, diversities, and unique aspects of the discourses of the peoples of Asia, Africa, Latin America, and other diasporic and indigenous cultures (Awayed-Bishara, 2018; Briscoe, Arriaza, & Henze, 2009; Carey, 1992; G.-M. Chen, 2004; Collier, 2000; Gavriely-Nuri, 2010; Gumperz & Levinson, 1996; Heisey, 2000; Kincaid, 1987; Kramsch, 1998; Mignolo, 1993; Miike, 2009; Pardo, 2010; Pennycook, 1998; Prah, 2010; Scollo, 2011; Shen, 2001; Shi-xu, 2005; 2009; 2012). Critical recognition in CDA itself has also been directed at the importance of taking a cultural, or multicultural, stance on studying different forms of discourses. In this respect, van Dijk (2001, pp. 95–96) gives an account from his long experience as a leading scholar in CDA and states:

> In my many years of experience as editor of several international journals, I have found that contributions that imitate and follow some great master are seldom original. Without being eclectic, good scholarship, and especially good CDA, should integrate the best work of many people, famous or not, from different disciplines, countries, cultures and directions of research. In other words, CDA should be essentially diverse and multidisciplinary.

What tends to weaken the CDA enterprise, in my view, is its set of distinctively Western values, terms, and ideas, albeit mobilized for the purposes of promoting social justice against the backdrop of specifically Western hegemonic forces. Specifically, international scholarship in the realm of social sciences in general and discourse studies in particular tends to be mainly Western, and to offer a universal image of discourses which are "not culturally neutral but themselves saturated with power and imbalance" (Shi-xu, 2005, p. 89). Despite the moral stance most CDA practitioners demonstrate as agents of social change, non-Western ideological paradigms do not seem to be influential in the theoretical architecting of the CDA program.

Non-White, non-Western, and Third World discourses and their cultural realities and experiences are often discredited, ignored, or disregarded in dominant Western cultural production through demeaning metaphors, narratives, and stereotypes (Spivak, 1988). In critiquing the dominance of Western ideologies in shaping theories of language in various academic contexts, Shi-xu (2005, p. 5) postulates that "on the one hand, the current theory of language, communication and discourse at an international level is largely western in perspective, whereby relevant concepts from non-western and Third World countries are vitally excluded." On the other hand, Western philologists and linguists have offered a long intellectual tradition in the study of the diversity of human languages whereby language is treated as varying in form and function from culture to culture, grounding the notion of so-called "linguistic relativity" (Sapir, 1949; von Humboldt, 1988; Whorf, 1956). These scholars propose that different people speak differently because they think differently, and that the reason for their different ways of thinking is because their languages offer them specific ways for describing the world around them (hence the notion of linguistic relativity). What I take as given in this volume, following Shi-xu (2005) and Butler (1992), is that cultural differences are instead at heart of power differences and thus, culture is a site for power struggle which becomes a culturally discursive struggle. The question is: How do we situate culture in the dynamic yet unbalanced power relations dominating the cultural politics of EFL discourse?

Situating Culture Within the Critical Study of EFL Discourse

Interest in the study of the cultural characteristics of national languages and their speakers coincided with the revival of nationalism in countries such as Germany and France. The Romantic notion that language is inseparable from culture was notably advanced by German scholars, such as Johann Herder (1744–1803) and Wilhelm von Humboldt (1762–1835), largely in reaction to the French military and political hegemony of the time. Against this backdrop, scholars started to pay attention to the diversity of the world's languages and cultures, a notion that was soon picked up in the United States by the linguist Franz Boas (1858–1942) and subsequently by Edward Sapir and his pupil Benjamin Lee Whorf (1884–1941). Studies in North America mainly focused on American Indian languages, and elaborated Whorf's views on the interconnectedness of language and thought, which later became framed as the "Sapir-Whorf Hypothesis." Kramsch (1998) notes that the Sapir-Whorf hypothesis encountered fierce controversy soon after Whorf formulated it in 1940, mainly on the basis of Whorf's claims that the linguistic structures in certain languages constrain what people can think or perceive. The implications of this claim in the positivistic climate of the time forced scholars to reject it "because it directly made the universal validity of scientific discoveries contingent upon the language in which they are expressed, [and so] it encountered the immediate scorn of the scientific community" (p. 12). Influenced by the structuralist thinking of the time, the link between a linguistic structure and a given cultural view had to be perceived as arbitrary. Henceforth, while a strong version of Whorf's claims that language determines its speakers' thoughts cannot possibly be accepted, a weaker version "supported by the findings that there are cultural differences in the semantic associations evoked by seemingly common concepts, is generally accepted" (p. 13). The saliency of discussing Whorf's claims on the indissociability of language and culture is not meant to reopen discussions on this link. Rather, that language and culture are closely connected compels us to identify the cultural context (e.g., of EFL users/themes/values/etc.) as essential complements to the meanings encoded in language. So what is it, then, about this "Western" interest in the diversity of human languages and cultures that makes it questionable when discussing the role English plays as the global language within "non-Western" contexts?

Regardless of how fascinated European and American scholars might be with the diversity of the world's languages and cultures, the overriding perspectives on the differences between Indo-European languages and cultures often reflect a binary distinction between the Indo-European or Western and a distinctive term of reference to the Other such as Non-European, Non-Western, Orientalist, Semitic, African, Asian, or American-Indian, etc. These binaries are frequently created through an ethnocentric – mainly Western-centric – set of conceptualized norms and values that tend to universalize human linguistic and social practices. Terms coined in the West such as "human rights," "democracy," "equality," or "freedom," for instance, are deployed, as Shi-xu (2012, p. 484) argues, as if they were universal, adjudicating the discourses of other cultural communities, governments or institutions [while overlooking] questions of whether there might be culturally different concepts and criteria of 'discourse', culturally divergent forms of discursive practice and local practical needs for discourse research.

From this it follows that despite being envisaged as a broad international project for combating ethnocentric and hegemonic forces of dominance and inequality, it might be useful to consider nuanced theoretical options for situating CDA adjacent to locally grounded paradigms that reflexively accentuate different non-Western cultural discourses. To offer alternative cultural discourses that may contest current, hegemonic EFL discourses that reproduce dominant ideas of native speakerism (Holliday, 2013; see also Chapter 1), Anglo-centrism, Self-Other distinctions, etc., we need to use a locally minded paradigm. A locally minded paradigm not only identifies different cultural values and norms that a non-Western group of learners have as part of their socio-linguistic repertoire. It also uses the cultural particularities of non-Western groups to coin alternative forms and practices for constructing a holistic, socially inclusive, and egalitarian EFL discourse. In the field of foreign language education, particularly English as a global/foreign language, there is a need to shift the goal "away from its focus on the development of native-speaker competence towards more realistic competencies to facilitate communication between speakers from a wide range of cultural backgrounds" (Sharifian, 2013, p. 2). Sharifian further notes that more than 80 percent of communication in English in the world is currently between the so-called "non-native" speakers of the language while Graddol asserts that "an inexorable trend in the use of global English is that fewer interactions now involve a native-speaker" (2006, p. 87). That said, research paradigms for studying the linguistic, cultural, or socio-political practices of users of English globally must by no means continue to be dominated by native-speaker models of American or British English. Rather, research in EFL education must be launched from a *local* point of departure through the lenses of professional scholars and experts who are capable of interpreting and applying locally oriented, and at the same time globally minded, forms of practices that might promote true intercultural competence. It is to these non-Western academic endeavors that the strand of discourse studies under the heading of Cultural Discourse Studies (CDS) directs itself. CDS is seen as

> [a] broad international project to create and practice a form of discourse research that is locally grounded (viz. exhibiting cultural identity and usefulness) and globally minded (viz. capable of engaging in international dialogue and showing global, human concerns). The argument will revolve round (a) the oft obscured cultural nature of discourse scholarship; (b) the actual cultural diversity and division of human discourses; and (c) the achievements, resources and conditions favorable for the construction of CDS.
>
> *(Shi-xu, 2012, p. 485)*

My goal in using CDS to reconstruct EFL pedagogy as a cultural discourse (see Chapter 6) is to enable different communities of practice to transform their discourses from mutual antagonism and often segregation (e.g., the opposing communities in the Israeli EFL context) to discourses of coexistence and collaboration. To this end, Shi-xu underscores some common principles explicitly required for the construction and practice of CDS models:

1. Be locally grounded with regard to culture-specific needs and perspectives.
2. Be globally minded with regard to culturally diverse perspectives and human concerns (especially coexistence, common prosperity, knowledge innovation).
3. Be susceptible to communicating with relevant international scholarly traditions in terms of concepts, theory, methods, terminology, etc.

The central task of this chapter so far has been to lay out the methodological and theoretical principles underlying the design of my research into the complexities of teaching English to speakers of other languages in its current Anglocentric and hegemonic context, and the reconstruction of EFL discourse in the service of a cultural politics of coexistence and common cultural prosperity that might challenge dominant hegemonic forces. I first explored the use of CDA as a tool in the critical analysis of EFL discourse and now I show how the methodological tools of CDS enable the other central task of this volume, namely, the task of reconstructing the EFL discourse.

In agreement with the methodological perspectives of both CDA and CDS, my goal as a researcher is to scrutinize processes of ideological domination in EFL educational discourses, and uncover discourses of cultural difference and discrimination. From a CDS perspective, I take an interventionist approach, and advocate for research that is oriented to transformative discourses, acting as a "compassionate, dialogical and critical researcher, while the researched is treated as [a] speaking agent, to be questioned, listened to and understood" (Shi-xu, 2012, p. 495). The reconstruction of EFL pedagogy as cultural discourse, then, must attempt to construct what Bhabha (1994, p. 57) describes as the "modes of political and cultural agency that are commensurable with historical conjunctures where populations are culturally diverse, racially and ethnically divided – the objects of social, racial, and sexual discrimination." From this it follows, then, that applying these two modes of research while studying EFL discourse brings together CDA and CDS in a coordinated, non-interrupted manner and constitutes methodological strategies that Shi-xu (2005) terms "political ethnography." In doing political ethnography scholars use two concrete strategies to conduct discourse research with cultural and political objectives that are both deconstructive and transformative:

> The first, termed 'deconstructive', directs researchers' attention to past and present discourses of cultural difference and discrimination and helps the researchers to undermine them through various discourse analytic

techniques. The second, named 'transformative', orients to potential, future discourses and suggests ways of initiating and advocating discourses of cultural harmony and prosperity.

(p. 73)

Globalization, international travel, and international academic programs are factors that play an influential role in shaping the academic identities of young discourse scholars from developing and non-Western countries, who experience Western cultures first-hand, while also practicing their own non-Western cultural norms. These scholars have the essential qualities and skills to construct culturally critical and innovative, or in-between-cultural (Shi-xu, 2005) concepts and perspectives. Shi-xu (2012, p. 493) underscores the saliency of the in-between cultural stance approach as he realizes that

> now there are increased and enhanced facilities and mechanisms for intercultural exchange, dialogue, and critique as well as collaboration, for example: international travel, the Internet, publications, translations, conferences, workshops, and international teaching and research programs. Given the new conditions and potentials for cross-cultural learning and critiquing, it would be reasonable to expect that there will be many more students of discourse research who become champions of multicultural scholarship.

Studying culturally diverse discourses through the critical lenses of both Western and non-Western scholars allows, then, for a scientific construction of culturally pluralistic and balanced knowledge that increases the chances of producing more egalitarian and socially just discourses. Applying the in-between cultural stance approach in reconstructing EFL cultural discourses requires paying close attention not only to the local context, which includes concerns about the researched (Blommaert, 1997), but also to the global context, which includes personal experiences and (multi)cultural insights (Bloor, 1978; Cappella, 1991). The in-between cultural stance is also a pragmatic approach, as it promotes the use of research strategies to accomplish the goals of cultural politics while integrating Western and non-Western concepts and issues. Concomitantly, "appropriate nonwestern methods are drawn upon as well, all for the sake of intercultural and international cohesion, communication and cooperation" (Shi-xu, 2005, p. 88). As Barker and Galasiński (2001, p. 46) suggest, cultural discourse researchers should produce knowledge, not as "a matter of getting a true or objective picture of reality," but as one of "creating tools with which to cope with the world." They illustrate this pragmatic approach and explain that

> since discourses of freedom and discourses of determination are socially produced for different purposes in different realms it makes sense to talk about freedom from political persecution or economic scarcity without the need to

say that agents are free in some metaphysical and 'underdetermined' way. Rather, such discourses are comparing different social formations and determinations and judging one to be better than another on the basis of our socially determined values.

(p. 47)

To conclude this section and schematize how the cultural approach to discourse proposed above (i.e. CDS) complements the critical approach to studying EFL discourse (i.e. CDA), I present Shi-xu's (2005, p. 88) three reasons for favoring the in-between cultural approach, which I rely on while reconstructing EFL pedagogy as cultural practice:

1. Help identify and challenge discourses of cultural imperialism in ordinary and professional life.
2. Focus research on the discourses of the subaltern or the disadvantaged in order to help them.
3. Help formulate and advocate discourses of cultural cohesion and prosperity.

While CDA functions as the diagnostic tool for identifying Anglo-centrism and cultural hegemony in EFL discourse, CDS serves to create an alternative EFL discourse that brings the West and the Rest into a pluralistic and multicultural dialogue with one other, thereby creating the conditions for transformation and social change.

In Chapter 3, Chapter 4, and Chapter 5, I will use methodologies drawn from CDA to critically analyze in turn EFL textbooks in Israel, students' responses to the cultural content of EFL texts and narratives, and policy documents and interviews with writers of EFL textbooks in Israel. Based on the theoretical framework offered in this chapter, I will provide a detailed methodological toolkit at the onset of each analytical chapter to link the analysis to its situated context. In Chapter 6, I will situate CDS methodologies within the framework of foreign language scholarship so as to offer a holistic, culturally critical model for reconstructing a transformative EFL pedagogy as cultural discourse. I will show that reclaiming non-Western voices in producing EFL cultural discourses, and increasing students' agency and reflexivity in EFL educational programs, might promote *global cultural consciousness, intercultural citizenship* (Byram, 2008; 2011; Kumaravadivelu, 2008; Risager, 2007), and *global citizenship*. Before doing so, it is important to start with an analysis of the ideological features of the current EFL discourse in Israel, which is the work of Chapter 3.

References

Althusser, L. ([1971] 2000). Ideology interpellates individuals as subjects. In P. Du Gay, J. Evans, & P. Redman (Eds.), *Identity: A reader* (pp. 31–38). London: SAGE Publications.

Austin, J. L. (1962). *How to do things with words: The William James lectures delivered at Harvard University in 1955.* Cambridge, MA: Harvard University Press.

Awayed-Bishara, M. (2015). Analyzing the cultural content of materials used for teaching English to high school speakers of Arabic in Israel. *Discourse & Society*, 26(5), 517–542. doi:26376399.

Awayed-Bishara, M. (2018). EFL discourse as cultural practice. *Journal of Multicultural Discourses*, 13(3), 243–258. doi:10.1080/17447143.2017.1379528.

Bakhtin, M. M. (1981). *The dialogic imagination: Four essays*. (C. Emerson & M. Holquist, Trans.). Austin, TX: University of Texas Press.

Barker, C., & Galasiński, D. (2001). *Cultural studies and discourse analysis: A dialogue on language and identity*. London: SAGE Publications.

Bhabha, H. K. (1994). *The location of culture*. New York: Routledge.

Blommaert, J. (1996). Language planning as a discourse on language and society: The linguistic ideology of a scholarly tradition. *Language Problems and Language Planning*, 20(3), 199–222. doi:10.1075/lplp.20.3.01blo.

Blommaert, J. (1997). Whose background? Comments on a discourse-analytic reconstruction of the Warsaw Uprising. *Pragmatics*, 7(1), 69–81.

Blommaert, J., & Bulcaen, C. (2000). Critical discourse analysis. *Annual Review of Anthropology*, 29(1), 447–466.

Bloor, M. (1978). On the analysis of observational data: A discussion of the worth and uses of inductive techniques and respondent validation. *Sociology*, 12(3), 545–552. doi:10.1177%2F003803857801200307.

Bourdieu, P. (1989). Social space and symbolic power. *Sociological Theory*, 7(1), 14. doi:10.2307/202060.

Bourdieu, P., & Wacquant, L. J. D. (1992). *An invitation to reflexive sociology*. Cambridge: Polity Press.

Briscoe, F., Arriaza, G., & Henze, R. C. (2009). *The power of talk: How words change our lives*. Thousand Oaks, CA: Corwin Press.

Butler, J. (1992). Contingent foundations: Feminism and the question of 'postmodernism.' In J. Butler & J. W. Scott (Eds.), *Feminists theorize the political* (pp. 3–21). New York: Routledge.

Butler, J. (1997). *Excitable speech: A politics of the performative*. New York: Routledge.

Butler, J. (1999). Performativity's social magic. In R. Shusterman (Ed.), *Bourdieu: A critical reader* (pp. 113–128). Oxford: Blackwell Publishers.

Byram, M. S. (2008). *From foreign language education to education for intercultural citizenship: Essays and reflections*. Clevedon: Multilingual Matters.

Byram, M. S. (2011). Intercultural citizenship from an international perspective. *Journal of the NUS Teaching Academy*, 1(1), 10–20.

Canagarajah, A. S. (1993). Critical ethnography of a Sri Lankan classroom: Ambiguities in student opposition to reproduction through ESOL. *TESOL Quarterly*, 27(4), 601–626. doi:10.2307/3587398.

Cappella, J. N. (1991). Mutual adaptation and relativity of measurement. In B. M. Montgomery & S. Duck (Eds.), *Studying interpersonal interaction* (pp. 325–342). New York: Wiley.

Carey, J. W. (1992). *Communication as culture: Essays on media and society*. New York, NY: Routledge.

Chen, G.-M. (2004). The two faces of Chinese communication. *Human Communication*, 7, 25–36.

Chen, J. J. (2005). Official knowledge and hegemony: The politics of the textbook deregulation policy in Taiwan. In Y. Nozaki, R. Openshaw, & A. Luke (Eds.), *Struggles over difference: Curriculum, texts, and pedagogy in the Asia-Pacific* (pp. 59–77). Albany, NY: State University of New York Press.

Collier, M. J. (Ed.). (2000). *Constituting cultural difference through discourse*. Thousand Oaks, CA: SAGE Publications.
de Certeau, M. (1984). *The practice of everyday life*. (S. Rendall, Trans.). Berkeley, CA: University of California Press.
de Saussure, F. (1959). *Course in general linguistics*. New York: Philosophical Library.
Derrida, J. (1978). *Writing and difference*. (A. Bass, Trans.). Chicago: University of Chicago Press.
Duff, P. A., & Uchida, Y. (1997). The negotiation of teachers' sociocultural identities and practices in postsecondary EFL classrooms. *TESOL Quarterly*, 31(3), 451–486. doi:10.2307/3587834.
Fairclough, N. (1989). *Language and power*. London: Longman.
Fairclough, N. (1992). *Discourse and social change*. Cambridge: Polity Press.
Fairclough, N. (1995). *Critical discourse analysis: The critical study of language*. Boston, MA: Addison Wesley.
Fairclough, N. (2001). *Language and power* (2nd ed.). London: Longman.
Fairclough, N. (2003). *Analysing discourse: Textual analysis for social research*. London: Routledge.
Fairclough, N., Mulderrig, J., & Wodak, R. (2011). Critical discourse analysis. In T. A. van Dijk (Ed.), *Discourse studies: A multidisciplinary introduction*, vol. 2: *Discourse as social interaction* (2nd ed., pp. 357–378). London: SAGE Publications.
Fairclough, N., & Wodak, R. (1997). Critical discourse analysis. In T. A. van Dijk (Ed.), *Discourse studies: A multidisciplinary introduction*, vol. 2: *Discourse as social interaction* (pp. 258–284). London: SAGE Publications.
Foucault, M. (1971). *L'ordre du discours*. Paris: Gallimard.
Foucault, M. (1972). *The archaeology of knowledge and the discourse on language*. (A. M. Sheridan Smith, Trans.). New York: Pantheon Books.
Foucault, M. (1980). *Power/knowledge: Selected interviews and other writings, 1972–1977*. (C. Gordon, Ed.). New York: Pantheon Books.
Foucault, M. (1986). *The history of sexuality*, vol. 2: *The use of pleasure* (R. Hurley, Trans.). London: Penguin Books.
Foucault, M. (1987). *The history of sexuality*, vol. 3: *The care of the self* (R. Hurley, Trans.). London: Penguin Books.
Foucault, M. (2001). *Fearless speech*. (J. Pearson, Trans.). Los Angeles, CA: Semiotext(e).
Fowler, R., Hedge, B., Kress, G., & Trew, T. (1979). *Language and control*. London: Routledge & Kegan Paul.
Gavriely-Nuri, D. (2010). The idiosyncratic language of Israeli 'peace': A cultural approach to critical discourse analysis (CCDA) . *Discourse & Society*, 21(5), 565–585. doi:10.1177/0957926510375934.
Gavriely-Nuri, D. (2016). *Israeli peace discourse: A cultural approach to CDA*. Amsterdam: John Benjamins.
Grace, G. W. (1987). *The linguistic construction of reality*. London: Croom Helm.
Graddol, D. (2006). English next: Why global English may mean the end of "English as a Foreign Language."London: British Council. Available at: http://englishagenda.britishcouncil.org/sites/default/files/attachments/books-english-next.pdf (accessed February 18, 2019).
Gramsci, A. (1971). *Selections from the prison notebooks* (Q. Hoare & G. Nowell-Smith, Trans.). London: Lawrence and Wishart.
Gulliver, T. (2010). Immigrant success stories in ESL textbooks. *TESOL Quarterly*, 44(4), 725–745. doi:10.5054/tq.2010.235994.
Gumperz, J. J., & Levinson, S. C. (Eds.). (1996). *Rethinking linguistic relativity*. Cambridge: Cambridge University Press.

Halliday, M. A. K. (1973). *Explorations in the functions of language*. London: Edward Arnold.
Halliday, M. A. K. (1978). *Language as a social semiotic: The social interpretation of language and meaning*. London: Edward Arnold.
Heisey, D. R. (Ed.). (2000). *Chinese perspectives in rhetoric and communication*. Stamford, CT: Ablex Publication Corporation.
Holliday, A. (2013). "Native speaker" teachers and cultural belief. In S. A. Houghton & D. J. Rivers (Eds.), *Native-speakerism in Japan: Intergroup dynamics in foreign language education* (pp. 17–28). Bristol: Multilingual Matters.
Jäger, S. (2001). Discourse and knowledge: Theoretical and methodological aspects of a critical discourse and dispositive analysis. In R. Wodak & M. Meyer (Eds.), *Methods of critical discourse analysis* (pp. 32–62). London: SAGE Publications.
Kincaid, D. L. (Ed.). (1987). *Communication theory: Eastern and Western perspectives*. San Diego, CA: Academic Press.
Kramsch, C. (1998). *Language and culture*. Oxford: Oxford University Press.
Kress, G. (1990). Critical discourse analysis. *Annual Review of Applied Linguistics*, 11, 84–99. doi:10.1017/S0267190500001975
Kress, G. (1993). Against arbitrariness: The social production of the sign as a foundational issue in critical discourse analysis. *Discourse & Society*, 4(2), 169–191. doi:10.1177/0957926593004002003
Kress, G., & Hodge, R. (1979). *Language as ideology*. London: Routledge & Kegan Paul.
Kumaravadivelu, B. (2008). *Cultural globalization and language education*. New Haven, CT: Yale University Press.
Kuzar, R. (2011). The subversive agent: Anatomy of personal ideological change. *Semiotica*, 2011(185), 223–234. doi:10.1515/semi.2011.040.
Labov, W. (1972). *Language in the inner city: Studies in the Black English vernacular*. Philadelphia, PA: University of Pennsylvania Press.
Lee, D. B. (2005). New ideologies of everyday life in South Korean language textbooks. In Y. Nozaki, R. Openshaw, & A. Luke (Eds.), *Struggles over difference: Curriculum, texts, and pedagogy in the Asia-Pacific* (pp. 117–129). Albany, NY: State University of New York Press.
Liu, Y. (2005). The construction of culture knowledge in Chinese language textbooks: A critical discourse analysis. In Y. Nozaki, R. Openshaw, & A. Luke (Eds.), *Struggles over difference: Curriculum, texts, and pedagogy in the Asia-Pacific* (pp. 99–115). Albany, NY: State University of New York Press.
May, T. (1996). *Situating social theory*. Buckingham: Open University Press.
Mignolo, W. D. (1993). Colonial and postcolonial discourse: Cultural critique or academic colonialism? *Latin American Research Review*, 28(3), 120–134.
Miike, Y. (2009). New frontiers in Asian communication theory: An introduction. *Journal of Multicultural Discourses*, 4(1), 1–5. doi:10.1080/17447140802663145.
Milani, T. M. (2007). Voices of authority in conflict: The making of the expert in a language debate in Sweden. *Linguistics and Education*, 18(2), 99–120. doi:10.1016/j.linged.2007.07.002.
Milani, T. M. (2008). Language testing and citizenship: A language ideological debate in Sweden. *Language in Society*, 37(1), 27–59. doi:10.1017/S0047404508080020.
Milani, T. M. (in press). Queer performativity. In K. Hall & R. Barrett (Eds.), *The Oxford handbook of language and sexuality*. Oxford: Oxford University Press.
Ndura, E. (2004). ESL and cultural bias: An analysis of elementary through high school textbooks in the western United States of America. *Language, Culture and Curriculum*, 17(2), 143–153. doi:10.1080/07908310408666689.
Pardo, L. (2010). Latin-American discourse studies: State of the art and new perspectives. *Journal of Multicultural Discourses*, 5(3), 183–192. doi:10.1080/17447143.2010.508526.

Pêcheux, M. (1975). *Les Vérités de la palice: Linguistique, sémantique, philosophie*. Paris: F. Maspero.
Pennycook, A. (1998). *The cultural politics of English as an international language*. London: Longman.
Pennycook, A. (2004). Performativity and language studies. *Critical Inquiry in Language Studies*, 1(1), 1–19. doi:10.1207/s15427595cils0101_1.
Prah, K. K. (2010). African languages and their usages in multicultural landscapes. *Journal of Multicultural Discourses*, 5(2), 83–86. doi:10.1080/17447143.2010.500467.
Reisigl, M., & Wodak, R. (2000). "Austria first": A discourse historical analysis of Austrian anti-foreigner petitions in 1992 and 1993. In M. Reisigl & R. Wodak (Eds.), *The semiotics of racism: Approaches in critical discourse analysis* (pp. 269–304). Vienna: Passagen Verlag.
Risager, K. (2007). *Language and culture pedagogy: From a national to a transnational paradigm*. Clevedon: Multilingual Matters.
Rorty, R. (1991). *Objectivity, relativism and truth: Philosophical papers*, vol. 1. Cambridge: Cambridge University Press.
Rorty, R. (1998). *Achieving our country: Leftist thought in twentieth-century America*. Cambridge, MA: Harvard University Press.
Said, E. W. (1978). *Orientalism*. New York: Vintage Books.
Sapir, E. (1949). *Selected writings in language, culture and personality* (D. G. Mandelbaum, Ed.). Berkeley, CA: University of California Press.
Schneer, D., Ramanathan, V., & Morgan, B. (2007). (Inter)nationalism and English textbooks endorsed by the Ministry of Education in Japan. *TESOL Quarterly*, 41(3), 600–607. doi:10.2307/40264392.
Scollo, M. (2011). Cultural approaches to discourse analysis: A theoretical and methodological conversation with special focus on Donal Carbaugh's Cultural Discourse Theory. *Journal of Multicultural Discourses*, 6(1), 1–32. doi:10.1080/17447143.2010.536550.
Searle, J. R. (1969). *Speech acts: An essay in the philosophy of language*. Cambridge: Cambridge University Press.
Sharifian, F. (2013). Globalisation and developing metacultural competence in learning English as an international language. *Multilingual Education*, 3(1), 7. doi:10.1186/2191-5059-3-7.
Shen, X. L. (2001). *Chinese grammar*. Nanjing: Jiangsu Education Press.
Shi-xu. (2005). *A cultural approach to discourse*. New York: Palgrave Macmillan.
Shi-xu. (2009). Reconstructing Eastern paradigms of discourse studies. *Journal of Multicultural Discourses*, 4(1), 29–48. doi:10.1080/17447140802651637.
Shi-xu. (2012). Why do cultural discourse studies? Towards a culturally conscious and critical approach to human discourses. *Critical Arts*, 26(4), 484–503. doi:10.1080/02560046.2012.723814.
Sinclair, J. M., & Coulthard, R. M. (1975). *Towards an analysis of discourse: The English used by teachers and pupils*. Oxford: Oxford University Press.
Spivak, G. C. (1988). Can the subaltern speak? In C. Nelson & L. Grossberg (Eds.), *Marxism and the interpretation of culture* (pp. 271–313). London: Macmillan.
Suaysuwan, N., & Kapitzke, C. (2005). Thai English language textbooks, 1960–2000: Postwar industrial and global changes. In Y. Nozaki, R. Openshaw, & A. Luke (Eds.), *Struggles over difference: Curriculum, texts, and pedagogy in the Asia-Pacific* (pp. 79–97). Albany, NY: State University of New York Press.
van Dijk, T. A. (1993). Principles of critical discourse analysis. *Discourse & Society*, 4(2), 249–283. doi:10.1177/0957926593004002006.
van Dijk, T. A. (1997). *Discourse studies: A multidisciplinary introduction* (vols 1 and 2). London: SAGE Publications.

van Dijk, T. A. (2000). *Ideology and discourse: A multidisciplinary introduction*. Barcelona: Pompeu Fabra. Available at: www.discourses.org/UnpublishedArticles/Ideology%20and%20discourse.pdf (accessed March 11, 2019).

van Dijk, T. A. (2001). Critical discourse analysis. In D. Tannen, H. E. Hamilton, & D. Schiffrin (Eds.), *The handbook of discourse analysis* (vol. 1, pp. 352–371). Oxford: Blackwell.

van Dijk, T. A. (2004). Racism, discourse and textbooks: The coverage of immigration in Spanish textbooks. Paper presented at the Symposium on Human Rights in Textbooks, Istanbul, Turkey: unpublished. Available at: www.discourses.org/Unpublished%20articles%20Teun%20A%20van%20Dijk.html.

van Dijk, T. A. (2006). Discourse and manipulation. *Discourse & Society*, 17(3), 359–383. doi:10.1177/0957926506060250.

van Dijk, T. A. (2008). *Discourse and context: A sociocognitive approach*. Cambridge: Cambridge University Press.

van Leeuwen, T., & Wodak, R. (1999). Legitimizing immigration control: A discourse-historical analysis. *Discourse Studies*, 1(1), 83–118. doi:10.1177/1461445699001001005.

Vološinov, V. N. (]1973] 1986). *Marxism and the philosophy of language* (L. Matejka & I. R. Titunik, Trans.). Cambridge, MA: Harvard University Press.

von Humboldt, W. (1988). *On language: The diversity of the human language structure and its influence on the mental development of mankind* (P. Heath, Trans.). Cambridge: Cambridge University Press.

Watts, R. (2001). Discourse theory and language planning: A critical reading of language planning reports in Switzerland. In N. Coupland, S. Sarangi, & C. Candlin (Eds.), *Sociolinguistics and social theory*. London: Longman.

Whorf, B. L. (1956). *Language, thought, and reality: Selected writings of Benjamin Lee Whorf*. (J. B.. Carroll, Ed.). Cambridge, MA: MIT Press.

Wodak, R. (1996a). Critical linguistics and critical discourse analysis. In J. Verschueren (Ed.), *Handbook of pragmatics* (pp. 201–210). Amsterdam: John Benjamins.

Wodak, R. (1996b). *Disorders of discourse*. London: Longman.

Wodak, R. (1997). Critical discourse analysis and the study of doctor-patient interaction. In B. L. Gunnarsson, P. Linell, & B. Nordberg (Eds.), *The construction of professional discourse* (pp. 173–200). London: Routledge.

Wodak, R. (2000). Does sociolinguistics need social theory? New perspectives on critical discourse analysis. *Discourse & Society*, 2(3), 123–147.

3
EFL TEXTBOOKS AS IDEOLOGICAL VEHICLES[1]

The chapter presents a critical discourse analysis of six English as a Foreign Language (EFL) textbooks used in Israeli high schools. In this context, the English curriculum is uniform for all learning populations, including Palestinian Arabs. The focus is on the dynamic between these Palestinian Arab learners, and the cultural content of the EFL textbooks, where the recurrence of seven discursive devices that might possibly serve as a means for shaping or (re)producing ideological values is discussed.

Introduction

The present chapter questions the cultural suitability of EFL textbooks in ways that might have implications for education and multiculturalism far beyond English learning in Israel. It presents a discursive analysis of these texts, which identifies and examines the ideological bias of narratives and texts used in them and verifies their cultural relevance for the target audiences they address. Although this chapter focuses on EFL, I situate myself within a larger framework of textbook analysis in Israel concerning other subjects, such as geography and civil science (see Nasser & Nasser, 2008; Peled-Elhanan, 2012; Podeh, 2000; 2002, as discussed in Chapter 1). Since research on language acquisition and cognitive development confirms that a thorough grounding in one's first language and culture enhances the ability to acquire other languages, literacies, and knowledge (Canagarajah, 1999, p. 2), I would argue that Palestinian Arab learners have difficulty in relating culturally to English curricular materials that assume an upper-middle-class Jewish exposure to US and/or Western cultures.

In Chapter 1, I argued that textbooks are ideological vehicles for transmitting dominant ideologies and perpetuating hegemonic discourses. In this chapter, I demonstrate how EFL textbooks promote intercultural understanding between Israel and the West, as well as among certain of Israel's diverse groups, while excluding the

Palestinian Arab minority. Subaltern Jewish groups, such as Ethiopian Jews, are not singled out for exclusion in the same way. My analysis will show that these textbooks tend to ignore the existence of Arabs, who are seldom so much as named, nor indexed through any cultural symbol. The few instances of representation are in fact *misrepresentations* of Arabs as underdeveloped, dependent, and traditionalist. In some cases, the standard European stereotype of the Bedouin, situated in the desert with camels, is invoked.

To analyze cultural bias in the EFL curriculum, I selected six textbooks used in Israeli high schools. Selecting the first two textbooks was guided by my first-hand experience with their content when I used them to teach EFL during my early career years as an English teacher in Arabic-speaking high schools. In fact, it was this experience that sparked within me a desire to unravel the dialectical relationship between Anglo-centric/Western ideologies and EFL pedagogical narratives. The factor that governed my selection of the other four textbooks was guaranteeing a representative selection of textbooks published by the two leading EFL publishing houses in Israel: Eric Cohen Books, and University Publishing Projects. In systematically analyzing them, I started from the principle that language shapes and is shaped by ideology, which in turn shapes attitudes and identities. Examining how these texts address (or fail to address) the issue of cultural diversity can demonstrate how their underlying ideologies shape learners' positionalities. The discourse analysis applied to the six EFL textbooks utilizes an integrated method, which combines models that share a theorization of an ideologically and socially motivated relationship between form and meaning. Based on Norman Fairclough's three-dimensional model (introduced in Chapter 2) I conducted a systematic text-oriented discourse analysis of various linguistic devices appearing in the texts, and how they construct learners' knowledge, shape their identities, and perpetuate dominant ideologies. Grammatical structures, lexical items, rhetorical techniques, types of discourse, and deictic words are understood as having significance beyond mere semantics, and as therefore open to closer examination.

Toward a Systematic Text-Oriented Discourse Analysis

The methodological model that I use in this chapter mainly uses tools from Critical Discourse Analysis (CDA) as presented in Chapter 2, and related models (Bucholtz & Hall, 2005; Lin, 2004; Tajfel & Turner, 1986; Wortham, 1996) that are useful for conducting a linguistic analysis of the cultural content of textbooks. The research questions guiding this part of the study are:

1. In what ways do EFL textbooks perpetuate and reproduce dominant ideologies within Israeli society?
2. Do cultural factors play a role in alienating Palestinian Arab learners from the content of EFL textbooks?
3. To what extent are EFL textbooks employed to construct a Jewish national identity and collective memory?

In order to answer these research questions I identified in the texts and then analyzed seven discursive devices:

1. The use of culturally distinctive names to refer to people or places (see Chiu & Chiang, 2012).
2. Pronoun usage in context (see Wortham, 1996).
3. The use of passive/active voice when referring to the Other (see Fairclough, 1992; van Dijk, 2006).
4. Explicit statements used to define the target audience of the text (for example, stating that "In our Western world …") that address a specific group, while excluding others (van Dijk, 2006).
5. Narratives about faraway cultures, and their roles as discursive devices in representing the Other and/or perpetuating Western stereotypes regarding the Other (van Dijk, 2006).
6. Assumed culturally specific prior knowledge in reading comprehension texts (see Lin, 2004).
7. The discursive construction of identities and collective memories (see Bucholtz & Hall, 2005; Tajfel & Turner, 1986; Wodak, 2002).

The evaluation of these discursive devices as diagnostic tools for assessing ideological bias and constructs is supported in the literature that underpins the methodological framework of this chapter.

Naming Practices

One of the ways to examine how texts represent different groups of people is to closely observe the naming practices related to characters and places, which sheds light on the ideological stance or position of those engaged in choosing the names. Naming a character in a text "Ariel" or "Mohamed," for example, is a discursive practice expressing an ideological choice. In their study of the "name rectification movement" of Taiwan's indigenous minority, Chiu and Chiang (2012) show that non-aboriginal society had long neglected issues related to this group, such as the loss of their culture, customs, and even ethnic or individual names, which contributed to a generalized national indifference towards them. It is important to note that one concern of the name rectification movement is

> the restoration of traditional aboriginal names for indigenous people's villages, landmasses, and bodies of water because these traditional names are of cultural, religious, and historical significance and they further define their identity within their territory … Thus, the restoration of the traditional aboriginal names given to geographical features will help indigenous people to reclaim their rights and redefine their position within Taiwan.
>
> *(p. 531)*

The authors further emphasize that the demand to be referred to by their indigenous names asserts that "just like other indigenous peoples elsewhere, Taiwan indigenous people deserve their own place in the world" (p. 532). It would be fair to expect, then, that in other contexts this intimate connection between naming and belonging might be observed, and that Palestinian Arab learners may also expect to see their ethnic names represented in school textbooks, as this metaphorical practice is an acknowledgment of their existence.

For the purposes of examining the representation of different ethnic groupings in EFL textbooks, I counted all the instances of names of people and places in each textbook, and classified the names into three categories: (1) Western/American; (2) Jewish-Israeli; and (3) Arab. Social identity theory posits that social categorization, which is the subjective process of classifying people into groups (through the use of ethnic names, for example) involves a basic distinction between the category containing the Self (the in-group or "us") and that which contains the Other (the out-group or "them") (Tajfel & Turner, 1986).

Indexical Pronouns

Analyzing the use of cohesive linguistic devices establishes the role(s) each clause or textual unit plays with respect to others. The use of personal pronouns, such as "we" or "they," among other kinds of deictic words, may point to an ideological position such as establishing an interactional in-group feeling, as opposed to an out-group feeling, creating a "Us" versus "Them" distinction through presenting "Us" in a positive and upgrading manner and "Them" (i.e. the Other) in a negative and degrading manner. Wortham (1996) terms these deictics "shifters," and explains:

> Personal pronouns ... refer to individuals or groups and thus contribute denoted content to what the participants are talking about. But they successfully refer by indexing some person or group that occupies a particular interactional role in the narrating event.
>
> *(p. 3)*

These linguistic "shifters" may create a referent group that is distinguished from other groups by means of including or excluding them. For instance, the pronoun "we"

> refers to some set of functions that include the speaker and some other(s). Consummated use of *we* establishes reference to that set – thus contributing to the anchoring of the speaker's footing, by presenting him or her as a central or defining member of a certain interacting group.
>
> *(p. 3)*

The use of pronouns is also evident in texts that deal with the relationship between dominant and dominated groups, majority and minority groups and – more specifically – between the "Western" and "Eastern" world. Such positive or negative presentations are often formulated on biased assumptions that serve the dominant group's ideological interests. Van Dijk (2006) has determined several strategic procedures governing the presentation of Self and the Other in discourse, claiming:

> The overall strategy of positive self-presentation and negative other-presentation is very typical in this biased account of the facts in favor of the speaker's or writer's own interests, while blaming negative situations and events on opponents or on the Others (immigrants, terrorists, youths, etc.).
>
> (p. 373)

Thus, the use of pronouns might play a forceful role in influencing the reader's attitudes, and can be strategically used by writers to implicitly express ideological positions or create in the reader a sense of belonging to the "in-group" or the "out-group."

Passive/Active Voice

Whether clauses are constructed in the active or passive voice reflects what kind of reader-text relationship the writer wishes to construct. The passive is used:

when the agent is known but is not the theme or topic;
when the agent is unknown and therefore omitted;
when the agent is already known and therefore omitted;
when the agent "is judged irrelevant or perhaps in order to leave agency and hence responsibility vague" (Fairclough, 1992, p. 76).

The motivation behind using the passive or active voice within a certain narrative depends on the perception of the individual subject as a receptive or free agent (see Chapter 2 for a discussion of the agentive role of the social subject). In his discussion of discourse and manipulation, van Dijk (2006, p. 361) distinguishes active from passive voice in a sentence based on what this assignment presupposes about subjects. Whereas assigning the subject an active role assumes a capacity to believe or act freely, assigning a passive role presupposes a lack of ability to understand real messages, and act accordingly.

It is thus imperative to pay attention to the use of the passive or active voice when analyzing texts that refer to the Other, as the choice of these grammatical features may reflect underlying assumptions about the characteristics of the religious, ethnic, disabled, gendered, or cultural group that are invoked. It is clear that grammatical forms affect readers' attitudes and ideological positions, functioning as a tool for maintaining or creating stereotypes and prejudices concerning the Other.

Constructing the Target Audience

If texts in English EFL courses are mainly targeted at Jewish learners, or attempt to construct Israeli Jews as intrinsically associated with Western cultures, then the way that the texts construct their target audiences would provide evidence of this. When texts explicitly address Jews, or associate Jews with the West or America, they are implicitly excluding Palestinian Arab learners (and to some extent other Jewish groups from Eastern origins, i.e. *Mizrachim*) who are not associated with the West but rather with the East and its large Arab culture, thus creating a Self (or We) versus Other (or They) distinction. Using phrases such as "our modern Western Culture" is an explicit way of including those who are associated with that culture, while excluding those who are not. Van Dijk (2006) offers strategies that analysts can employ in order to uncover how writers load linguistic signs with ideological messages in discourses of the Self and the Other. One of the strategies used by writers to produce "local meanings of Our/Their positive/negative actions" is by "being explicit/implicit" (p. 373). When writers positively present the Self (i.e. we) and/or negatively present the Other (i.e. they), the tendency is to use explicit terms of reference (e.g. "westerners, American, Israelis, etc." or "non-westerners, Indians, Chinese, Bedouins, etc.," respectively). Negative presentation of the Self and/or positive presentation of the Other is more likely to be done implicitly, without explicitly stating who the actors are. Through analyzing the recurrence of these strategies in textbooks, I will explore how these practices function as cultural gatekeepers, preventing minority students from relating to these texts, and perpetuating their sense of being outsiders.

Representing the Narratives of Remote Cultures

The EFL curriculum states that one of the main principles underlying English language teaching is the inclusion of culture as a significant component of presenting language to learners. So including narratives about other cultures and peoples in English textbooks meets the teaching requirements of the curriculum, and cultures from remote places, including India and Pakistan, are duly represented in the texts. Although this is ostensibly a presentation of a variety of cultures, whether an egalitarian picture emerges is a question for analysis. I examine how these cultures are represented using van Dijk's (2006) strategies for analyzing discourse about the Other:

1. *Overall interaction strategies*: positively presenting the Self and negatively presenting the Other.
2. *Lexical selection*: positive words for Us, negative words for Them.
3. *Rhetorical figures*: using metonymies and metaphors emphasizing Our/Their positive/negative properties (p. 373).

Culturally Specific Prior Knowledge

In the field of second/foreign language reading, the interaction of the reader and the written text has been recurrently investigated from the perspectives of both cognition and meta-cognition. A meta-cognitive perspective on reading emphasizes the reader's "need to be aware of what is involved in the process of reading and of utilizing effective reading strategies to enhance their reading ability" (Lin, 2004, p. 9; see also Carrell, 1989; 1991). In order to enhance reading abilities, Lin (2004) considers the recognition of EFL readers' cultural prior knowledge as a guiding factor in improving reading comprehension. In reading English texts, comprehension depends on the learner's ability to connect new information with culturally specific prior knowledge that the writer assumes they have, though this might not necessarily be the case. That is, when writing texts, writers base newly-presented information on prior knowledge that is presumably already known to the reader. However, prior knowledge of New York's Central Park or the Yankees baseball team, for example, is not necessarily shared by all readers, and instead is highly culturally specific. In her research, Lin investigated the effects of culturally specific prior knowledge on Taiwanese EFL high school seniors' English reading comprehension. Her analysis endorses the positive influence of learners' own culturally specific prior knowledge on their reading comprehension. Lin concludes that this knowledge is pivotal to enabling learners (in her study, Taiwanese senior high school students) to achieve a broader understanding of English texts. Culturally distant knowledge may thus impede readers' comprehension, and even cause them to lose interest.

To what extent the culturally specific information presented in EFL textbooks caters to the diverse learning populations in Israel and their multi-layered cultural milieus is another focal point in my analysis. The manner in which culturally specific information is presented to English learners in Israel raises a fundamental and complex question: Should English be taught as a foreign language by "domesticating" it, or by preserving its Anglo-centric hegemony? Whereas the former transforms English into an "alien" medium in order to suit the cultural milieu of the people learning it (Akere, 2006, p. 2), the latter presents English through an Anglo-centric lens, that is, through mainly exposing the EFL learner to American and British culture. Determining which approach should be adopted as part of the language policy and planning in Israel and/or other EFL contexts is clearly a multifaceted issue that I will deal with more comprehensively in Chapter 5 and Chapter 6. Here, I will argue that materials should be designed so that they cater to the specific cultures of the learners (i.e. be "locally grounded") while placing English in its broader, international context (i.e. be "globally minded"). What I am suggesting, then, is neither pure domestication, nor pure preservation of the Anglo-centrism of English, but rather a balanced dynamic between the two approaches.

Constructing Identities and Collective Memories

One way identity is linguistically marked is through the use of certain discursive devices, such as the use of indexical pronouns (as discussed earlier) or the use of certain lexical items that aim to unite a group of people under one national or ethnic identity. Examples would be the Israeli flag, or praying in a synagogue on the Sabbath, etc. For Bucholtz and Hall (2005), identity is seen as emergent, constructed through discursive interaction where speakers situate themselves in social relationships with others. The identities that emerge from engaging in discourse are dynamic, mutable, and malleable, in the sense that the development of one's identities is a process through which the context defines the identity. Identity construction is thus a social process, and not an individual one (see also Frogner, 1999).

Through the narratives used in EFL textbooks, national identities are bound to emerge, and collective memories to be maintained. A national identity may emerge when a learner associates him/herself with a character who "usually joins his grandfather when he goes to the synagogue on Shabbat" (Maor & Ziv, 2009, p. 66) or with a youngster who "finished his army service and is now going to travel" (Cohen, Loney, & Kerman, 2006, p. 31). Collective memories may also be maintained when Israeli Jewish learners read about the Holocaust and about how some symbolic items, which the late Israeli astronaut Ilan Ramon carried with him into space, "represent the six million people *we* lost in the Holocaust" (Komet & Partouche, 2006, p. 48; my emphasis). The inculcation of these and other semiotic resources such as the Israeli flag, celebrating Purim or Hanukah, or referring to places in Hebrew but with English transliteration, may all function as building blocks in identity construction.

In the analysis that follows, I will pay close attention to these seven discursive devices in order to answer my specific research questions: To what extent do they function as ideological means for reproducing and perpetuating a discourse of inequality, a lack of fair multicultural representations, or even discriminatory values?

Data Collection and Data Analysis

The six EFL textbooks in the corpus are approved by the Ministry of Education, published by two different publishers, and distributed to various Israeli high schools. They are listed in Table 3.1. The analysis will be presented according to the order of the discursive devices I presented above.

Naming Practices

Among all the names used in the researched textbooks (506 names of people and 191 of places), Western/American names were the most dominant (70 percent of

TABLE 3.1 Textbook sampling

Textbook	Author(s)	Publisher	Level
Results for 4 Points	Judy Cohen, Naomi Loney and Sue Kerman	Eric Cohen Books	Proficiency level, stages two to three
Build Up	Judy Dobkins	Eric Cohen Books	Intermediate level, stages one to two
High Points	Evelyn Ezra	Eric Cohen Books	Proficiency level, stages two to three
Ten	Cindy Komet and Debi Partouche	Eric Cohen Books	Proficiency level, stage one
Zoom	Ziva Maor and Micaela Ziv	University Publishing Projects	Proficiency level, stage one
Dimensions	Hanny Turgeman and Rita Zaltzman-Kulick	University Publishing Projects	Proficiency level, stage one

the occurrences). The assumption that most textbook writers and designers associate English culture mainly with the United States and the United Kingdom is compatible with this high prevalence. Similarly, other researchers have found that locally produced English textbooks contained mostly British and Anglo-American cultural values, rather than globally oriented materials (Shin, Eslami, & Chen, 2011). Furthermore, most of the texts or activities that dealt with real-life situations such as writing a letter to a friend/relative abroad, complaining about a social condition or discussing a social problem, instantiate problems prevalent in major international metropolitan cities (such as New York, London, Los Angeles, and Tel Aviv, etc.). Conversely, representation of characters or states of affairs from peripheral areas was significantly less prominent. This observation is crucial for scrutinizing the notion of the "global" in EFL discourses, and for offering new discursive routes for designing transformative EFL materials, as I will show in Chapter 6.

Israeli Jewish names of people and places (149 and 53, respectively) were used in almost 30 percent of the cases. One prevalent linguistic practice for presenting Jewish names (especially of places) was through English transliteration of the Hebrew, despite the availability of an English alternative. For example, *Kinneret* or *Tveria* is used instead of Tiberius, *Akko* instead of Acre, and *Agam* Hula instead of Hula Lake. This linguistic practice was also employed to name Jewish organizations or social customs such as *Galgal Bema'agal* to refer to dancing in wheelchairs, *Magen David Adom* (Red Star of David or Red Magen David) to refer to Israel's national ambulance service, *Matkot* to refer to the paddleball game, *Ulpan* to refer to institutes for intensive Hebrew study for immigrants, and *Rosh Hashana* to refer to the Jewish New Year.

Finally, some of the texts use words that, despite being considered English words, are only used in Jewish/Israeli contexts, such as *Kibbutz* or *Moshav*, referring to the collective settlements that are associated with modern Israel and early Zionist movements that are the settings for certain events or narratives in the texts. For example, one character states: "We can go spend some time with my cousins on *Kibbutz Sde Boker*" (Cohen et al., 2006). Israeli Jewish learners may easily engage with such narratives, and experience an in-group feeling.

As opposed to the extensive Western/American and Jewish-Israeli names used, the study revealed a near-total avoidance of Arab names. Fewer than 1 percent of the names in the textbooks could be considered "Arab": only six out of 506 personal names, and only two out of 191 place names. The contexts in which they were used were also noteworthy, as I shall now explain.

The first name (Muhammad; one occurrence) is used to refer to an Indian Muslim from Bangladesh, who is a professor of economics and a Nobel Prizewinner (Ezra, 2011, p. 40); Muhammad is clearly not an Arab. The second and third names (Mahmoud and Miriam; one occurrence each) are used to refer to Bedouins of the Negev. The two are discussed as members of Bedouin society, without mentioning any details associating them with the Palestinian Arab minority in Israel, such as the fact that their native language is Arabic, or that they form a part of this large minority. The implications of not referring to Bedouins as "Arabs" in the only two incidences in which Arabs might implicitly have been mentioned raises serious questions about how these textbooks present this minority to Israeli learners. The narratives in which these two characters are presented depict Bedouin society as underdeveloped and traditionalist, and associate Bedouins with the desert, and camels. Similar to the Indian "Muhammad," both "Moussa" and "Rokia" (supposedly Arabic names) are used (one occurrence each) to refer to children from Mali, who are Muslims, but not speakers of Arabic. Again, the narrative depicts their environment as poor, underdeveloped, extremely needy, and dependent on the "good-hearted and generous" West for support. It is striking that so many of these personal names in Arabic do not index actual Palestinian Arabs living in Israel.

The final Arabic name, "Samira," is also interesting. The relevant text (Dobkins, 2008, p. 37)) mentions students from Herzog School acting as volunteers; one of them is named Samira. It soon becomes obvious that Herzog School is not an Arab school, so including a girl with an Arabic name (Samira) among eight Western and Jewish names without bothering to explain why she studies in a Hebrew-speaking school (which is in general an unusual occurrence) begs an explanation. The fact that Israel has two separate schooling systems for its Jewish and Arab citizens impedes, in my view, genuine processes of learning about and appreciating the Other. The text with "Samira" thus could have offered a different, even desirable, narrative where Jews and Arabs are encouraged to learn in the same schools, turning the text from a tool for reproducing the status quo of distance between the two populations to one for effecting social change. Adequately presented, then, a text about a Palestinian Arab student studying in a Jewish school could have offered a new ideological challenge for Israeli learners, Jews and Arabs alike.

The last point to be made in this section concerns the naming of Miriam's village, which in the text is called *Tel Sheva*. Miriam lives in an Arab village in the south that is called, in Arabic, *Tal as-Sabi*. The meaning of *Tal* is height and *Sabi* means seven which is Sheva in Hebrew. The choice of referring to a Bedouin Arab village by its Hebrew name rather than its Arabic name further demonstrates the seemingly deliberate avoidance of designating Arab localities as Arab. *Tel Sheva* is thus not only not an Arabic place name, but a deliberate camouflage of one. Note, for comparison, the use of the Arabic name (transliterated as *Tel as-Sabi*) in the English Wikipedia as a counterpart of the Hebrew Wikipedia *Tel Sheva* (spelled in Hebrew), a website that lies beyond the scope of influence of the Israeli education system.

The two other place names in Arabic were both of Druze villages (*Beit Jan* and *Daliat Al Carmel*). The presentation of such names, as is the case with the Bedouin one, fails to associate these names with the Arab culture or minority. Had the writers of these texts mentioned that Druze or Bedouins are Arabs, who live in Israel, they would have been treated as representatives of the Palestinian Arab minority.

The naming practices in the six English textbooks suggest three specific conclusions. First, the position of the United States and other European English-speaking countries as the "homelands" of English culture is re-established, since almost 70 percent of the representative characters and places in the textbooks are American or European. Second, the choice of names in the textbooks is viewed through a Jewish perspective of the history of the Jewish people in the Land of Israel. This view perceives Israel as a modern state that is both a part of the "West" and a Jewish-Zionist nation. Western/American and Jewish names recur frequently, while Arabic names are incredibly rare. Finally, the existence of the Palestinian Arab minority in Israel is linguistically erased. Where Arabic names are used, they either do not refer to Arab Palestinians, or ignore the reference to Arab Palestinian people. Namely, the consistent avoidance of using the term "Arabic" or "Arab" suggests a deliberate avoidance of addressing the Palestinian Arab minority. Palestinian Arabs are not synonymous with Bedouins who live in the desert and guide tourists on their camels. Bedouins, like Palestinian Muslims, Christians, and Druze, form part of the ethnic, indigenous minority referred to as Palestinian Arabs who live in Israel, or sometimes as "1948 Arabs."

Indexical Pronouns

Establishing an interactional in-group or a nonreciprocal out-group feeling may be achieved through the use of the pronouns "we" or "us," which might indicate a desire to include a certain group of people while excluding others. In my analysis, I encountered numerous usages of the pronoun "we" that might be interpreted as ideologically relevant and which, intentionally or not, include Israeli Jewish learners and exclude Palestinian Arab ones.

It is worthy of mention that analyzing the use of singular pronouns such as *I* versus *he/she*, for example, complements the analysis of the plural pronouns *we/they* as components in constructing Self-Other dichotomies. Furthermore, the use of the direct pronoun *you* to address readers may also be used to create an in-group or out-group feeling, especially if what "you" are being asked to do or think about is unfamiliar, or assumes particular cultural reference points. One teaching unit requests of students, for instance, to create a project entitled "Israel" in which they are asked to look into issues such as the languages of the native countries of immigrants, their Hebrew instruction experience in the *Ulpan* upon immigrating to Israel, and their opinion on the status of Hebrew in Israel in light of an increasingly varied linguistic repertoire (Turgeman & Zaltzman-Kulick, 2008). All of these questions are directly formulated by using the pronoun "you." However, in this case, "you" obviously refers to Jewish learners who have either immigrated themselves, or whose families historically immigrated to Israel. Although the pronouns are used in questions, it is clear that "you" is not used with Palestinian Arab learners in mind who, together with the rest of their ancestral families, belong to the indigenous population who predates the establishment of the State of Israel. Because they and their ancestors were born on the land, the *Ulpan* experience, for example, is irrelevant.

In *Zoom*, the indexical pronouns have been repeatedly used in ways that undoubtedly create an in-group feeling in Israeli Jewish learners, and an out-group feeling in Palestinian Arab learners. In a text discussing the topic "Making Friends," which is accompanied by a photo of an Ethiopian girl, "us" is used in order to form an in-group relationship between Israeli and Ethiopian Jews, who are encouraged to accept the Ethiopian minority and help them integrate into Israeli society and culture. Furthermore, students are encouraged to think about what they can do in order to help these immigrants assimilate into Israeli society, such as teaching them Hebrew or helping them with homework. Unlike the attempts to encourage the assimilation of Jewish immigrants that EFL texts seem to reinforce, the socio-legal agenda between Jews and Palestinian Arabs in a nation state as Israel, is that of non-assimilation (Karayanni, 2018, p. 26). All of these practices are performed, thus, within a specific practitioner community that may share the experience of teaching Hebrew to immigrants, and have internalized the significant ideological role of Jewish immigration (*Aliya*) to Israel. Again, it is simply not possible that Palestinian Arabs would be included in this community. The same theme (i.e. encouraging Israeli youth to volunteer to help new immigrants) is also found in other textbooks (Dobkins, 2008, for example) which suggests that the forming of in-group feelings among Israeli Jewish learners, and out-group feelings in Palestinian Arab learners, is in fact a norm in EFL teaching in Israel.

In other contexts, students are asked to relate personal experiences orally or in writing and are given examples such as "*We* love to watch the schoolchildren in their *Purim* parade" or "*I* usually join *my* grandfather when he goes to the *synagogue* on *Shabbat*" (Maor & Ziv, 2009; my emphasis). The practices performed by these subjects (*we* and *I*) are of an exclusively Jewish nature emphasized by referring to a collective Jewish practice during Purim or praying in a synagogue on the Sabbath.

In all six books, noteworthy pronoun use in depicting characters in the context of their army service was recurrent. The theme of one story, "Hospital Windows" (Maor & Ziv, 2009), is people encouraging one another through ordeals (a universal theme) and for that purpose two men are depicted conversing during their stay in a hospital. The story presents two men (presented as "they") and the common ground they share (families, wives, and children) and also the time they served in the army, which does not serve any purpose in promoting the universal theme of the story other than stating that these two representatives did army service, namely, fulfilled their civic Jewish duties. Andy, "My brother," "We," and "I" are all repeatedly described in the textbooks as finishing or intending to finish their army service, and then travel or go on to university. It is worth clarifying that compulsory enlistment in the Israel Defense Army includes citizens over the age of 18, who are Jewish, Druze, or Circassian; Palestinian Arab citizens are not conscripted. It would therefore be fair to conclude that these pronouns work to include Israeli learners who belong to the group serving in the army, while excluding those who do not.

The most prominent use of pronouns as a discursive device for forming in-group or out-group feelings was in the text involving an interview with the late Israeli astronaut, Ilan Ramon (Komet & Partouche, 2006, p. 47). The text highlighted the central role of Ramon's Jewish national identity through facts such as his having been born to Holocaust survivors, having served in the Israeli Air Force, and having participated in famous Air Force attacks, among other things. All of these details were presented as reasons why "*we* can all look up to him" (Komet & Partouche, 2006; my emphasis). However, those who can look up to Ramon for these reasons are only those for whom these facts are harmonious with what they perceive as essential in forming their membership in the Zionist collective (see the discussion in Chapter 2, and Kuzar, 2011, on the interpellation of subjects). In the interview, Ramon also uses the pronoun *we* to exclusively address Jewish people – who even include "Jewish communities all over North America" – in talking about his intention to take symbolic Jewish items with him into space to "represent the six million people *we* lost in the Holocaust" (Komet & Partouche, 2006, p. 47, my emphasis).

Ramon's use of the pronoun *we* to refer to the six million people lost in the Holocaust strengthens the national and historical ties that Jewish people have with the Holocaust, a major constituent of national Jewish identity. The sentence could have been written in the middle voice (medio-passive) by omitting the pronoun: "Some of them are going to represent the six million people lost in the Holocaust." The use of "we" puts emphasis on the loss of six million people as being the loss of Jewish people alone, as opposed to a loss for all of humanity. Students of all backgrounds should be able to relate to the Holocaust from a humanistic perspective, and realize the implications of this atrocity, while sympathizing with the impact of this tragedy on the Jewish people specifically. However, when some students are treated as "outsiders" in school textbooks, whose ostensive aim is to teach all students about the Holocaust, they are pre-emptively excluded from forming this attitude.

The last point to relate to in this section is the manner in which EFL narratives geographically divide the globe into two distinctive worlds that are indexed as *Here* (the West) as opposed to *There* (the East or the Developing World). Through indexical use of locative pronouns/adverbial deictics (*here* vs. *there*), two images may be imprinted on learners' minds: an image of developing countries (i.e. poverty, hunger, and a vicious cycle), as opposed to an image of Westerners' constant "desire" to assist these countries (i.e. being constantly encouraged and reminded to work for the benefit of Third World people). Such a dichotomous image is ideological as it might instill a feeling of superiority in the Israeli learner that is actually based on an illusion. This ideological dichotomy, Said (1978) postulates, creates an image of a degenerate and passive East that the West needs in order to sustain itself as active and more vital.

The examples presented in this section demonstrate how the use of indexical pronouns points to the ideological underpinnings of the text and distinguishes positive-Self from negative-Other groups. The *Self* vs. *Other* narratives used in EFL textbooks give Europeans and Westerners the feeling that they can "advance securely and unmetaphorically upon the Orient" as a topic of learning (p. 3). When Israeli learners – who are likely to view themselves as modern Westerners – are asked by a school textbook to categorize the world into two groups – the Self-helping and the Other-helped – they are interpellated by an ideology that is directly guiding them to occupy a superior position. Namely, students are basically offered an ideologically-oriented challenge in which they are asked to categorize the world into a world of *We*, who are modern, good-hearted, and always-ready rescuers versus a world of *They*, who are underdeveloped, "caught up in a vicious circle of poverty" (Ezra, 2011, p. 40), and dependent. Students, unfortunately, are not motivated to reflect on negative aspects of Western hegemony and control over other countries, and hence the agentive aspect of their interpellated subject is not stimulated to subversively act to change these dominant Western conventions. As a result, only what these dominant ideologies are interested in preserving is perpetuated and reproduced. Furthermore, the Anglo-centric nature of certain narratives tends to highlight the Western individual's ability to choose freely, argue, and struggle against any attempts to restrict his/her freedom (Kuzar, 2011). In other words, young Western individuals (with whom Israeli Jewish individuals are associated in these textbooks) are presented as rational and coherent, demanding, for example, the right to choose their spouses (Ezra, 2011), push for more freedom from their parents (Komet & Partouche, 2006), and/or fight against a law that sets a curfew on all teenagers (Turgeman & Zaltzman-Kulick, 2008). However, this same apparently "coherent" and "rational" Western individual is interpellated by these passages reminding him/her to perpetuate some dominant Western features guided by people dictating the ideological nature of these textbooks. It could be argued that there is a clash of views concerning the way the individual learner is perceived in English textbooks.

Passive/Active Voice

The narratives and texts referring to the Other (non-Western, non-Jewish, or otherwise non-conforming) make disproportionate use of the passive voice. Such characters (whether African-American, Bedouin, or members of other minority groups) achieve success only if another explicitly or implicitly mentioned agent (usually American, British, or European) intervenes in order to change the course of their destinies. By comparison, inspiring stories about people who originated from similar conditions but who are members of majority groups are depicted in the active voice, as agents of their own change. An example of such a distinction may be found in the EFL textbook, *Results for 4 Points* (Cohen et al., 2006), in which two juxtaposed texts describe teenagers who have overcome failure. The first character, Ryan, is a black school "dropout" in Britain who is explicitly referred to in the text as belonging to a minority group. The second is Liz, a white, homeless teenager from New York. Ryan is depicted as follows:

> As part of a remarkable social experiment, Ryan Williams, a black teenage dropout, *was placed* in one of Britain's top boarding schools to see how he would cope... Ryan excelled.
> It wasn't always so ... he might easily have ended up in jail. Then fate intervened. Ryan's mother *was approached* by Pepper Productions, a British television company and *was asked* if her son could take part in a TV series called *Second Chance*.
> What this demonstrates is that in the right environment, children's lives *can be changed*.
>
> (p. 106, my emphasis)

Ryan's success, then, was determined by someone else's initiative (Pepper Productions) and he was accepted into one of Britain's top schools not due to his own resourcefulness, or that of his mother, but because of somebody else's intervention. Ryan's excellence is constructed as determined by an outside force, Pepper Productions, which gave him the opportunity to excel, assigning the boy himself a passive role.

As opposed to Ryan's passive representation, Liz Murray, a white New Yorker who was also headed for failure, is described in the active voice, as demonstrated in the following excerpt:

> Liz Murray *went* from living on the streets of New York City to winning a scholarship to Harvard University ... She *had dropped* out of school and *was living* on the streets; *sleeping* in subways ... Liz *had always imagined* having a better life. With her mother gone, she *began* to realize that it was up to her. 'I *got* the sense that my life was in my own hands ... that at the end of the day, whatever I *did* or *did not do* with my life *would stick* to me... so I *went* back to school.'
>
> (p. 113; my emphasis)

The succession of active verbs in this excerpt depicts Liz as an energetic, motivated, and self-determined young woman, who is moved by inner forces, and not dependent upon external ones. Throughout the text, Liz's decisions are unaffected by anything but herself and her will to change the status quo. As opposed to Ryan, who is referred to as a "black ... dropout," she herself made the decision to drop out of school, and then she also decided to go back to school to resume her education. Ryan, as mentioned earlier, "was placed" back in school after his mother "was approached" by Pepper Productions.

The use of active/passive voice in the two examples, of almost "minimal pairs," illustrates how a writer's choice of a certain grammatical feature (i.e. active or passive voice) may reflect underlying assumptions regarding certain religious, ethnic, disabled, gendered, or culturally different groups. Thus, choosing grammatical forms may affect readers' attitudes and ideological positions, functioning as a tool for maintaining or creating stereotypes and prejudices concerning the Other. Members of minority groups must depend on the intervention of *good-hearted* white people, who are "always prepared" to offer them "the right environment," so that every black child's life (like Ryan's) "can be changed."

Another example of how the passive voice constructs the Other is in an article about a young Bedouin woman who is defined at the beginning of the article as follows: "Miriam Abu-Raki'eh is not *your* typical entrepreneur. A Bedouin woman from Tel Sheva, five kilometers northeast of Beersheba ..." (Ezra, 2011, p. 54; my emphasis). The pronoun "your" interpellates a readership for whom a Bedouin woman is clearly atypical as an entrepreneur. Miriam is described as an exception, not like "most Bedouin women who *are not allowed*" (Ezra, 2011) to do what they want. Miriam managed to succeed in creating her own business, called "Daughter of the Desert," despite living in a patriarchal society where "marriages *are arranged* according to Bedouin tradition" (Ezra, 2011). Although Miriam is initially described as a young woman with initiative, we learn later that

> chance intervened in Miriam's life. Her father used to raise and trade horses. In the course of business, the family had developed a friendship with a woman from England. It was she who ultimately made it possible for Miriam to come to England, where she studied marketing for three years.

Although Miriam herself, as opposed to the other Bedouin women in her society, is not directly depicted in the passive voice, she is definitely assigned a passive role when "chance" intervenes in her life course. Had it not been for the British woman, Miriam could probably not have "made it" as a "non-typical entrepreneur" since "it was she [the British woman] who ultimately made it possible for Miriam" to be taken away of her traditional society, where she would presumably have entered into an arranged marriage, like all, supposedly, other Bedouin women.

These examples are a small sample of the general use of the passive in the EFL textbooks in order to refer to the Other. This usage tends to construct the Other as traditionalist, underdeveloped, dependent, and lacking agency. Some other examples are:

- "Many of the villagers *were caught up* in a vicious cycle of poverty" (Ezra, 2011, p. 40).
- "women in Jobra [a village in Bangladesh] break out of the desperate situation they *were trapped in*" (p. 40).
- "Rokia *is presented* as a victim of a larger global hunger" (p. 68).

The use of the passive voice in the EFL textbooks thus clearly depicts people of other ethnic, racial, or cultural groups as passive and non-initiating, and therefore perpetuates a negative image of the Other that is opposed to a positive image of the Western Self. It is also important to emphasize how "fate" or "chance" are presented as the agents responsible for success stories involving these people. We have seen how fate and chance intervened in the life of both Ryan (the black dropout) and Miriam (the young Bedouin woman) and how in both cases "fate" was represented by British people. We could fairly question, then, the "good" intentions of supposedly presenting the success of minority people, whose success depends on the "intervention" of a "British" or "Western" individual. This may also be seen as ironic, as the "Westerner" is referred to as *fate*. The simple question that we may ask ourselves is whether these representative characters would still have made it, had "fate" not intervened.

To further elaborate the point I raised at the end of the last section about the construction of the individual learner, the use of the active/passive voice, similar to the ideological use of indexical pronouns, might prevent students from taking agentive stances that question or oppose social inequalities and injustices. More specifically, the idealistic state of the Western individual does not include characters who might be interpellated by the ideological conventions of their native culture while subversively fighting against some of its norms. This was the case with Miriam, who indeed struggled against her society's prejudice against women, and yet managed to succeed. Despite being subversive, Miriam was not given full credit for her agentive initiative, which was rather attributed to the "intervention of fate" in the form of a British woman. In a follow-up reading activity, students are asked to think about the way women are treated in Bedouin society, as opposed to modern societies, and about having the right to choose one's spouse, as opposed to traditional arranged marriages. Therefore, we can again conclude that students are not motivated to think of Bedouin society, in this case, outside the narrative of patriarchy, lack of education, women's oppression, and traditionalism. Therefore, they are interpellated into perpetuating dominant western ideologies concerning the image of the Bedouin (or "Arab") (Said, 1978). Miriam is a definitive example of a subversive agent going against the conventions of her society, but she is not presented as a stimulus motivating readers to change the ideas they hold about her society. For them, she is *non-typical* and *an exception*.

Constructing the Target Audience

Van Dijk (2006) argues that explicit statements often signal local meanings. For example, making explicit that something or someone is "Western," "American," or "Jewish" indicates what can be taken for granted, and what must be stated upfront, in a particular cultural context. Israeli Jews might tend to make explicit their association with "modern" Western culture, and thereby evoke an in-group sense of belonging. The otherness of Palestinian Arabs, on the other hand, may be engendered through associating the Arab world and its chiefly (though of course not exclusively) Islamic culture with non-Western "backwardness," and evoke a sense of exclusion for Arab learners. Phrases such as "in our modern Western world" thus potentially alienate those who are less likely to see themselves as belonging to that world. In order to determine whether a text utilizes explicit statements in defining its target audience, I analyzed the contexts in which words such as "Western," "American," "Israeli/Jewish," "Eastern," "Arab," or "Palestinian" were used.

One editorial text entitled "You and the people around you: International Teen Magazine" (Turgeman & Zaltzman-Kulick, 2008) discusses international teen issues for the ostensible purpose of finding common ground. However, the text opens by explicitly linking questions to places: "Did you know that in the *United States*, teenagers under the age of 18 ... Did you know that in the *United Kingdom*, teenagers are ..." (p. 32; my emphasis). The editorial exclusively discusses issues involving American and British teenagers (regardless of what these issues are), undermining its claim to be a truly "International" teen magazine. One would think that truly international coverage of teenage issues would discuss problems from slightly further afield, including parts of the world characterized by different social, cultural, or religious customs and conventions, rather than two countries as closely linked as the United Kingdom and the United States.

The sheer prevalence of these countries in the textbooks suggests they play a culturally hegemonic role that the authors are invested in reproducing. This serves to fix in the minds of learners Israel as a supporter of Western – and chiefly American – hegemony. The assertion of the special link between Israel and the West is evident in texts such as "Israel often imitates American trends" (Ezra, 2011, p. 102) or in creating an explicit bond between Israeli Jews and Americans/Westerners by stating, for example, that "David is writing a letter to his American cousin, Jason" (Maor & Ziv, 2009, p. 16). A simple statement such as "We are visiting my grandparents in London this week" (Dobkins, 2008, p. 27) is another example. This emphasis on the fact that Israeli Jews have blood relations in the West appears in the EFL textbooks to make a clear statement: Israel is part of the West. It may also be argued that in creating such a close bond between Israel and America, or Britain, an even closer bond is created among certain mainstream Israeli Jewish groups – who are probably also upper-middle class – to whom America or Britain (metonymically representing Europe) is their homeland country or culture.

These examples reveal a uniformity in the ideological purpose that these explicit statements are meant to serve. They are used in narratives informing students of the folklore, history, and fairy tales of America and Europe. Other texts foreground class and/or gender debates in the West through stating that "in the United States, for every two men who receive a college degree, three women receive one," or that "young people in Western societies expect and demand the right to choose their own wife or husband" (in Ezra, 2011, pp. 56, 96). In these instances, American and Western societies are compared to Eastern "traditional" societies. In the former case, the statistics about women's education in the United States were presented following the text on Miriam (the Bedouin woman), who was an exceptional case in her traditional society, where woman are not given equal opportunities for education. The latter case was also presented in an interactional activity in which students were supposed to reflect on how marriages are performed and maintained in Western as opposed to traditional societies by highlighting the free choice of Westerners compared to the arranged (imposed) nature of marriages in Eastern or traditional societies. Finally, Jews were repeatedly connected to European or American communities through the discursive use of explicit statements, such as "this issue of our magazine for *Rosh Hashanah* is going to Jewish communities all over North America" (Komet & Partouche, 2006, p. 47).

In conclusion, the use of statements that explicitly specify West/Western, Israeli, Jewish, American, or the like, aims at defining the target audience of certain texts. The Palestinian Arab learning population is not, however, defined as part of the target audience; a conclusion that is based on the lack of statements that explicitly use terms such as Arab/East/Palestinian in the EFL textbooks. The explicit statements used in EFL textbooks have an ideological tendency to associate Israeli Jewish learners with Western and mainly American cultures, and therefore; to create a positive Western Self as opposed to a negative non-Western Other, and to promote an in-group feeling among Israeli – mainly upper-middle-class – Jewish learners and an out-group feeling among Palestinian Arab, and to a certain extent other Jewish, learners.

Representing the Narratives of Remote Cultures

Including culture as a significant component of language learning is required by the official English curriculum, and is implemented throughout the six textbooks. While there are a number of discussions of remote cultures in India, China, and Pakistan, no actual discussion of the local Palestinian Arab culture is presented. As already presented, the only two examples refer to stereotypical reductions of Bedouin culture that erase the Arab identity of Bedouin people. In one of the teaching units, entitled "A World of Stories," the theme is the universal role of storytelling and fairy tales in different cultures. The unit highlights the common features of storytelling and the universal values appearing in this literary genre, values such as love, hate, jealousy, and betrayal. The unit's main objective seems to be to increase students' intercultural awareness. Fairy tales and folktales from China, India, and Ethiopia are presented. These are juxtaposed with popular Western fairy tales such as Snow White and Cinderella.

One text reviews the history of fairy tales, informing students that the best-known fairy tale, Cinderella, can be traced back to ninth-century China. When adapted for Western audiences by the German Brothers Grimm, the students are told, these tales are presented without their "darker and more terrifying elements" (Turgeman & Zaltzman-Kulick, 2008, p. 95). It is implied that there is a dark aspect of Chinese culture, something perverse that cannot be adopted by the West undiluted. The example provided to support this claim in the text is that in the original Chinese version of Cinderella, the older stepsister cannot get her big toe into the glass slipper, so her mother hands her a knife and tells her to cut it off, since once she is queen, she will no longer need to walk. The daughter does as she is told. This scene associates violence and mutilation with a murky Eastern Other that, plausibly, is not merely Chinese. Brutality and subservience are commonly associated with the Orient in general in Western cultural production (Said, 1978). When learners read about these negative violent images as deriving from the East and rejected by the West, they assign negative and positive values respectively. The use of such discursive strategies may perpetuate prevailing Western stereotypes regarding other cultures, which depict them as inferior.

Elsewhere, students read an Indian tale about reincarnation, as well as an Ethiopian tale. Both narratives represent the people of these cultures as primitive, traditionalist, and superstitious, which is implicitly opposed to the civilized, modern, and rational West. The main character in the Indian tale is a "guru," who is portrayed in a drawing (next to the story) wearing nothing but a piece of fabric only covering his waist and another wrapped around his head (in the traditional Indian manner) and sitting on the ground. He lives in a barn and dreams that he is going to be reincarnated as a pig, therefore requesting his favorite disciple to slaughter him once this happens. However, when this does indeed come to pass, the pig suddenly speaks and asks him not to do so because his life as a pig is actually better.

The description of the Indian character, his portrait, and the message conveyed by this tale (i.e. that living as a pig is preferable to living as a human being in India) all carry a cultural message, which is also problematic. Comparing the two manners of existence that is introduced by the figure of the guru sparks a fundamental philosophical question that brings to mind John Stuart Mill's debate on whether "it is better to be a human being dissatisfied than a pig satisfied; better to be Socrates dissatisfied than a fool satisfied" (Mill, 1993, p. 10). The visual representation of the Indian guru and his choice to remain a "happy pig" as described in the text offer a counter-philosophy, that this guru espouses. To argue that the text might have intended to engage students in a philosophical debate on individual conceptions of the good life is hard to make without any textual clues indicating that students are expected to so do. This does not seem to be the case in this text. Neither the text nor the follow-up activities offer such an intellectual challenge to discuss what human happiness is or whether it is better to be a happy pig than an unhappy

Socrates. It could be argued, then, that the failure to link the image of the guru to such a philosophical debate presents the Other culture (in this case, Indian) as inferior, dehumanized, miserable, and no better than living as an animal. These associations are important and powerful, as students consider texts and textbooks an authoritative sources, and tend to accept what appears in them as informative knowledge.

As for the presentation of Bedouin culture in the English textbooks, it is worth mentioning that the two examples (either directly or indirectly) associate Bedouin characters with the desert and camels. Although this is not made explicit in the textbooks, it needs to be clarified for readers who are not familiar with the demographical fact that Bedouins in Israel are Muslim Arabs. In his discussion of the Arab image in the minds of Western image-makers, Hamada, (2001). argues:

> The fear of Islam and Muslims is a major factor in the production of the negative Arab image in the west, most specifically in the United States. This is the case since, in much of the writing about Arabs, there is confusion concerning 'Arabs' and 'Muslims'. Consequently, to many if not most western peoples the terms 'Arab' and 'Muslim' are interchangeable. One often gets the impression that Arabs and the desert are always synonymous – or at least they belong to each other.
>
> *(p. 9)*

Numerous studies involving Western images of Arabs have also revealed "a strong anti-Arab bias as reflected in the public's negative stereotypes of Arabs – their society, culture, and institutions" (p. 7). As was discussed above, the Bedouin entrepreneur Miriam, who is described as non-typical, assumes the stereotypical title "daughter of the desert." A narrative in *Building Blocks* entitled "Desert camel tours in the Negev" opens as follows: "On our tour, we use the desert's most ancient form of travel – the camel" (Dobkins, 2008, p. 10). It is in this context that we are introduced to "Mahmoud," who works as a guide for tourists in the desert. The narrative describes a scene in which Western travelers are touring the desert on camelback, guided by Mahmoud, who wears a *galabiya* (Arabic for a long cloak) and an *iqal* (Arabic for a white head scarf), which are traditional, folkloric Arabic clothing (as the picture accompanying the text shows). The text is accompanied by a photograph showing the travelers (Western-looking in clothes and appearance) on camelback accompanied by a Bedouin guide, who is leading the camels and carrying a shepherd's crook.

Given that representations of Arabs are so rare in the textbooks, the stereotypical image of the Arab presented here is especially significant. It is not that Bedouin culture is somehow unworthy of representing the Palestinian Arab minority, but rather that they are presented in a way that accords most closely with the stereotype of backward traditionalism, without mentioning any other groups. Not only is the large Arab minority as a whole misrepresented in this book; Bedouins themselves have rapidly become urbanized, and today lead more "modern" lifestyles. The representation of Mahmoud thus invokes the Bedouin past more than its present or future.

In conclusion, while the textbooks present Western culture in a positive light, non-Western cultures are presented as backward and permanently stuck in the past. Because (as was argued earlier) the textbooks work to associate their audience with the West (and not the East), a Negative-Other group is reproduced simultaneously with a Positive-Self group (van Dijk, 2006). The EFL textbooks thus tend to construct positive Western cultural narratives in opposition to negative non-Western narratives, perpetuating and reproducing negative and dominant stereotypes about non-Western cultures, while avoiding almost entirely the representation of Palestinian Arab culture.

Culturally Specific Prior Knowledge

As explained briefly above, the prior cultural knowledge that students need to have so they can read and understand the texts in EFL textbooks is grounded mainly in upper-middle-class Jewish exposure to Western and American cultural production. In this section, I discuss the role this knowledge plays as a cultural gatekeeper preventing Palestinian Arab learners (and perhaps other Jewish learners) from relating to these English passages, and consequently from fully comprehending them. The textbook authors, who are mostly native English speakers, use their knowledge of Western culture, which is indeed not available to all English learners.

Culturally specific prior knowledge entails familiarity with common Western or American cultural symbols, starting with knowledge of specific locations (such as Fifth Avenue), famous people (such as Abraham Lincoln), movies or TV programs (such as *Friends*), and ending with knowledge of abstract notions such as "Murphy"s Law" or the idea that "Berkeley" is "progressive." When texts mention the names of supposedly well-known American or Western personalities, such as Abraham Lincoln, Stephen King, or Stephen Hawking, without offering a biographical note to explain who they are, the underlying assumption is that they are well known to everybody. The comprehension questions that follow reading texts often rely on students' knowledge of these figures that is not contained in the texts themselves. It should be noted, moreover, that some English teachers in the Arabic-speaking schools may themselves not be familiar with these people or concepts. Even if they are, the process of explaining every detail might make EFL an exhausting experience, frustrating both learners and teachers.

Other texts focus on topics dealing with the history, lifestyle, and/or other social-cultural aspects of the United States or Britain. For example, in a text about the American Great Depression of the 1920s, places such as Columbus Circle, Fifth Avenue, and Central Park are mentioned without explaining their place in the geography of New York. Familiarity with these and other American localities and cultural symbols is shared between people whose English-language cultural consumption is oriented around the United States, which includes only specific Israeli learners: those from upper-middle-class backgrounds, or those who have gained exposure to these settings through traveling, meeting relatives/visitors from abroad, or who share a personal admiration for or a desire to learn more about American culture.

The assumption of this cultural familiarity also reproduces a class bias, which discriminates against all Israelis who are not part of the established, West-oriented middle class. The sheer intensity of Western/American cultural references in the textbooks, which often constitutes the basis for comprehending English passages, presents an insensitive, one-dimensional, and naïve view of EFL learners.

The cultural reference points of the textbooks analyzed were thus chiefly drawn from Western culture and ideology. Teaching English through the use of narratives depicting one sector of privileged people, who share similar speech practices, customs, lifestyles, and behavior, constructs an image of English being associated with these commonalities. The exclusiveness of these narratives may well increase a sense of exclusion, or even hostility, among people who do not associate with mainstream Western culture. The culturally specific prior knowledge required by the English textbooks unfairly rewards those with a high degree of exposure to Western/American contexts. It would thus be fair to conclude that these textbooks assume a cultural common ground of Western-American prior knowledge based on upper-middle-class Jewish exposure to US and Western culture.

Constructing Identities and Collective Memories

As noted earlier in Chapter 1, school textbooks are used as agents for producing and perpetuating national identity and collective memory. In a conflict-ridden place such as Israel, and especially since the Jewish ethno-nation is a mixture of people from all over the world with hardly anything in common, Zerubavel (2002) posits that questions of collective and individual identities are controversial, and can often become heated arguments, or even "history wars."

Textbook writers tend to include materials that comply with the dominant ideology of educational policy-makers (Yiftachel, 2006). These materials include ideas, symbols, practices, and historical names and figures that are the foundation of Jewish-Zionist national identity and collective memory. Textbook writers are workers in the field of re-contextualization, and thus contribute to the perpetuation and reproduction of already existent features of identity and memory (Bernstein, 1996).

The reoccurrence of the theme of national military service in the EFL textbooks demonstrates the way that learners are interpellated as involved in the reproduction of a specifically Jewish national identity. Jewish protagonists and their relatives who have to finish their army service before traveling or studying are often foregrounded. Every practice of traveling, learning, or decision-making presented in these textbooks is conditioned by completing army service. While reading these narratives, Israeli Jewish youngsters, who will soon be drafted into compulsory army service, may first form an in-group feeling with characters who are about to start or finish their army service; second, they might internalize that this structural order (i.e. finishing army service, traveling, and then studying) is the normative way of leading a real Jewish life in Israel, and is thus the core of their national Jewish identity. In other words, a Jewish national identity emerges through presenting army service as the core of the linguistic depiction of this idealistic structural order within Israeli society.

Taken together, when a text states that "many of Israel's political leaders have come from *the army*, for example, Moshe Dayan, Yitzhak Rabin, and Ezer Weizmann" (Cohen et al., 2006, p. 60), learners internalize the idea that in order to make it up the ladder in Israel, one needs to start in the army, just as Ilan Ramon said: "The State of Israel decided that the first one [astronaut] would be from *the Air Force*" (Komet & Partouche, 2006, p. 47). As a result of forming such a political and ideological position, any person who does not abide by this structural order (i.e. Palestinian Arabs, or other Jewish groups) might be treated with indifference and hostility. On the other hand, Palestinian Arab learners, who do not serve in the Israeli army, have different ways of constituting their national identity as Palestinian Arabs living in Israel. The problematic aspect of dealing with the issue of army service among Palestinian Arabs is their common rejection of the role the Israeli army plays in treating Palestinians in the Occupied Territories.

Similarly, creating a collective memory based on Jewish and national ideological symbols is done through the reading of narratives that repeatedly remind Jewish learners of values or facts that constitute their collective memory as Jews. In a text about the Israeli performing artist *Yossi Banai* (Maor & Ziv, 2009, p. 48), the narrative highlights how growing up in his neighborhood (Jerusalem's *Mahane Yehuda*) affected his performance. The text states: "Throughout his impressive career he always told stories about growing up in Jerusalem and even sang about it in 'Me, Shimon and little Moishe'" (Maor & Ziv, 2009). The song carries nostalgic overtones of longing for Jerusalem as embodied in a description of Banai's childhood neighborhood, *Mahane Yehuda*. The linguistic choice of phrases such as "that colorful neighborhood" and the choice of biblical Hebrew names (*Shimon*: Simon and *Moishe*: Moses) are all features used in Israeli-Zionist narratives, according to Peled-Elhanan (2012), to unite Jewish Israelis, who "have come from the remotest corners of the world, with nothing in common except their ancestors' religion" (p. 8). The whole narrative is ideologically shaped and produces a feeling of Zionist belonging in Jerusalem. It is worthy of mention that the text states that Banai was born in 1933, prior to the establishment of the State of Israel. But the narrative refrains from mentioning this fact and depicts Banai's childhood neighborhood, *Mahane Yehuda*, as an entity dating from ancient history. The reality of Jerusalem's neighborhoods is, in fact, far more complicated than this fanciful description would suggest. The debate over Jerusalem is an incendiary issue in the Israeli-Palestinian conflict, mainly due to the fundamental role played by Jerusalem in the three main religions.

The last point to be made in this section involves lexical choices that might create a Jewish national bond. Examples would be words and phrases relating to the Holocaust, such as "Holocaust survivor," "Auschwitz," "Holocaust Remembrance Day," "commemorating the Holocaust," "annual trips to Poland," "Holocaust deniers," and so on. All of these terms unite the Jewish people by one shared collective memory that aims at keeping the memory of the Holocaust central to Jewish-Zionist identity. Other narratives use terms such as "the Israeli flag," "synagogue," "Purim," "kosher," and so on, which may cause the Jewish learner to identify passionately when reading these narratives and engaging in the discussion activities that follow them. These passionate feelings experienced by Jewish learners may be experienced as alienating by Arab learners, who may not relate to or even understand the symbolic significance of such words. My contention is that the presentation of these Jewish symbols could be better interpreted and accepted for consideration by the Arab learners had the EFL textbooks not erased Palestinian Arab words, symbols, and historical memories. Providing an egalitarian representation of the Self and the Other is the principle that should govern the architecture of EFL textbooks, as I will argue in Chapter 6.

Analysis of the ideological roles of English narratives has revealed prominent use of the army service issue as a major constituent of Jewish national identity and repeated use of Jewish/Zionist notions as major constituents in the Jewish collective memory. It could be fair to conclude that through the use of such narratives, the EFL textbooks perpetuate and reproduce one national Jewish identity and collective memory, and provide narratives that include Jewish learners as an in-group and exclude Palestinian Arab learners as an out-group.

Conclusion

The cultural suitability of English textbooks has been examined in this part of my study in an attempt to check whether their cultural content caters to the Palestinian Arab cultural milieu. Discourse has been viewed as a special practice which is imbued with power and ideology, and therefore, a discourse analysis of the English textbooks has been conducted. Textbook analysis has shown how through the reoccurrence of Western and basically American and Jewish culturally based issues, the textbooks interpellate English learners as Western-oriented Jewish-Zionist subjects, thus contributing to the reproduction and perpetuation of Western and Jewish hegemony. Besides serving as a tool for perpetuating and reproducing dominant hegemonic ideas, English textbooks in Israel reinforce the marginalization of the Palestinian Arab minority.

To sum up, I should note that students learn from their schoolbooks and mostly "learn to present interpretations as facts, to insert personal views into seemingly neutral representations; in short they learn the language of power" (Coffin, 1997, cited in Peled-Elhanan, 2012, p. 231). However, textbooks are duty-bound to offer learners a language that represents facts and views of other people. This chapter has presented preliminary concerns regarding the ideological nature of the language used to teach and learn English in Israel. In Chapter 4, I examine how the cultural content of EFL texts shapes and constructs learners' identities and ideological stances about the Other.

Note

1 The author gratefully acknowledges SAGE Publications for publishing an earlier version of this chapter in *Discourse & Society*. Awayed-Bishara, M. (2015). Analyzing the cultural content of materials used for teaching English to high school speakers of Arabic in Israel. *Discourse & Society*. May (2015), 1–26. https://doi.org/10.1177%2F0957926515581154.

References

Textbooks

Cohen, J., Loney, N., & Kerman, S. (2006). *Results for 4 points*. Ra'anana: Eric Cohen Books.
Dobkins, J. (2008). *Build up*. Ra'anana: Eric Cohen Books.
Ezra, E. (2011). *High points*. Ra'anana: Eric Cohen Books.
Komet, C., & Partouche, D. (2006). *Ten*. Ra'anana: Eric Cohen Books.
Maor, Z., & Ziv, M. (2009). *Zoom*. Tel Aviv: University Publishing Press.
Turgeman, H., & Zaltzman-Kulick, R. (2008). *Dimensions*. Tel Aviv: University Publishing Press.

Works cited

Akere, F. (2006). The English language in Nigeria: The sociolinguistic dynamics of decolonization (pp. 2–16). Paper presented at the Conference of the Nigerian English Studies Association, University of Ilorin.
Bernstein, B. (1996). *Pedagogy, symbolic control and identity: Theory, research, critique*. London: Taylor & Francis.
Bucholtz, M., & Hall, K. (2005). Identity and interaction: A sociocultural linguistic approach. *Discourse Studies*, 7(4–5),585–614. doi:10.1177/1461445605054407.
Canagarajah, A. S. (1999). *Resisting linguistic imperialism in English teaching*. Oxford: Oxford University Press.
Carrell, P. L. (1989). Metacognitive awareness and second language reading. *The Modern Language Journal*, 73(2), 121–134. doi:10.2307/326568.
Carrell, P. L. (1991). Strategies reading. In *Georgetown University Roundtable on Language and Linguistics* (pp. 167–178). Washington, DC: Georgetown University Press.
Chiu, S., & Chiang, W. (2012). Representations of the name rectification movement of Taiwan indigenous people: Through whose historical lens? *Language and Linguistics; Taipei*, 13(3), 523–568.
Fairclough, N. (1992). *Discourse and social change*. Cambridge: Polity Press.
Frogner, T. (1999). European identity: A perspective from a Norwegian European, or a European Norwegian. In T. Jansen (Ed.), *Reflections on European identity* (pp. 73–76). Brussels: European Commission.
Hamada, B. I. (2001). The Arab image in the minds of western image-makers. *The Journal of International Communication*, 7(1), 7–35. doi:10.1080/13216597.2001.9751897.
Karayanni, M. (2018). Multiculturalism as covering: On the accommodation of minority religions in Israel. *The American Journal of Comparative Law*, 66(4), 831–875. doi:10.1093/ajcl/avy039.
Kuzar, R. (2011). The subversive agent: Anatomy of personal ideological change. *Semiotica*, 2011 (185), 223–234. doi:10.1515/semi.2011.040.

Lin, L. (2004). Effects of culturally specific prior knowledge on Taiwanese EFL students' English reading comprehension. PhD thesis. University of Victoria, Victoria, BC.

Mill, J. S. (1993). *Utilitarianism: On liberty; considerations on representative government; remarks on Bentham's philosophy*. (G. Williams, Ed.). London: Everyman's Library.

Nasser, R., & Nasser, I. (2008). Textbooks as a vehicle for segregation and domination: State efforts to shape Palestinian Israelis' identities as citizens. *Journal of Curriculum Studies*, 40(5), 627–650. doi:10.1080/00220270802072804.

Peled-Elhanan, N. (2012). *Palestine in Israeli school books: Ideology and propaganda in education*. London: I.B. Tauris.

Podeh, E. (2000). History and memory in the Israeli educational system: The portrayal of the Arab-Israeli conflict in history textbooks (1948–2000). *History and Memory*, 12(1), 65–100. doi:10.1353/ham.2000.0005.

Podeh, E. (2002). *The Arab-Israeli conflict in Israeli history textbooks, 1948–2000*. Westport, CT: Bergin and Garvey.

Said, E. W. (1978). *Orientalism*. New York: Vintage Books.

Shin, J., Eslami, Z. R., & Chen, W.-C. (2011). Presentation of local and international culture in current international English-language teaching textbooks. *Language, Culture and Curriculum*, 24(3), 253–268. doi:10.1080/07908318.2011.614694.

Tajfel, H., & Turner, J. C. (1986). The social identity theory of intergroup behavior. In W. G. Austin & S. Worchel (Eds.), *Psychology of intergroup relations*. Chicago, IL: Nelson-Hall.

van Dijk, T. A. (2006). Discourse and manipulation. *Discourse & Society*, 17(3), 359–383. doi:10.1177/0957926506060250.

Wodak, R. (2002). Fragmented identities: Redefining and recontextualizing national identity. In P. Chilton & C. Schäffner (Eds.), *Politics as text and talk: Analytic approaches to political discourse* (pp. 143–172). Amsterdam: John Benjamins.

Wortham, S. E. F. (1996). Mapping participant deictics: A technique for discovering speakers' footing. *Journal of Pragmatics*, 25(3), 331–348. doi:10.1016/0378-2166(94)00100-00106.

Yiftachel, O. (2006). *Ethnocracy: Land and identity politics in Israel/Palestine*. Philadelphia, PA: University of Pennsylvania Press.

Zerubavel, Y. (2002). The "Mythological Sabra" and Jewish past: Trauma, memory, and contested identities. *Israel Studies*, 7(2), 115–144.

4
STORIED SELVES
Analysis of EFL Learners' Cultural Representations

This chapter examines how the cultural content of EFL textbooks constructs the identities, global cultural consciousness, and intracultural/multicultural understanding of English language learners. Based on 12 hours of recorded interviews with 30 Jewish and Arab high school EFL learners that focused on their description and understanding of four texts in authorized Israeli EFL textbooks, the analysis suggests that certain cultural representations work to complicate identity construction processes, hindering the development of globally/locally aware language learners open to learning about and accepting the Other.

Introduction

Previous studies have focused on the textual and/or visual representation of specific cultural groups in EFL textbooks, generally through applying either quantitative or qualitative methodologies. Analysts have counted the number of times that nations, well-known figures, or places, among other cultural tokens, are mentioned; they have also critically analyzed texts in terms of Self/Other representations. What has not been examined, however, is the manner in which learners exposed to these texts might negotiate and be influenced by their underlying ideological content (Weninger & Kiss, 2013, p. 7). Mindful of a common critique of Critical Discourse Analysis (CDA) – that it is not sufficiently oriented toward the analysis of pedagogical texts – this chapter offers a perspective on how this important analytical tradition might be used to analyze learning and meaning-making processes in educational environments. I contend that, as an analytical tool, personal narratives – or *storied selves* – can be viewed as an interface between discourse and meaning-making, discourse and the reproduction of hegemonic ideologies, and between discourse and social change. Methodologically speaking, I investigate possible ways in which EFL discourse shapes and constructs processes of meaning-making and identity formation among learners in actual learning situations. My presupposition is that textbooks can play a pivotal role both in perpetuating hegemonic ideologies and negative cultural representations of the Other, and in transforming preconceived ideas and promoting mutual understanding and respect. To investigate this assumption, I focus on the discursive practices of learners while they interact with EFL texts in order to examine how their own practices foster notions of Self/Other, and how they represent and negotiate their identities and textual understanding through language. As EFL is taught globally, insights into the meaning-making and identity construction processes of EFL learners from different national, linguistic, cultural, and ethnic backgrounds are crucial. I would argue that they are even more so in conflictual educational settings.

EFL Discourse and Learning Processes

The major shift in the status of English from the local language of English-speaking countries to the global language of communication, academe, commerce, and world politics has motivated a revisiting of the issue of cultural representation in EFL textbooks (e.g. Awayed-Bishara, 2015; Gray, 2010; Lee, 2009; Yamanaka, 2006; Yuen, 2011). In line with current scholarly approaches, culture is understood as a complex and transnational phenomenon (Risager, 2007) requiring teachers of EFL to move beyond the mere teaching of language structures and vocabulary. Within the notion of promoting so-called "21st century skills" (Trilling & Fadel, 2009), learners are expected to learn how to become critically reflective (Kumaravadivelu, 2008), politically conscious and engaged (Byram, 2011), and cosmopolitan (Rizvi, 2005). Thus, *global cultural consciousness* and *intercultural citizenship* have been key words – at least since 2000 – as they are the major outcomes of EFL pedagogies that aim to play a transformative role (Byram, 2008; 2011; Kumaravadivelu, 2008). Against this backdrop, I analyze whether the cultural content of EFL texts promotes intercultural awareness and reflexive thinking, and whether an *intracultural* understanding of the Other is advanced by EFL materials.

For this purpose, and in accordance with the line of analysis I initiated in Chapter 3, I approach the question of EFL ideologies from a different angle: that of the learners' perspectives. I examine the extent to which what is often considered a *neutral* yardstick by textbook writers, i.e. global English, may not be neutral at all, but might become an ideological vehicle for local interests and concerns. In the case of Israel, I argue that English might serve a pro-Zionist and Western-oriented agenda. Discourse analysis of English textbooks used in Israeli high schools demonstrates how the recurrence of Western – specifically American and Jewish – cultural tokens ideologically position English learners as Western-oriented, Jewish, and Zionist subjects, contributing to the reproduction and perpetuation of Western and Jewish hegemony (Awayed-Bishara, 2015). Concomitantly, English textbooks both elide the identity of the Palestinian Arab minority, its culture and traditions, and misrepresent and marginalize its members.

By shifting the focus from the textbooks to the learners themselves, this chapter aims to investigate how EFL discourse is reproduced, negotiated, and contested by high school students from the Jewish majority, and the Palestinian Arab minority, in Israel. As the English curriculum is uniform across populations, EFL educational discourse could potentially function as a tool for bringing Jewish and Palestinian Arabs closer. However, this would require a reconstruction of EFL pedagogy around goals, such as transformation and social change, and such an objective could only be achieved through offering egalitarian and positive representations of the Self and the Other (Awayed-Bishara, 2018). I will discuss the details of these transformative EFL pedagogies at length in Chapter 6. To illustrate how this might be facilitated, I will first do the groundwork of demonstrating how culture and ideology are major constituents of EFL discourse in Israel. I will then show how CDA of the discursive construction of EFL learners' "storied selves" serves to assess their growth as critical/reflective thinkers, intraculturally, and/or multiculturally conscious citizens.

"Storied Selves" and Identity Politics in the Israeli Educational System

In Chapter 1, I presented the complexity Palestinian students face while learning English in a state-controlled educational system that serves the interests of hegemonic Israeli politics. In this chapter, I focus on *how* EFL learners' "storied selves" are discursively constituted, while relating to the cultural content of EFL texts used in the Israeli context. I specifically ask: How do EFL learners narrate themselves as insiders/outsiders, superior/inferior, or subjects/agents when relating to EFL texts? The cultural content of the materials they have access to through EFL textbooks may, to a certain extent, determine the stories they tell about who *they*, or the *Others* they read about, are. Learners' authoring of themselves may be in alignment with the textbook's depiction of who they or the Other are (e.g. "positive Self" or "negative Other") or in reaction against these textual constructions. The construction of counter-narratives shows how learners represent themselves in relation to other people in order to reframe their identities. The notion of *storied selves*, then, marks the processes whereby people arrive at a sense of selfhood and identity (Luttrell, 1997). A socially-situated identity involves a process of conveying a perceptible "kind of person" performing a "certain kind of act" (Gee, 2009, p. 13). Regarding the ways learners react to messages provided in EFL textbooks, Rogers and Elias (2012) suggest that "cultural models and situated identities often include multiple, fluid, and unstable relationships that form [an individual's] sense of self" (p. 260).

In the Althusserian perspective of identity as institutionally determined, individuals have no say about the nature of their identity (Althusser, 2000). Identity is seen as a predetermined act where "there is no core quality to our identity which exists outside the time and place of our existence" (Suleiman, 2011, p. 50). Palestine's poet laureate, Mahmoud Darwish, describes the complexity of Palestinian identity: "What about identity? I asked. He said: self-defense ... Identity is *the child of birth*, but at the end, it"s *self-invention*, and not an inheritance of the past. I am *multiple* ... Within me an ever new exterior" (Darwish, 2005, cited in Butler, 2012, p. 218).[1]

In this regard, the use of phrases such as "I was born an Arab" may shed light on the way identity is imposed on people, not least those who live in societies characterized by power hierarchies in which they are assigned dominant/subordinate relationships. Novel identities may, however, emerge as people enter into processes of socialization, resulting in new identity definitions different from or complementary (sometimes even contradictory) to their initially imposed identity.

Contrary to the fixed notion of identity, I see identity as relational, and as part of a process of ongoing construction through linguistic interactions. Similarly, Bucholtz and Hall (2005) see identity as a construct that is situated in discourse, and that surfaces within an interaction as two speakers engage in discourse. Speakers' identities are seen as dynamic, mutable and malleable, situated in a social relationship with other people that emerge through interaction. In line with this fluid notion of identity, I examine EFL learners' identity formation as part of a process of ongoing construction through linguistic interactions. Within such an ongoing dialogic interaction, one may recognize certain power asymmetries. Realizing that the constitution of social identity is enmeshed in these power relationships (Hall, 2000, p. 17) "compels us to accept that groups will define themselves and be defined in terms of dominance and subordination" (Suleiman, 2011, p. 50). Thus, identity construction involves a process of othering (Blommaert, 2005) or "differentiation from what is not" (Wodak, de Cilla, Reisigl, & Liebhart, 1999, p. 3). Within the Israeli-Palestinian context, "the acceptance of one group's identity and aspiration for national self-determination is often interpreted as necessarily invalidating the identity of the other – given the extent to which each group desires a monopoly on political and territorial control" (Hammack, 2006, p. 6). Reading EFL texts containing ideological messages might cause EFL learners – in our case, both Jewish and Palestinian Arab – to reconsider their present conceptions of Self and Other. Against this backdrop, I investigate how EFL learners socially situate their identities in ways that either reinforce the messages conveyed by EFL textbooks, or act subversively against them. Before delving into detailed analysis of interviews with EFL learners, I first want to reintroduce the four EFL texts (which I analyzed in detail in Chapter 3) employed in this study, followed by some methodological reflections on research design.

The Four EFL Texts

Analysis of EFL narratives and texts referring the Self or Other (who might be Western/non-Western, Jewish/non-Jewish, or majority/minority) indicated that such characters are often represented as examples of success stories (see Chapter 3). In contrast to members of majorities, members of minorities are depicted either grammatically in the passive voice or through other devices that obscure agency, thus emphasizing that their success was determined by another explicitly or implicitly mentioned agent (usually American, British, or European) who intervened and changed the course of their destinies (Awayed-Bishara, 2015). An analysis of the use of active/passive voice, lexical selections, or personal pronouns examines whether a writer's overall choice of a certain linguistic feature reflects underlying assumptions regarding the characteristics of particular religious, ethnic, disabled, gendered, or culturally different groups (Awayed-Bishara, 2015; 2018; Fairclough, 1992; van Dijk, 2006).

The first text presents the story of Ryan, who is described in the passive voice and is referred to in the text as "a black teenage dropout" who was "at the edge of the criminal world" until he "was placed in one of Britain's top boarding schools" by "a British television company" (Cohen, Loney, & Kerman, 2006, p. 106). In juxtaposition to Ryan, the same textbook presents a narrative about Liz Murray, who is described in the active voice. Liz managed to progress from being homeless to winning a scholarship to Harvard. Although Liz is white, as can be seen by the accompanying illustration, the text refrains from stating this, as opposed to the explicit use of the term "black" to describe Ryan. Throughout the text, Liz's decisions are unaffected by anything but her own agency and her will to change the status quo.

The third text describes a Bedouin woman who (like all Bedouins) is an Arab, but is not referred to as such in the text. Miriam is described as an exceptional young Bedouin woman and a "non-typical entrepreneur," who was not like "most Bedouin women who are not allowed" to do as they wish. Miriam manages to create her own business called "Daughter of the Desert," despite living in a patriarchal society where "marriages are arranged according to Bedouin tradition" (Ezra, 2011, p. 54). Although Miriam, as opposed to the other Bedouin women in her society, is not directly depicted in the passive voice, she is assigned a non-agentive role in the "intervention of chance" in her life course. Had it not been for a British woman, Miriam could probably not have made it as a "non-typical entrepreneur" since the text states "it was she [the British woman] who ultimately enabled Miriam" to go to England and study marketing.

The fourth text presents a Self-narrative in the form of an interview with the late Israeli astronaut, Ilan Ramon, in which his Zionist and Jewish identity is highlighted through the use of words describing his army service, his being the son of Holocaust survivors, and his Jewish patriotism. The recurrence of army service in English textbooks demonstrates the way these textbooks interpellate students through an *inner voice* repeatedly reminding them of those elements constituting Jewish national identity. Jewish protagonists or their relatives are often represented as completing their army service before traveling or studying (Awayed-Bishara, 2015).

Research Design

The analysis in this chapter is based on a corpus of 12 hours of recorded interview data collected from 30 Jewish and Arab high school EFL learners. In the interviews, learners describe and interpret their understanding of the four texts described above. Focusing on how learners actually interact with these texts sheds light on the processes of identity construction provoked by reading these texts. All interviews were conducted in the interviewees' first language – which was either Hebrew or Arabic – and are presented here in English translation. The research sample represents various national/ethnic and religious groups who reside in various towns/cities in northern Israel. Table 4.1 illustrates the distribution of the interviewees (identified by pseudonyms) based on age, gender, nationality, and religion. The interviews were for the most part structured, and in some cases (with the consent of the students and their parents) interactions between students were recorded. The latter generally took place after the individual interviews, and took the form of an extended group discussion on the topic of the interview.

CDA (Fairclough, 1992; van Dijk, 2006; Wodak, 2011; Wodak & Fairclough, 2010) was employed to analyze students' responses and to examine processes of identity formation among EFL learners. Conducting a CDA of students' responses to the four texts required examining their use of certain ideologically-motivated discursive devices. First, according to van Dijk (2006), lexical selection may allude to the manner in which a speaker represents other groups or differentiates the Self from the Other. For example, the use of personal pronouns, such as "we" or "they," alongside other types of deictic words, may guide analysts to uncover a possible ideological position, such as establishing an interactional in-group feeling as opposed to an out-group feeling or creating a "we" versus "they" distinction through presenting "us" in a positive and upgrading manner and "them" (i.e. the Other) in a negative and degrading manner (Awayed-Bishara, 2015; van Dijk, 2006; Wortham, 1996).

Different views about the "universes of discourse" (Marcuse, 1964) described in EFL texts may also be evoked, as Jewish and Palestinian Arab students hold different (if not opposing) views regarding the shared space in which they live. Subsequently, worldviews are "the outcome of given texts and discourse worlds" (Filardo-Llamas, 2015, p. 281). Moreover, a text might function as a linguistic and

TABLE 4.1 Distribution of interviewees based on age, gender, ethnic, and religious affiliation

Pseudonyms	Age	Gender	Ethnicity	Religion	Number
Layana, Maria, Rula, Reema	16–17	Female	Arab	Christian	4
Rami, Afif, Sari, Ameer, Fadi	16–17	Male	Arab	Christian	5
Yara, Mira, Eman, Ahlam	16–17	Female	Arab	Muslim	4
Tasnim, Amina, Ranya	16–17	Female	Arab/ Bedouin	Muslim	3
Adam, Ahmad, Ali, Rawad, Wajdi	16–18	Male	Arab	Muslim	5
Avishag, Yael, Tami, Chen	16–17	Female	Jewish	Jewish	4
Omer, Etai, Uriah, Edo, Itzik	16–17	Male	Jewish	Jewish	5
Total					30

multimodal stimulus contributing to the construction of a point of view (Sweetser, 2012, p. 3). In this respect, recontextualization plays an important role because parts of a text that previously appeared in a different context are reiterated and thereby endowed with new meanings (Filardo-Llamas, 2015). Through recontextualization, then, each student makes a distinct statement about the way the Other is presented in these texts.

Speakers may also discursively construct a "face," which Goffman (1967) defines as an image "pieced together from the expressive implications of the full flow of events in an undertaking" (p. 31) and "the positive social value a person effectively claims for [her/himself] by the line others assume [s/he] has taken during a particular contact" (p. 5). Speakers will thus attempt to advance or minimize "face-threatening acts." According to Brown and Levinson (1987), "the desired minimization of face-threatening acts compels speakers to utilize several strategies that range from not committing face-threatening acts (FTA) at all to committing these acts without mitigation" (p. 60). Through utilizing diagnostic tools appropriate to assessing how the aforementioned discursive devices construct ideological positions, I intend to show in the following analysis section how the subjects of this study undergo complex identity construction processes as a result of exposure to the four EFL texts.

Hypothesizing that educational discourse, and more specifically EFL discourse, is imbued with power and that ideology plays an important function on EFL learners' identity formation, the analysis provided in this chapter seeks to answer following three research questions:

1. What images of the "Other" do EFL school texts (re)produce or perpetuate in learners' narratives?
2. What kind of in-group/out group relations do EFL school narratives enable/constrain among English learners?
3. What other identity processes emerge from the reading of EFL school narratives?

Findings and Data Analysis

EFL and Global Cultural Consciousness: Creating Agents or Interpellating Subjects?

This section examines how EFL textbooks help to create individual agents with subversive inclinations, but also interpellates subjects, who are subconsciously subjugated by the dominant ideologies propounded in some texts. The following excerpt demonstrates how Yara, a 16-year-old female Palestinian Arab student, undergoes an ongoing transitional process of the construction of Self after reading the text about Ryan (the "black teenager"):

> [In] the environment in which Ryan lived, everybody was like him because he was influenced by them and it's normal that those surrounding him will be like him. I mean, if I were surrounded by good people, let's say, they would also affect me positively, but what was going on there was negative.

Yara's initial position regarding this text is based on a clear distinction between the Self (i.e. "I") who is "positively" affected by her relatively advantaged environment as opposed to the Other (i.e. "Ryan") who is negatively affected (indicated by "was negative") (van Dijk, 2006). However, as the interaction proceeds, Yara goes on to state:

> Nowadays, the idea about black people has changed. We see black people who are educated, who are better, even better than whites. They have finally overcome the situation they were in.

Yara uses "nowadays" in order to draw on an idea that was previously mentioned by Rami (another interlocutor) who mentioned how "black people are discriminated against." By recontextualizing this previous idea about black people, she presents *her* idea that "black people ... are educated" or "black people are even better than whites." In this way, Yara is implicitly hinting at the possibility that some people may still have prejudiced attitudes towards black people. It is even likely that she herself is internally conflicted about such attitudes, as indicated by her final statement "they have finally overcome the *situation* they were in." The absoluteness in her tone may allude to a desperate attempt to fight the voice constantly telling her how she needs to understand the phrases she is reading in the text, such as: "Ryan was at the edge of the criminal world." Her *unrealistic* statement (i.e. that black people have finally overcome these prejudices) alludes to the way texts may problematize rather than advance the issue of accepting the Other when a learner starts casting doubt on what is presented in texts, as may be seen in the following excerpt:

> [They] told us that Ryan's environment included criminals and I want to believe that this is something negative but then I remind myself of what I personally know about black people and I don't like it, I don't accept it, 'criminals' is negative.

Yara explains how the statement "Ryan was at the edge of the criminal world" is meant to affect how she constructs her position regarding "black people." First, having used the words "criminals" and "crime," she explicitly states that these words create a "negative" attitude that this statement is forcing on her by saying "and I want to believe this is something negative." Yara then elucidates her position that regardless of how the text affects her, a "negative" attitude is not what she wants to construct. By saying that she must rely on her personal knowledge about "black people," Yara consciously tries to activate in her subjugated self an "agentive" rejection of this image offered by the text of "black people being criminals," as she says: "I don't like it, I don't accept it, 'criminal' is negative."

An analysis of Yara's responses to the text about Ryan reveals a constant shift differentiating a "positive Self" from a "negative Other," then going against and hence doubting negative representations coming from a textual source. Further shifts in Yara's grappling with questions of identification can be seen in the following excerpt:

> [But] when I read such a text I feel sorry for them. I feel it's possible that those who are rich should help these people out and take them out of this environment. I mean, America is considered a country that has enough to help these people.

Ultimately, Yara constructs a position about "black people" in which she feels "sorry for them" and implores Western countries and specifically "America" to help them out. In other words, the discourse about Ryan presented in this text interpellated Yara into reproducing and perpetuating the idea that such people, as a minority, are deprived and in need of the West (more specifically Whites) to help them manage in this world. Even though Yara seems to be struggling between her conflicting selves, the subject position she finally constructs about "black people" remains and is summoned by what the text is implicitly indicating.

Do EFL Textbooks Enable the Construction of Intracultural/ Multicultural Understanding?

The Israeli EFL curriculum explicitly claims to encourage multiculturalism and pluralism by presenting texts about other cultures and peoples. This does not seem to manifest itself in authorized English textbooks, where other cultures are either totally marginalized (such as Palestinian Arab culture in Israel) or misrepresented (as in the case of Indian and Chinese cultures) as inferior to Western cultures (Awayed-Bishara, 2015).

While reading the text about Miriam, Hebrew speakers displayed a lack of familiarity with Arab or Bedouin identity – struggling to describe or identify people who probably live a few miles away from them:

OMER: [An] Arab is not a Bedouin. It is a kind of a community.
ETAI: Somebody who came from Arab countries.
OMER: No. Not at all, because that is not the same. It is like Jews, Muslims, Christians, there are also Bedouins and Druze. This is like a division in Islam, a trend in Islam, to anyone who was born to a Muslim mother. It is like Moroccans and Ashkenazim.

Etai, and particularly Omer, are unable to define either "Arab" or "Bedouin." Omer asserts that "an Arab is not a Bedouin" and then defines Bedouins as a "community" that is not Arab. Moreover, Omer equates the "community" of Bedouins with other "communities" residing in Israel such as "Jews," "Christians," and "Muslims," but realizes afterwards that there is a connection between Bedouins and Muslims, and decides that they have split from Islam and that a Muslim is a person whose mother is a Muslim. Omer does not really know what constitutes Muslim identity – nor even its formal definition, which is patrilineal – and hence, draws on the closest case he knows of, namely, through *recontextualizing* how Jews are matrilineally defined.

The distinctions made by Omer raise a number of serious issues within the Israeli-Arab context. First of all, the Jew-Christian-Muslim distinction implies that Omer, like many other Israeli Jews, mistakenly assumes that Christians and Muslims are two distinct ethnic groups, whereas in fact both religious groupings mostly identify as Arabs and are considered as such by the state (at least officially) as Arab citizens in Israel. The term "Arab" has until recently appeared on the identity card of every Arab citizen in Israel, regardless of religious affiliation. Arab members of the Knesset, as well as scholars and intellectuals (such as Edward Said and Azmi Bishara), who are Christian, have always been categorized as Arabs, not to mention Palestinian. Nonetheless, such a distinction characterizes the prevalent position most Israelis have regarding the national affiliation of the Christians in Israel/Palestine, which EFL textbooks seem to reinforce. Many Israelis believe that the Christian citizens of Israel are not Arabs and that the term "Arab" is only associated with Islam. This claim is supported by the following excerpt, in which one of the Jewish interviewees states that Miriam is an Arab, which prompts his classmate to assert that she is Muslim:

ETAI: She is an Arab.
OMER: A Muslim. A Muslim because …
ETAI: The *hijab*. It shows.

Many Christian Arabs, however, reject such a position, since the category "Arab" constitutes a major element in constructing their national identity. Table 4.2 shows examples of how the Arab interviewees defined themselves, either directly or indirectly, throughout the interviews. For them, "being an Arab" constitutes a fundamental element in the identity construction of all Arab interviewees, regardless of religious affiliation. It is imperative to state that some of the interviewees express their rejection and resentment of how the texts they read depict "Arabs" as being only Muslims, or as being only Bedouins without even referring to them as Arabs at all.

One Christian interviewee states that presenting a woman wearing the *hijab* is meant to convey that Arabs are only Muslims, and that this practice reinforces tendencies to exclude Christians from the Arab collective, not only among foreigners and Israelis, but among other Arabs as well:

94 Storied Selves

TABLE 4.2 Examples of national identity discourse construction among speakers of Arabic

	National identity construction	
Christian Arabs	Muslim Arabs	Muslim-Bedouin Arabs
We 1948 *Arabs* need to get the rights of our people [Jerusalem and West Bank Palestinians] back ... (Layana)	I am an *Arab* who is a Muslim. (Ali)	We are all *Arabs*. (Ranya)
They go on trips to Poland ... so they remember [the Holocaust] ... and keep talking about it ... it is like when *Arabs* go to Jerusalem or Bethlehem ... and we see the wall ... (Layana)	He doesn't represent me as an *Arab* ... they said an Israeli ... and talked about Israeli things. (Wajdi)	I am an *Arab* who lives in occupied Palestine ... a Bedouin and a student. (Amni)
... there they put them in concentration camps with official stamps ... some of *my people* [Palestinian Arabs outside the green line] ... are also dying under cannons or their houses are destroyed over their heads. (Fadi)	Let's say that we are Israelis and they talked about us in general ... as an Israeli society ... Yes, I mean if they talked about a lot of traditions that both Jews and *Arabs* share. (Adam)	I am an *Arab*, Palestinian, a Bedouin who lives in the state of Israel. (Tasnim)
I don't eat Kosher ... all of us *Arabs* we don't keep Kosher. (Rula)	As an *Arab*. Yes. she represents me. (Eman)	I am an *Arab*... a Palestinian. (Tasnim)
I was born an *Arab*, then I am 1, 2, 3, 4 ... (Rami)	That we are *Arabs* ... both of us. (Ahlam)	As an *Arab* I say that ... (Amini)
... why as *Arabs* they would have these stereotypes about us and I'm not like that at all ... I mean ... I don't have an ID card yet. (Rami)	Being an *Arab* ... I feel offended. (Rawad)	Bedouins are *Arabs* ... (Tasnim)
	We, the *Arab* minority, are ...'(Ahlam)	

YARA: The name Mahmoud makes it easier for foreigners to understand that he is an Arab.
RAMI: What they want to say is that an Arab is a Muslim.
YARA: But the majority of Arabs are Muslims; those in Qatar and Saudi Arabia are Muslims. This is why we are Arabs ... [Yara did not finish what she started].
LAYANA: The thing is that we can barely convince the Arabs that there are Christians who are Arabs, let alone convince foreigners.

The three respondents agree that, in the Arab context and in Israel, there is an attempt to Islamize everything that is Arab. Following Rami's rejection of Yara's statement, she asserts that "the majority of Arabs are Muslims." There is a shift in Yara's performance of Self after this point as she tries to cope with the emergence of a different Self-Other distinction. Up to this point, Yara, Rami, and Layana co-construct the Self-narrative of an Arab learner who needs to cope with the ideological dilemmas presented in the English texts. Conversely, when Yara uses the pronoun "we," she differentiates herself as a Muslim by saying "this is why *we* … are Arabs" from her friends Rami and Layana, who are Christians and who do not apparently accept the way Yara defends this practice (i.e. Islamizing Arab identity). Similar conflicts in the Self are made even clearer by Layana when she goes against Rami's statement by saying that the practices Yara is defending are making things difficult for her (i.e. Layana as Other) as a Christian. Her statement, "We can barely convince Arabs that there are Christians who are Arabs" demonstrates the complexity of constructing her national identity. On one hand, she recurrently associates herself with the Palestinian Arab people on both sides of the Green Line by stating, at a different point in the interview: "[It] is like when *we* go to Jerusalem or Bethlehem, and *we* see the separating wall … *We* 1948 Arabs need to get the rights of *our* people back."

On the other hand, when discussing whether Arabs sympathize with the Holocaust, Layana argues that unless Israel acknowledges the pain of "*my* people" and the mistakes it committed against them, she will not be able to acknowledge the pain of the Holocaust. The use of "*my*" evidently constructs an in-group feeling with the Palestinians in the Occupied Territories. While discussing the Bedouin woman, Miriam, we notice a shift in Layana's identity construction that rejects being categorized, labeled, and/or described as dependent or passive:

> Arabs are not only those wearing the *hijab* … But why, why do you [addressing the writer of the textbook] choose a specific thing such as the *hijab*? You could have chosen any other Arab.

By addressing the writer, Layana is acting critically, even subversively, since she rejects the attempt to categorize Arabs as Muslims wearing the *hijab*. She voices her discontent with the writer's choice because not only does she not see Miriam as representative, she is also made to feel part of an out-group. Her shifting identity as an Arab and as a woman is evident in the following excerpt, in which she criticizes the example given in the text of the role the Englishwoman plays in offering the Bedouin woman the chance of her life by taking her to London to study marketing:

> But this is not what generally happens! Maybe [Miriam] would have made it if the Englishwoman hadn't arrived! It is not exceptional! As opposed to every woman who cannot make it, there are maybe ten Arab women who can make it on their own because they want to. I intend to study. I can succeed without anybody's help.

Layana rejects the text's depiction of the Arab woman as passive, dependent, or unmotivated, and argues that Miriam's success is not "exceptional," as was stated in the text. For her, it is commonplace, and not dependent on "chance." Miriam could also have "made it" without the Englishwoman, just like many other Arab women do. At this point, Layana's out-group feeling caused by the *hijab* earlier is replaced by an in-group feeling based on the desire to defend Miriam, and give her credit for her own success, first, for being a woman and, second, for being an Arab woman. She is aware of the fact that some Arab women have difficulties ("for every woman who can't") but she rejects the way they are depicted in the text as passive, controlled by their fathers or brothers, and subjected to traditional arranged marriages. Yet, her conflict with the values presented in the text about Miriam's society again causes her an out-group feeling, as she says:

> She doesn't represent me in any way! First, *I* don't live in an environment where people marry without knowing the person they marry, *we* have nothing of that sort of marriage and *I* don't live in the desert, and my traditions are different from her traditions.

Layana explicitly distances herself from arranged marriages, living in the desert, and being dependent. Conversely, she underscores her agentive role in making her own decisions, in choosing her spouse, and in defining her goals in life. Through the use of "I" versus "she," Layana differentiates herself as free, independent, and active, as opposed to Miriam, who is constrained by "traditions," dependent on "chance," and passive. Layana's attitude toward the way EFL textbooks depict Arabs and their culture manifests a kind of inner conflict among possible selves.

An interview with Jewish EFL learners regarding the text on Miriam illustrates how this text reinforces negative stereotypes about Arabs in general, and Bedouins in particular:

URIAH: I think that she represents most of the population, the Bedouin community, because most of the Bedouin community is still … It is a relatively closed religion, closed within itself and they don't, almost nobody knows, it is like similar to the Druze a bit and …

[Uriah seemed to be struggling with how to express his views about Miriam, which explains the incomplete sentences in the excerpt.]

YAEL: The Druze are not like that at all …
URIAH: No. That they also split from Islam and there is, let us say, there is … most Bedouins are still …
YAEL: Living in tents and keep three camels and have ten women! Is this what you are trying to say?
URIAH: Yes [he laughs]. Most Bedouins have a number of women. I don't know whether they live in tents and this, but most of them do! There is a great

importance given to the tradition of arranged marriages ... I think that there is almost no Bedouin women who goes out to study.

This excerpt illustrates how negative stereotypes about other groups are reinforced in EFL texts. Uriah, a 16-year-old Jewish EFL learner, starts his turn with non-fluid speech, indicating his difficulty in determining who Bedouins are. First, it is a "population," referring maybe to the whole Arab population to whom he relates as Bedouins, and then, it is a "community" and finally he states that they are a "community closed in itself" that split from Islam and that nobody knows anything about. His supposedly stated "fact" about the similarity between Bedouins and Druze ironically reflects his ignorance of this group (Bedouins are Muslims; there was no split from Islam, etc.). Yael, on the other hand, is conforming neither with what the text is suggesting nor to what Uriah is reproducing. Through co-constructing the conversation, Yael makes explicit what Uriah seems to believe but is initially hesitant to declare, perhaps out of respect for the researcher, namely, that for him Bedouins (and perhaps even Arabs in general, given his confusion in the previous turn) "are still living in tents and keep three camels and have ten women." Once Yael had constructed this statement for him, he laughed sarcastically and confirmed that this was indeed what he meant to say. He then elaborates on the way he sees Bedouins: the men are traditionalists and womanizers; the women are uneducated. Uriah makes the sweeping generalization that "there is almost no Bedouin woman who goes out to study." The stance that Uriah takes regarding Bedouin women has serious implications for our approach to the way that other cultures are described to learners in a school textbook. In this case, the negative description of Miriam's cultural environment in general seems to have had an impact on readers that outweighs the representation of her story on an individual level – as a "non-typical entrepreneur" who studied marketing in England for three years (Awayed-Bishara, 2015). Yael, as opposed to Uriah and the other Jewish interviewees in the study, however, displays some agentive resistance in response to the article about Miriam. The following excerpt shows her impression of the text, and reflects her resistance to the negative generalizations about the Other. "They present the Bedouin population as an old-fashioned and undeveloped population ... We can see that these were obstacles, her father and the environment because these things impede ..." Yael didn't finish her sentence.

To conclude this section: the reactions of both Jewish and Arab EFL learners to the text about Miriam indicate that the textbook has failed to advance intra/multicultural understanding of the Other. For Jewish students, a text about an Arab woman is supposed to introduce them to the Other's culture, and to provide them with adequate information about the beliefs, characteristics, customs, and identity associated therewith. Instead, most of them were more concerned with whether the character was an Arab, a Bedouin Arab, a Muslim, or only a Bedouin. Apart from their failure to teach members of the majority about the Other, who constitute 20 percent of Israel's population, EFL texts also seem to function as a means of dividing the different groups who constitute the Palestinian Arab minority against each other. The constant shifts in Layana's positions toward Bedouins and Muslims reflect the everyday conflict that Palestinian Arab citizens living in Israel must cope with in their relationship with other Arabs with different religious and cultural affiliations. The complication of these identity constructions, however, serves the interests of the state, which is constantly threatened by unification inside the Arab minority. Perhaps the best example to support such a claim is how Israel's prime minister, Benjamin Netanyahu, following the establishment of the first United Arab Party, called upon Jewish citizens of the country during the elections in 2015 to go out and vote because "Arab voters are heading to polls in droves" (Zonszein, 2015). As state-controlled apparatuses, EFL textbooks both interpellate Jewish students into subject positions with negative attitudes about the Other residing in Israel, while placing Arab students in a position that perpetuates ideologies of religious rifts that maintain the state's preferred division among the Arab citizens (into, for instance, Christians, Muslims, Druze, and Bedouins).

EFL Texts: Prompting Globally Aware Learners?

The ideologically constructive role of the EFL narratives examined in this research seems to affect Hebrew speakers differently from Arabic speakers. For most Hebrew speakers, the texts about Miriam (mainly the issue of arranged marriages) and Ryan (mainly the issue of underachievement and dropping out of school) evoked a feeling of superiority, as exemplified in the following excerpt by Omer (Hebrew speaker):

> [We] grew up in an environment that is much more supportive and in favor of investing more in studies. Our parents are affluent and can help us with private tutoring, they are capable of providing us with education.

Through recontextualizing the text's description of Ryan's environment, Omer constructs a positive self-narrative that is juxtaposed with the negative Other-narrative presented by the text regarding minorities in general and "black people" in particular, since the text about Ryan opens by stating, "This story will raise serious questions. Questions about how schools deal with 'no-hope' pupils. Questions about why schools have failed to meet the needs of *minority* pupils" (Cohen et al., 2006, p. 106; my emphasis). As opposed to "no-hope" pupils among minorities and the "black teenage dropout," Omer depicts how he and other members of the majority group (indicated by "*we*") are privileged to have grown up with parents who invest more in studies, are financially affluent, and capable of giving their children what they need in order to succeed in school. The same feeling of superiority was also aroused following the reading of the text about Miriam, when Omer expresses his views about how young Western people demand the right to choose their spouses as opposed to arranged marriages in Eastern societies.

I think that we were born into this and this is how things should be. I am going to live with my wife for the rest of my life and not my parents. So, I think that it is quite 'retarded' when the parents are the ones who choose [spouses].

Omer clearly believes that his culture is just the way things should be. He makes a clear distinction between his views about his own culture (indicated by "*we*") which is essentially modern, free, and rational (to him, after all, "this is how things should be") as opposed to the other culture that he sees not only as old-fashioned, but also as "retarded." I have translated the Hebrew word that Omer uses (*mefager*) as "retarded" – but, unlike the English word, it also has the connotations of "primitive" or "backward." Through negative lexical selections (van Dijk, 2006) and the use of the pronoun "we," Omer assumes a degrading attitude regarding the Other's culture as described in the text by stating that his culture's way of doing things embodies "how things should be." It is pivotal to note that Ali, a Palestinian Arab student, when reacting to the text about Miriam also uses the Arabic word for "retarded" (*mutakhalif*), which has similar connotations to *mefager* in Hebrew. He uses "they" to refer to the Jewish writers, and "we" to refer to Arabs, in his statement: "*They* are saying that *we* are a retarded and backward society." Table 4.3 indicates similar responses by Arabic speakers in this regard. Comparing these statements with those expressed by Hebrew speakers demonstrates how such texts tend to instill feelings of superiority as opposed to feelings of resentment (even humiliation) among Hebrew and Arabic speakers, respectively.

Following Omer's turn, Avishag, whose mother is Moroccan (i.e. of North African Jewish origin), concurs with Omer's normative statements.

TABLE 4.3 Examples of responses showing superiority/resentment

Hebrew speakers	*Arabic speakers*
• It is [Jewish] modernism versus [Arab] conservatism. (Edo) • *They* [Bedouins] are in this thing, *they* are still to a certain degree like the stereotype. (Uriah) • *We* also choose *our* spouses and for me this is not even a question. (Omer)	• *They* are comparing *us* with the West. (Ali) • This is not the image *I* want about Bedouins. (Rula) • *Our* parents arrange *our* bride/groom for *us*. (Adam) • *We* are the third world and *they* are the first world. (Ali) • *They* have civilization and *we* are Bedouins. (Layana) • *They* [English] are the god and *we* learn from *them*. (Wajdi) • It is as if *we* live in a world in which *we* cannot progress unless *we* look at the other world. (Ranya) • *We* do not exist in the world of entrepreneurs. (Rami) • *They* see *us* as living in a bubble. (Rula)

AVISHAG: I feel the same. My grandmother got married in an arranged way, she was 11 and he was 25. It was in Morocco, not that this is a Western country.
OMER: Your grandfather is ... from ...
AVISHAG: Yes. So, it is not something normal that is supposed to happen. They got into an arranged marriage. This is strange. This is not something that is supposed to happen.

Omer's incomplete sentence "your grandfather is ... from ..." may allude to the uneasiness caused by Avishag's face-threatening acts (FTA). The fact that Avishag's grandparents underwent an arranged marriage situates the "retarded" practice, which is attributed to the Other by Omer, in a manner that threatens the Self. As Jews, Avishag and her grandparents are part of the *We* that Omer considers superior and more rational. The fact that her ancestors took part in this "retarded" practice potentially tarnishes the image of the Self that Omer has constructed. Avishag attempts to minimize the threat of her FTA by committing FTAs with mitigation (Brown & Levinson, 1987) by making it clear that the arranged marriage took place in a non-Western context. Subsequently, Avishag attempts to neutralize the FTA by stating that arranged marriage "is not normal ... strange ... [and] it is not supposed to happen." Avishag's discursive strategies pragmatically foster Omer's feelings of superiority towards non-Western cultures.

Another discursive device that is similarly used to instill a feeling of superiority is the constant mention of army service in Israel's EFL textbooks. When discussing this issue, Omer again uses the word "retarded" to describe every Israeli citizen who does not do army service, including anyone "who is an Arab or Ultra-Orthodox, Bedouin, etc." These examples further illustrate the manner in which EFL textbooks interpellate Jewish students into reproducing and perpetuating hegemonic discourses about the Other. Whereas such narratives reinforce feelings of belonging and self-worth among Jewish learners, they reinforce feelings of alienation and marginalization among Palestinian Arab learners. Following the reading of the text about the late Israeli astronaut Ilan Ramon, Rula, a Palestinian Arab student, states

> [They] enjoy their presence in the army and for me they are killing our people. They talk of the army as if it is a lovely thing and when I see such a thing in a text, I stop concentrating on this text.

This excerpt demonstrates what Hammack (2006) says about the opposing views held by Jews and Palestinian Arabs about national symbols. Through the use of *I/our* as opposed to *they/their*, Rula excludes herself from the Other-narrative of "army service" by means of interdiscursivity. Namely, the statement, "they are killing my people," reflects elements in the prevalent discourse of the Israeli-Arab conflict among Palestinian Arabs who usually condemn military actions in the Occupied Territories. Rula's self-exclusion from the depiction of the army as a lovely thing expresses how she perceives the *presence* of the army as a moral obstacle that stands between her and the schoolbooks on which she is trying to "concentrate." The following excerpt describes how the EFL texts about army service contributed to Rula's experience of alienation:

> [It] is as if these books were not mine and as if I can't study with these books. They would always have stories about children who were Jews, always. All the names in our books were Jewish names. They used to write the names in Arabic. Every time I see something about the army, I feel like a stranger because it is Jewish.

Rula puts the EFL textbooks in their larger educational context as she draws on similar past experiences with other textbooks used in Israeli schools. The English textbooks that are supposed to promote global values through presenting other cultures are in fact continuous with an educational context that frustrates a fair and equal learning opportunity. Stating that reading about army service makes her feel like a "stranger" confirms Yiftachel (2006), Yonah (2005) and Peled-Elhanan's (2012) findings, that Arabs are marginalized in Israeli schoolbooks, just as they are excluded from Israeli cultural discourse and social life. Referring to the recurrent use of Jewish names in textbooks and the way they are transliterated into Arabic is also compatible with the finding regarding the dominant presence of Jewish names in English textbooks, which may be contrasted to the absence of Arabic names, and suggesting an intentional policy of marginalization (Awayed-Bishara, 2015).

The choice of words in EFL discourse is socially and ideologically motivated (Fairclough, 1992) in a way that hampers learners from confronting accepted cultural beliefs about the Self and the Other. Within such ideologically unbalanced educational settings, it is hard to see how EFL discourses could serve to achieve what Kumaravadivelu (2008) describes as "promoting global cultural consciousness in the classroom" (p. 189). For Hebrew speakers, words such as "arranged marriage," "black dropout," and "no-hope pupils," reflect a reality making clear distinctions between a "positive" Self and a "negative" Other. For Arabic speakers, these same words reflect a reality of marginalization and alienation, reproducing the discourse of state victimization.

Young EFL Critics: Jewish and Palestinian Arab Learners on Educational Policies

During the interviews, some EFL learners strongly urged writers, educators, and the Ministry of Education to address pitfalls in EFL textbooks. Learners – whether Hebrew or Arabic speakers – mainly addressed the way in which EFL materials depict other people and their cultures. The international status of English, acknowledged in the curriculum, appears to promise young learners access to academic and professional success by means of multicultural and global education. Conversely, when students encounter incidents in which English alternatively promotes Western and Israeli-Jewish hegemonies, negative attitudes toward English and those involved in these practices are apt to surface.

Palestinian Arab learners perceived EFL texts such as the one about Miriam as an extended act – one among many – aimed at reinforcing marginalization and inequality. Ranya, a Palestinian Arab EFL learner, offers a deep critique:

> [The] things that they mention are incorrect, incorrect! It is not only a matter of a racist story that we can simply ignore or choose not to study; it hurts. Isn't it enough: the marginalization, and all of the inequality, and the Judaization of the villages?

Ranya accuses textbook writers of conveying "incorrect" information, which, in her eyes, is a separate matter and even more dangerous than spreading "racist" stories about Arabs that she clearly abhors, but is perhaps accustomed to. Note that the repetition of the word "incorrect" is meant to underscore a problem other than a widespread racist discourse in Israel in the face of which many Palestinian Arabs have developed counter-measures of disregard, what one might think of as a *thick skin*. Although one might claim that such a strategy functions as an everyday survival tool in a country that is dominated by right-wing and extremist ideologies, it also has serious ethical and psychological implications for identity formation. Cheater (1999) explains how the marginalization of minority groups is closely connected to the concept of disempowerment, and can be explained in terms of ignorance, intimidation, or negative stereotyping. Within educational contexts, Ranya is alluding to a practice of discursive manipulation that aims at perpetuating negative stereotypes about Arabs, or totally ignores their existence, in either of which case, according to Rania, the result is that it "hurts." This excerpt also expresses what is often a repressed identity that Palestinian Arabs construct regarding issues of displacement and land confiscation (spelled out as the "Judaization of villages") and unequal rights (referred to as "inequalities").

Struggling between the repressed identity that exists alongside their other multiple identities enables individuals of this minority to maintain a fair level of normalcy in a lifestyle characterized by:

1. speaking one's mother tongue (i.e. Arabic), but conducting daily matters in the state's official language (i.e. Hebrew) (e.g. in education, work, medical services, shopping, etc.);
2. having one history, but learning and teaching their children a history that invalidates their own;
3. seeing themselves as "victims," while their "victimizers" construct them as "the problem";
4. justifying their existence while having no control over the fact that they were born in the same conflictual place;
5. perceiving various religious and cultural differentiations that obstruct their selves;
6. above all, being officially framed as second-class citizens in a country that lawfully defines itself as a Nation State of the Jewish People.

Table 4.4 lists examples of similar responses that criticize current writing practices in EFL textbooks and their impact on identity/position construction. So, inspired by the above texts Palestinian Arab EFL learners seem to construct a subject position of marginalization nurtured by the dissonance and disregard created by EFL materials that misrepresent Arab culture and communal practices, misrepresent other cultures (e.g. African) as inferior, and center Jewish identity through glorifying army service.

For some Jewish EFL learners, reading the selected EFL texts also evoked critical positions regarding certain writing practices. The following excerpt reports an interaction that took place after the structured interview where Edo, Uriah, and Yael continued discussing the way Ryan and Miriam are described in the texts:

EDO: These are sanctions put in place by society that if writers don't mention that he is black, something will happen to you but it is these things that society imposes on us and that we impose on ourselves, to socially categorize a person who is different ...

TABLE 4.4 Examples of responses critiquing writing practices in EFL textbooks by speakers of Arabic

- I feel as if they are saying something about all blacks, a kind of generalization. (Layana)
- The way they describe things; they could have taken any child. I mean, it shouldn't have been a black [child]. (Rami)
- The bottom line is that I don't like this sentence appearing in the text about Ryan. (Rami)
- They are attributing certain (random) characteristics to people who are black. (Adam)
- I mean, human beings can be like that [rude, unmanageable, etc.] but why did they specifically choose a black person? (Eman)
- They are trying to divide us. (Ranya)
- ... why do they do this division and separation? (Rula)
- ... and the Judaization of the language that it is Tal Asabia ... why write it Tel Sheva? (Rula)
- It feels as if there are no Arabs in Israel. (Ahmad)
- It hurts. There are other people living here. They were displaced and are asking to return and they [Israelis] tell them that there isn't place for them while others are told "yallah" come. I mean the *Aliya*. (Wajdi)
- ... from a humanistic point of view, these stories [referring to the story of Ryan and critiquing the use of the term Black] can happen to everyone, a normal thing. (Tasnim)
- If someone, an outsider, reads this article, they will say that Arabs in Israel are Bedouins. (Ali)
- But ... why do you choose something as specific as the *hijab* ... why do you specify? (Layana)
- When was this textbook written?' [Sarcastically stated, suggesting that the textbook is outdated in terms of the information it presents about Arabs.] (Wajdi)
- I feel as if this textbook is too old, as if it was written 50 years ago. (Wajdi)
- What they want to say is that an Arab is a Muslim. (Rami)
- Instead of saying Miriam the Arab, they said Miriam the Bedouin. (Ahmad)
- They must bring something that represents the majority [of the Palestinian minority]. (Adam)
- But we are the opposite of that, not like what is written in this text. (Rula)
- I feel as if there is no room for us; they don't even mention us ... (Rami)
- They need to show both sides ... when they get to a level where they can acknowledge my pain. (Layana)

URIAH: "Black" has to be mentioned as it helps us understand the text better because if he is black, then why shouldn't they expel him from school, and why shouldn't he behave in such a way? I noticed some differences between the two texts, with Ryan, they focused more on how the company helped him. But they said how determined Liz was [i.e. the white American teenager who made it from being homeless to winning a scholarship to Harvard] how she took herself into her own hands …

For Edo, referring to a character as "black" or "Bedouin" reflects how societies deal with difference, an act of what Foucault (1989) calls "problemization." Problemization refers to practices aimed at making being different a problem, rather than simply a feature of diversity. Edo criticizes the way EFL textbooks treat the Other as a "problem" – rather than simply as different. In support of Edo, Uriah also explains how categorizing people as belonging to other groups preconditions readers to form their understanding of these people, as when writers identify a character as "black," so it makes sense that he is expelled from school when he is considered as being on the brink of entering the criminal world. Uriah also criticizes the differences he notices in describing members of minorities as opposed to members of majorities when he makes a clear distinction between his impression of Ryan and Liz. While Uriah views Ryan as a passive subject, he views Liz as an active agent. The following excerpt by Yael further supports this finding, as she makes a similar observation:

[It] shows the perspectives of whoever wrote this book that he intentionally chooses texts in which minorities are always those who need help and a white woman who is also found at the same low and inferior position manages to overcome everything on her own. These are the author's perspectives.

For Edo, identifying the other as different is a compelling social practice (spelled out as "sanctions"), since people who choose not to abide by this convention are liable to face sanctions. These sanctions are imposed on individuals who do not take part in the reproduction of dominant or mainstream ideologies. Table 4.5 displays how Hebrew speakers criticize other writing practices in EFL textbooks.

The following and final excerpt by Edo summarizes how framing people according to certain stereotypes is misleading. It refers to multi-modal texts, where authors include images that supposedly *represent* certain groups to accompany the narrative about them. An example of this is a narrative that portrays a scene in which Western travelers are wandering in the desert on camelback, guided by a Bedouin Arab wearing a *galabiya* (a long cloak) and an *iqal* (a white head scarf), traditional Arabic clothing. A photograph accompanies the text that shows the travelers (Western-looking in clothes and appearance) on camelback accompanied by a Bedouin guide, who is leading the camels and carrying a shepherd's crook. Edo argues that such practices can be misleading, as people may be persecuted based on outer appearances that reproduce stereotypes about the Other. "[It] could

TABLE 4.5 Examples of responses critiquing writing practices in EFL textbooks by speakers of Hebrew

- It says "a black teenage dropout" … couldn't have they written something like "a 15 years old teenage who is kicked out of school" [he laughs] or anything … (Edo)
- They associate him with a certain group [i.e. Black] but this is a story that can happen to anyone … (Uriah)
- … so this fear of that which is different is the result of a stigma that we acquired. (Edo)
- It is not fair they said he is black … (Yael)
- Having written "West" also shows something about the difference; it is modernism versus conservatism. [Critiquing the way texts associate the West with modernism.] (Edo)
- It is a kind of a value ladder that they are situating here: what is more important for you to state? The fact that he is black is maybe the thing that they rush into stating. (Yael)
- It could be that there is something that is a little bit stereotypical. (Uriah)
- They present the Bedouin population as an old-fashioned and undeveloped population. (Yael)
- They undermine Bedouins as a people. (Edo)
- Everybody says "accepting the other, accepting the other …" but this is a kind of fear, a kind of "ah, he's black so I don't want to be anywhere near him … maybe because of his skin color …" (Avishag)

also be that because someone is blond and has blue eyes, they will say that he is Russian or Romanian or German even though he is a Muslim or the other way around. These stereotypes are dangerous."

The critical positions constructed by Jewish EFL students following the reading of the EFL texts demonstrate their understanding of, and objection to, the misleading use of stereotypes when representing the Other, prioritizing Western over Eastern practices, and failing to educate students to accept the Other. The analyses offered by the learners themselves in Table 4.4 and Table 4.5 demonstrate an emerging level of agency among both Arab and Jewish learners manifesting their reluctance to approve of some of the values and ideas the EFL texts are propounding, potentially rendering EFL as a unique educational setting for bringing about social change.

Conclusion

This chapter presented extensive evidence of how EFL learners construct their identities in relation to the cultural content of four texts that appear in authorized EFL textbooks. Using CDA, I underlined the discursive contours of EFL learners' storied selves manifested through the use of recontextualization, indexical pronouns, and lexical selections. An analysis of how learners actually negotiate meaning/identities while reading EFL texts challenges current pedagogical notions regarding the transnational role of culture in promoting global cultural consciousness and intercultural citizenship. Anglo-centric and local hegemonic ideologies dominate the way other cultures are represented in EFL textbooks, thus shaping the way learners from multiple cultural, linguistic, and national backgrounds might relate to such representations. Taking Israel as a case study, an analysis of how learners discursively relate to EFL cultural content indicates that most Hebrew speakers demonstrate how superior they feel toward others, how they lack knowledge about them, and how fully they accept the legitimacy of the Jewish-Zionist values promoted in EFL texts. Conversely, most Arabic speakers display an understanding of their marginalized position in the Israeli educational system and other spheres, how cultural and religious narratives may contradict national narratives within their Palestinian Arab community, and how they construct their positionality as victims of discrimination.

The way students responded to the texts they read in English should raise serious questions about the way EFL discourse deals with issues of diversity and cultural difference. Findings suggest that cultural representations in EFL textbooks affect identity construction processes, hindering the development of globally aware language learners who are open to learning about and accepting the Other. Such EFL materials seem to undermine the development of critical learners who are capable of taking an ideological stand regarding local/global conflicts, cultural diversity, and Otherness, as they fail to offer students a window through which they can successfully construct a new reality. The way most EFL learners in this study narrated their Self-identities and stances regarding the Other calls for an intervention that focuses on promoting learners' critical sense and agency when reading texts about the Other. A process of empowerment whereby minority members are granted a "voice" in EFL textbooks may also provide counter-narratives to hegemonic narratives in the EFL context in Israel and elsewhere.

All in all, the role played by some young Jewish and Palestinian Arab EFL learners who critically read the questionable EFL texts presented to them definitely reveals an emerging process of agency. Nevertheless, whether these results might serve as a means of effecting social change is unclear, as many EFL learners – both Jews and Arabs – still appear to be led by inner voices interpellating them into reproducing the status quo desired by dominant groups in Israel upholding Jewish-Zionist and Western hegemony, on the one hand, and Palestinian Arab marginalization, on the other. Interpellation notwithstanding, the examples of learners' agentive capabilities presented in this chapter will guide the arguments I make in Chapter 6 regarding possible critical and transformative EFL pedagogies. Such pedagogies mainly depend on authoring the agentive perspectives of learners (e.g. those studied in this chapter) and considering their reflexive interpretation while reading English texts. These young EFL "critics" have spoken out against what might be a major obstacle in achieving a more promising future for the citizens of this state. It is up to policy-makers to either give them a legitimate voice or continue to maintain their current policy of oppression and indifference. In Chapter 5, I critically examine how EFL policy and practice in Israel are intertwined, and whether they address the challenges EFL learners tackle when learning English.

Note

1 See also what Darwish writes in "Contrapuntal": available at: http://mondediplo.com/ 2005/01/15said

References

Textbooks

Cohen, J., Loney, N., & Kerman, S. (2006). *Results for 4 points*. Ra'anana: Eric Cohen Books.
Ezra, E. (2011). *High points*. Ra'anana: Eric Cohen Books.

Works cited

Althusser, L. (2000). Ideology interpellates individuals as subjects. In P. Du Gay, J. Evans, & P. Redman (Eds.), *Identity: A reader* (pp. 31–38). London: SAGE Publications.
Awayed-Bishara, M. (2015). Analyzing the cultural content of materials used for teaching English to high school speakers of Arabic in Israel. *Discourse & Society*, 26(5), 517–542. doi:26376399.
Awayed-Bishara, M. (2018). EFL discourse as cultural practice. *Journal of Multicultural Discourses*, 13(3), 243–258. doi:10.1080/17447143.2017.1379528.
Blommaert, J. (2005). *Discourse: A critical introduction*. Cambridge: Cambridge University Press.
Brown, P., & Levinson, S. C. (1987). *Politeness: Some universals in language usage*. Cambridge: Cambridge University Press.
Bucholtz, M., & Hall, K. (2005). Identity and interaction: A sociocultural linguistic approach. *Discourse Studies*, 7(4–5), 585–614. doi:10.1177/1461445605054407.
Butler, J. (2012). *Parting ways: Jewishness and the critique of Zionism*. New York: Columbia University Press.
Byram, M. S. (2008). *From foreign language education to education for intercultural citizenship: Essays and reflections*. Clevedon: Multilingual Matters.
Byram, M. S. (2011). Intercultural citizenship from an international perspective. *Journal of the NUS Teaching Academy*, 1(1), 10–20.
Cheater, A. P. (1999). *The anthropology of power: Empowerment and disempowerment in changing structures*. London: Routledge.
Fairclough, N. (1992). *Discourse and social change*. Cambridge: Polity Press.
Filardo-Llamas, L. (2015). Re-contextualizing political discourse. *Critical Discourse Studies*, 12 (3), 279–296. doi:10.1080/17405904.2015.1013478.
Foucault, M. (1989). *The archeology of knowledge*. (A. M. Sheridan Smith, Trans.). London: Routledge.
Gee, J. P. (2009). *An introduction to discourse analysis: Theory and method* (2nd ed.). New York: Routledge.
Goffman, E. (1967). *Interaction ritual: Essays on face-to-face behavior*. Garden City, NY: Anchor Books.
Gray, J. (2010). The branding of English and the culture of the new capitalism: Representations of the world of work in English language textbooks. *Applied Linguistics*, 31(5), 714–733. doi:10.1093/applin/amq034.

Hall, S. (2000). Who needs identity? In P. Du Gay, J. Evans, & P. Redman (Eds.), *Identity: A reader* (pp. 15–30). London: SAGE Publications.

Hammack, P. L. (2006). Identity, conflict, and coexistence: Life stories of Israeli and Palestinian adolescents. *Journal of Adolescent Research*, 21(4), 323–369. doi:10.1177/0743558406289745.

Kumaravadivelu, B. (2008). *Cultural globalization and language education*. New Haven, CT: Yale University Press.

Lee, K.-Y. (2009). Treating culture: What 11 high school EFL conversation textbooks in South Korea do. *English Teaching: Practice and Critique*, 8(1), 76–96.

Luttrell, W. (1997). *School-smart and mother-wise: Working-class women's identity and schooling. Perspectives of gender*. New York: Routledge.

Marcuse, H. (1964). *One-dimensional man: Studies in the ideology of advanced industrial society*. Boston, MA: Beacon Press.

Peled-Elhanan, N. (2012). *Palestine in Israeli school books: Ideology and propaganda in education*. London: I.B. Tauris.

Risager, K. (2007). *Language and culture pedagogy: From a national to a transnational paradigm*. Clevedon: Multilingual Matters.

Rizvi, F. (2005). Identity, culture and cosmopolitan futures. *Higher Education Policy*, 18(4), 331–339doi:10.1057/palgrave.hep.8300095.

Rogers, R., & Elias, M. (2012). Storied selves: A critical discourse analysis of young children's literate identifications. *Journal of Early Childhood Literacy*, 12(3), 259–292. doi:10.1177/1468798411417370.

Suleiman, C. (2011). *Language and identity in the Israel-Palestine conflict: The politics of self-perception in the Middle East*. London: I.B. Tauris.

Sweetser, E. (2012). Introduction: Viewpoint and perspective in language and gesture from the ground down. In B. Dancygier & E. Sweetser (Eds.), *Viewpoint in language: A multimodal perspective* (pp. 1–22). Cambridge: Cambridge University Press.

Trilling, B., & Fadel, C. (2009). *21st century skills: Learning for life in our times*. Hoboken, NJ: John Wiley & Sons.

van Dijk, T. A. (2006). Discourse and manipulation. *Discourse & Society*, 17(3), 359–383. doi:10.1177/0957926506060250.

Weninger, C., & Kiss, T. (2013). Culture in English as a Foreign Language (EFL) textbooks: A semiotic approach. *TESOL Quarterly*, 47(4), 694–716. doi:10.1002/tesq.87.

Wodak, R. (2011). Complex texts: Analysing, understanding, explaining and interpreting meanings. *Discourse Studies*, 13(5), 623–633. doi:10.1177/1461445611412745.

Wodak, R., de Cilla, R., Reisigl, M., & Liebhart, K. (1999). *The discursive construction of national identity*. (A. Hirsch & R. Mitten, Trans.). Edinburgh: Edinburgh University Press.

Wodak, R., & Fairclough, N. (2010). Recontextualizing European higher education policies: The cases of Austria and Romania. *Critical Discourse Studies*, 7(1), 19–40. doi:10.1080/17405900903453922.

Wortham, S. E. F. (1996). Mapping participant deictics: A technique for discovering speakers' footing. *Journal of Pragmatics*, 25(3), 331–348.

Yamanaka, N. (2006). An evaluation of English textbooks in Japan from the viewpoint of nations in the inner, outer, and expanding circles. *JALT Journal*, 28(1), 57–76.

Yiftachel, O. (2006). *Ethnocracy: Land and identity politics in Israel/Palestine*. Philadelphia, PA: University of Pennsylvania Press.

Yonah, Y. (2005). *In virtue of difference: The multicultural project in Israel*. Tel Aviv: Hakibbutz Hameuchad and Van Leer Jerusalem Institute.

Yuen, K.-M. (2011). The representation of foreign cultures in English textbooks. *ELT Journal*, 65(4), 458–466. doi:10.1093/elt/ccq089.

Zonszein, M. (2015). Binyamin Netanyahu: 'Arab voters are heading to the polling stations in droves.' *The Guardian*, March 17. Tel Aviv. Available at: www.theguardian.com/world/2015/mar/17/binyamin-netanyahu-israel-arab-election (accessed April 30, 2019).

5
EFL POLICY DISCOURSE
Global and Local Perspectives

This chapter scrutinizes notions of "local" and "global" in EFL policy documents through a critical analysis of its constituent discourses. Specifically, it examines the intersection between the promotion of English as *the* global language, the situation of EFL within Anglo-centric frameworks, and the construction of the local learning populations to which EFL policies are directed. Insofar as the English curriculum in Israel is uniform for both Hebrew and Arabic speakers, this chapter sets out to investigate critically whether EFL policy discourse works to reproduce social injustices and educational inequalities, or instead promotes equal and just educational opportunities.

Introduction

This chapter explores the interplay between politics and language policy from the premise that language is inherently political. As political projects, language policies are largely driven by the ideologies, attitudes, and beliefs of various stakeholders, including government officials with specific political agendas. In multilingual contexts, such policies may work to disadvantage ethnolinguistic minorities – such as the Palestinians in Israel – and perpetuate social differentiations and injustices. In tandem with the work of other scholars who study the role of ideology in shaping language policies (e.g. Krzyżanowski & Wodak, 2011; Kymlicka & Grin, 2003; Milani, 2008) I consider that there is a need to critically respond to how such policies shape the process of *learning* languages at local and global levels. Contrary to how political and ideological agendas take precedence over educational needs and priorities when it comes to designing and implementing language policies (Kymlicka & Grin, 2003), this chapter illuminates the challenges and possibilities for work in the opposite direction. I argue that educational needs and linguistic equality should be prioritized in multilingual contexts, both locally and globally.

My overriding concern is not just to understand how social differentiation and injustices are reproduced through such ideological state practices in a way that disadvantages minority students and their languages. Rather, this chapter sets the ground for ways to explore how such language policies can also be contested.

In terms of EFL language policies in Israel, the National English Curriculum (Ministry of Education, 2018) states in its introduction that any approach to teaching English must take into consideration the major shift in its status as *the* global language. English no longer solely belongs to the United States of America or Britain, as "the speakers of English whose mother tongue is another language already vastly outnumber the English native speakers, and their relative number continues to grow" (p. 7). The curriculum also states that it is intended for the diverse learning populations in Israel, including learners whose first language is Hebrew (i.e. Jews), English (i.e. Jews who are native speakers of English), Arabic (i.e. Palestinians), or any language other than Hebrew (i.e. immigrants). Against this backdrop, the questions I want to address in the present chapter are:

- To what extent are stated EFL policies in Israel as spelled out in national curricula and other official documents compatible with their implemented practices?
- How do language policies in Israel, and more specifically language educational policies, deal with the diversity of learners' needs and their different linguistic repertoires in a manner that offers every learner an equal opportunity to learn English?

Relying on Althusser's (1971) notion of ideological state apparatuses, I will argue that those questions are ultimately connected to ideological practices, and notions of native speakerism (Holliday, 2013) and professionalism. Such questions can be answered with the aid of a theoretical framework that captures the subtle links between policy text(s), ideological state practices, and notions of native speakerism/ professionalism in EFL. Before delving into textual analysis of policy documents, let me shortly revisit some of the theoretical underpinnings I mentioned in Chapter 1, and which I shall apply here.

Theoretical Underpinning of EFL as an Ideological Discourse

The findings in the two previous analytical chapters on the cultural content of textbooks and students' responses to EFL cultural narratives have suggested the ideological orientation of EFL discourse in relation to global and local factors. At the global level, the Anglo-centric and Western perspectives dominant in the textbooks undermine the very notion of "global" and suggest, thus, a critical examination of their socio-political genesis in language policy discourses. At the local level, EFL textbooks have been shown to contribute to the further marginalization of minority learners and their cultures, as well as of those who are not associated with dominant Western cultures. From this it follows that assessing the degree of Anglo-centrism, and marginalization of non-Western learners, in policy documents might deepen our understanding of EFL discourse as a cultural practice. My aim is to scrutinize the level of compatibility between policy and practice in order to gain some insights into what needs to be (re)considered and (de)constructed in order to achieve a transformative EFL pedagogy.

In Chapter 1, I illustrated the special status of English, and how it is unequally situated in Israel in relation to both Hebrew (the language of the majority) and Arabic (the language of the minority). Just as with other subjects, the choice of EFL curricular materials is administered and determined by educators and government officials with mainstream Jewish-Zionist views (Yiftachel, 2006). These texts interpellate various social actors (teachers, learners, inspectors, school principals, textbook writers, etc.) into subject positions that reproduce particular ideologies constellated around Israel as a nation-state. The National English Curriculum thus serves as an ideological state apparatus (Althusser, 1971) that actively represses through the direct policing of subjectivity, while demarcating the realm of acceptable ideology.

Aside from its function as an ideological vehicle, the complexity of teaching English to speakers of Arabic also interacts with the diglossic nature of Arabic (Ferguson, 1959) – that is, the fact that, for Palestinian learners, English comes fourth after spoken Arabic, Modern Standard Arabic, and Hebrew. In tandem with my general focus in this volume on the way Palestinian learners tackle their EFL learning experience, this chapter questions whether the National English Curriculum considers the specific conditions under which Arabic speakers learn English. More specifically, I examine whether Arabic speakers really have equal opportunities to achieve the high level of English that is institutionally required to facilitate their academic and professional advancement. The complexity that immigrant students in Israel also face while learning English is equally important to consider, and insights from my analysis of the Palestinian Arab case might be similarly applied to these cases. However, specific attention to the way other groups learn English in Israel needs to be critically examined in future research.

The last, but central, point I consider in my analysis here is how EFL policy discourse constructs the notion of native speakerism, and how it situates the native speaker of English in relation to other non-native groups. In Chapter 1, I situated the notion of native speakerism within broader international EFL frameworks, illustrating how the concept of the "native speaker" is still controversially undertaken in English education scholarship (Byram, 2008; Davies, 2003; Kramsch, 1998; 2015; Sharifian, 2013). Native speaker competence is still treated as the international norm, despite the fact that globally English is spoken by more non-native than native speakers (Davies, 2003; Jenkins, 2000). This tendency continuously drives many English teachers and policy-makers to fix their attention on the "native speaker" level as the standard against which they design their curricula and assess their students, often overlooking how the native speaker as an ideal might be no more than a "fine myth" (Davies, 2003, p. 197). It is my intention in this chapter to examine whether the ideological dominance of native speaker models constitutes a hegemonic discourse of native speakerism within the architecture of EFL policy in Israel. I argue that if we consider the shift that English is undergoing as the global language, then native speakerist discourses need to be examined against the background of non-native discourses regarding the pedagogical perception of a learner's competence. To examine how the notion of non-native competence is often ideologically accounted for when designing and policing EFL teaching, let me set some notions of Anglo-centrism against those of domestication.

EFL Ideologies: Anglo-Centrism Versus Domestication

One of the prevailing means of teaching English is through presenting learners with English-speaking cultures. The manner in which cultural content is presented to English learners who come from different cultural backgrounds is often intertwined with notions of the "domestication" and/or "Anglo-centrism" of English. A language is domesticated, according to Onyemelukwe and Alo (2015), when "it takes on and retains the respective local colors appropriate to the various ethno-cultural milieu where it has been domesticated" (p. 2). Whereas domestication transforms English into an "alien" medium in order to suit the cultural milieu of the people learning it (Akere, 2006, p. 2), the other approach presents English through an Anglo-centric lens, that is, through exposing the EFL learner mainly to American and British culture.

Teaching English is also caught up in the neoliberal conception of which skills are necessary for people to converse in the *global market* with native speakers of English *and* with native speakers of other languages who speak English, and to practice in *local* cultures of consumerism and social media platforms commonly held in English. Scholars estimate that more than 80 percent of communication involving English in the world is now between so-called "non-native" speakers of the language (Sharifian, 2013). Graddol (2006, p. 87) observes that "an inexorable trend in the use of global English is that fewer interactions now involve a native-speaker." It is obvious that participating in global and local cultures of consumerism/communication through the use of English is not grounded in belonging to a particular national culture. Specifically, speakers of different languages learn English today not merely to "become educated users of the language, to communicate with native speakers and to read the literature written by and for native speakers" (Kramsch, 2015, p. 410). Rather, they do so in order to learn how to function between languages through acquiring cross-cultural skills "as global communications have become more and more multimodal and multilingual and potential interlocutors are not necessarily monolingual native nationals but other multilingual non-native speakers" (Kramsch, 2015). How these observations shape the learning of English and other languages in Anglophone countries is also crucial for understanding the globalization of English.

Considered as a whole, globalizing English poses serious challenges to the promotion of multilingual ideologies among native speakers in Anglophone countries who are interpellated by monolingual English-only ideological practices. Under neoliberalism, the role other languages play in the market, in businesses, and in global testing is almost totally marginal, rendering English as the one practical language one needs to invest in learning. In their editorial for a special issue of *Language and Intercultural Communication*, on the topic of Education and the Discourse of Global Neoliberalism, which is worth quoting at length, Gray, O'Regan, and Wallace (2018) describe the tension between English and other languages as follows:

> The global spread of English, which is itself a 'global' industry, has in turn created the conditions in which internationalized capital and national education systems across the world not only excessively valorize English, but also in which the nations of the Anglophone core excessively valorize monolingual instrumentalism. In the UK and the US, for example, the global spread of English has led to an active disinterestedness in the learning of other languages, since the popular perception is that 'everyone speaks English'. In the process, often with the explicit encouragement of right-wing agitators in the political establishment and the Fourth Estate, English native speakers have been made more monolingual, and with it, more insular and lacking in intercultural curiosity, as the election of Donald Trump in the US and the UK's Brexit vote have shown.
>
> *(p. 475)*

In this respect, one should bear in mind that English shapes the construction of neoliberalism as a political enterprise not only as a "market-based and governmentally-authoritarian phenomenon" (p. 471), but also as a linguistic and intercultural phenomenon. The changing context of English use, both locally and globally, is complicated by the prevalent notion of language and culture as representing two sides of the same coin (Nault, 2006). In the field of language education in general and foreign language education in particular, the language-culture link is central for advancing the learner's true proficiency in a target language as proficiency is conditioned upon familiarity with the culture associated with that language (Bhabha, 1994; Hinkel, 1999; Jiang, 2000; Kramsch, 1998; Nault, 2006; Witherspoon, 1980).

This problematic language-culture link that arises in discussions of English education issues and the global role English plays in neoliberal markets bring to the surface some critical questions with which this book is centrally concerned:

- Which culture(s) is English, supposedly the global language, most closely associated with?
- How do English teachers or textbook writers relate the changing context of English use at local/global levels to the fact that English is also the national language of dominant world powers, such as the US or the UK?

From a pedagogical perspective, how could the teaching of English to speakers of other languages offer a balanced cultural experience between the Anglocentric nature of English, and its inevitable global nature? If English no longer belongs to one or two countries, then teaching English might be expected to consider new forms of English that are being used in countries all over the globe, and the domestic cultures of those associated with these forms. Suffice it to say here that any attempt to offer some answers to the complex questions above seems only possible if we critically examine how the notion of "global" is constructed in EFL discourse.

Whether EFL policy-makers translate their understanding of the globalizing change in contexts of English use into actual practices is the focus of the policy analysis I will present. My point of departure in critically questioning English ideologies in EFL policy discourses is the simple fact that non-native speakers, sometimes also non-western "Other" speakers, bring with them their own cultural experiences, languages, beliefs, and value systems into the learning of English. What concerns me, then, is the way these learners (including speakers of Arabic in Israel) tackle an English learning experience that is heavily saturated with Anglocentric and Western values (see Awayed-Bishara, 2015). Nault (2006) notes that

> The culture-bound nature of ELT [English Language Teaching] materials can sometimes present serious dilemmas in language classrooms because images and concepts that appear natural or harmless to the average Western reader, for example, may be viewed as intrusive and/or demeaning by people from other backgrounds.
>
> *(p. 322)*

In line with what Spolsky and Shohamy (1999) report regarding the large number of native speakers in the EFL enterprise in Israel, Alptekin (1993) points out that

> Most textbook writers are native speakers who consciously or unconsciously transmit their views, values, beliefs, attitudes, and feelings of their own English-speaking society – usually the United States or United Kingdom. As such, when learners acquire a new set of English discourse as part of their evolving systemic knowledge, they partake of the cultural system which the set entails.
>
> *(p. 138)*

The US and the UK are clearly dominant world powers and major sites of native English usage. It therefore makes some sense to introduce familiarity with American or British cultures into the English-teaching environment. However, this must be done while also keeping in mind that, in the eyes of many learners, English is valued for the access it gives them to various global activities (political, academic, commercial, etc.) and not for any familiarity they might gain with its native speakers' Anglo-centric perspectives. To live up to the notion of English as the language of the world and its diverse multicultural speakers, Kramsch and Sullivan

(1996) suggest a language pedagogy that combines both "*global* appropriacy" and "*local* appropriation." Canagarajah (1999) views such pedagogy of *appropriation* as a promising method that enables "students to appropriate the dominant codes and discourses according to their needs and interests" (p. 186). It is essential, then, that any EFL "methodology of a global nature should be sensitive to local socio-cultural conditions" (Luk, 2004, p. 248), so that learners of different cultural backgrounds accept rather than reject new cultural content.

Methodology and Data

Similar to the two previous analytical chapters, this chapter uses tools and methods from Critical Discourse Analysis (CDA) to analyze policy papers regarding the teaching/learning of EFL in Israel. Generally speaking, "CDA aims to investigate critically social inequality as it is expressed, constituted, legitimized, and so on, by language use" (Wodak & Meyer, 2009, p. 10). I developed a broad understanding of EFL language educational policy through analyzing the following documents (many of which appear on the Education Ministry's "Stay Up-to-Date" official website):[1]

1. The National English Curriculum (Ministry of Education, 2018).
2. An official document entitled "Teaching English in Israeli Schools" (Ministry of Education, 2016).
3. Various policy documents from the English Inspectorate's desk.
4. Interviews I conducted with EFL textbook writers.

Four textbook writers responded to my emails and agreed to talk to me either in person, or through email correspondence. All participants requested anonymity, and I therefore do not state their names, affiliations, or the publishing houses they work(ed) for. Participants were asked to describe the process of writing a textbook from the stage of receiving a publishing contract, to the final authorization from the Israeli Ministry of Education for the finished textbook. Three writers stated that they initiated the submission of a textbook proposal; the fourth reported being approached by a publishing house. Three reported being native speakers of English, originally from North America and Britain, while the fourth reported being a non-native speaker of English. The interviews in person were semi-structured, and not tape-recorded as no permission to record was granted. Field notes were taken during the interview and subsequently analyzed. Excerpts from email records will also be presented for analysis.

Below, I will present critical analysis that offers a new way of viewing English language education in Israel, and opens new windows onto a pedagogy that claims to encourage students to "cross cultural and discursive borders" (Canagarajah, 1999, p. 186). The relevance and importance of offering a new approach to English language education in Israel will be practically developed in Chapter 6. Based on the assumption that diversity needs to be accounted for in EFL education, and that

Anglo-centrism alone, without a measure of domestication, is unjust, I pose the following research questions:

- To what extent does the National English Curriculum in Israel – which is uniform for Hebrew and Arabic speakers – take into account learner diversity?
- Do language policy and EFL language educational policies in Israel provide equal opportunities for mastering English to all learners?
- To what extent is the EFL policy discourse in Israel Anglo-centric?

Through undertaking a critical discourse analysis of the policy documents and interviews with textbook writers, I hope to shed light on the policy and planning issues around EFL in Israel that could also have serious implications for education and multiculturalism far beyond the learning of English in Israel.

Analysis of Documents

Analysis of the documents reveals high levels of inconsistency, and even incompatibility, between what is explicitly stated in them, and the manner in which their fundamentals are implemented in the various sectors. Below, I will demonstrate some of the inconsistencies between the stated language educational policies (LEP) (as they appear in the National English Curriculum, entitled *Teaching English in Israeli Schools*, documents from the Inspector's desk, and interviews with EFL textbook writers) and their practices in the field.

The National English Curriculum: Uniform or Segregating?

One of the crucial observations in the English curriculum is the definition of target English learning populations. The curriculum states: "The English Curriculum in Israel sets out the expected standards for the teaching of English in Israel, in schools under the supervision of the Ministry of Education. This includes all sectors: *secular, religious, Arab, Druze, and Bedouin*" (Ministry of Education, 2018, p. 7; my emphasis).

However, not all the above-mentioned sectors operate under the supervision of the Ministry of Education. The "religious" (meaning Orthodox Jewish) sector is a notable exception. The attitudes toward English teaching in religious schools are varied and complex. According to Baumel (2003), while some religious groups (particularly ultra-orthodox) are reluctant to teach English in schools (some *Haredi* groups), others (*Hasidic* or *Habad*) permit and even encourage the teaching of English for "pragmatic" reasons, as "it will act as a linguistic conduit to allow religious knowledge to spread outwards" (p. 57). Baumel also points out gender differences in determining who should and who should not learn English. Ultra-orthodox schools operate under the umbrella of various educational entities such as the *Hinuch Atzmai* or the *Shas* system, which determine curricular policies compatible with the ideological and cultural needs of those groups. In many cases, these school systems also produce their own teaching materials and textbooks. Baumel further demonstrates that

> These schools often use English textbooks developed by the *Beit Ya'akov-Hinuch Atzmai* educational system, which are usually very similar to their secular and modern-religious counterparts, including vocabulary, grammar, reading comprehension, and unseen texts, but only those suitable for a Haredi lifestyle. Pictures of boys and girls appear in these textbooks; however, they are dressed *appropriately*.
>
> (p. 60; emphasis in original)

It seems, then, that the ultra-Orthodox sector operates according to a special LEP with "variations in student body, curriculum, matriculation policy and certification" (p. 57). This LEP *domestically* suits the ideological and cultural milieus of a religious sector for which the curriculum (i.e. their special curriculum) is a text that exhibits the dominant tone of the prevalent social or educational discourse of a particular society or population (Pinar, Reynolds, Slattery, & Taubman, 1995). One may then fairly ask: Why does the curriculum refrain from stating that certain groups of EFL learners follow special curricular programs? An even more pertinent question is: Why is the general LEP in Israel so tolerant toward the special cultural and ideological needs of the ultra-orthodox sector, to the extent that they are allowed to design their own LEP, while the needs of other groups may be safely ignored?

The second point that arises from the analysis is the division of the Arabic-speaking target learning population into Arab, Druze, and Bedouin – a questionable and problematic move, for two reasons. First, unlike in the Jewish sector, all Arabic-speaking populations must adhere to the same English curriculum. Why would the Arabic-speaking community be discursively divided into the ethnic subsections of Arab, Druze, and Bedouin, while the Jewish community is not ethnically divided into Ashkenazi, Sephardi, Ethiopian, etc., but only into secular and religious? Second, and more crucially, the "Arab, Druze, and Bedouin" division is not equivalent to the "secular and religious" division. In fact, the category of "Arabic speakers" *does* include "Druze" and "Bedouins" but the Ministry of Education seems to discursively and deliberately discern between these groups. Such "divide and rule" policies clearly serve the interests of dominant Israeli-Zionist ideologies mostly threatened by unification of the various groups comprising the Palestinian minority (i.e. Christians, Muslims, Bedouins, and Druze). More importantly, such apparently "multicultural" accommodation that the state "allows" among its Arab minority acts as nothing more than a covering (Yoshino, 2002) for the state's socio-legal practices against the assimilation of Palestinian Arabs within the Jewish nation-state. In anticipation of the possible "multicultural" justification for the ministry's division of the Arab minority into various sub-groups, I invoke Karayanni's (2018) observation "that the covering offered by multiculturalism is instrumental for the nation-state constellation as it masks its incompetency to offer an inclusive identity for all its citizens, especially for those who do not belong to the ruling majority" (p. 3).

So, cultural diversity and religious diversity among English learners (i.e. Jews and Arabs, both religious and secular) are explicitly acknowledged by the Ministry of Education in the text. Nonetheless, other than acknowledging how the curriculum is also intended for speakers of Arabic (in a total of only *two* lines in 114 pages), the curriculum refrains from offering any special attention or guidelines to the complex linguistic challenges speakers of Arabic face when learning English, such as reference to the diglossic aspect of their mother tongue and its impact on learning a foreign (and fourth) language. It is also revealing that the entire issue of "Learner Diversity," stated as central to the curriculum's rationale, is only dealt with on one page divided into three sections. The first section is a short paragraph that defines what "Learner Diversity" means:

> As a result of the diversity existing in the classroom, there are groups of learners who, for various reasons, will reach the Foundation, Intermediate, and Proficiency Levels at different times and not necessarily at the grade levels mentioned in Section Two. Therefore, the implementation of the curriculum for these learners is different and requires special attention.
> *(Ministry of Education, 2018, p. 110)*

Subsequently, the curriculum states,

> These populations include:
> Learners who are *native speakers* of English, or have grown up in a bilingual home or have lived or studied in an English-speaking environment.
> Learners who are *native speakers of Arabic*, whose school learning load includes Modern Standard Arabic as well as Hebrew and English.
> Learners who are new immigrants, and need to learn Hebrew as a second language and English as a foreign language.
> Learners who, as a result of socio-economic circumstances, are inadequately prepared for schooling.
> Learners who have special needs; such learners with hearing and vision problems ...
> *(Ministry of Education, 2018; my emphasis)*

Following this specification of learners who require special attention, only *two* populations are given "more detailed guidelines" in two documents entitled: "Adapting the English Curriculum for *Students with Disabilities*" and "Guidelines on the Teaching of *Native Sspeakers of English*" (Ministry of Education, 2018; my emphasis).

Delving into other official documents to see whether guidelines for the other three diverse groups are provided elsewhere (i.e. other than in the curriculum itself) reveals how the English Inspectorate completely disregards Palestinian Arab EFL learners, who form a major part of the EFL target audience. In other words, whether through the links offered in the curriculum or through direct access to the official website, no guidelines whatsoever are provided for the teaching of English to Arabic speakers. In contrast to the lack of such guidelines, the English Inspectorate presents a link in its main page (under the title "Inspector's desk") called "Native Speakers." The link entitled "Native Speakers" and the document "Teaching English in Israel" both appear on this official ministerial website (Ministry of Education, n.d.). These two links offer some insights into how the Ministry of Education constructs the role of the native speaker of English within EFL teaching and learning in Israel.

The Superior Native Speaker

Analysis of the online document entitled "Native Speakers" on the official website of the English inspectorate casts light upon the use of various discursive practices to segregate native speaker (hereinafter NS) teachers and learners from non-native speakers (hereinafter NNS) and to situate them in a superior position. This is discursively achieved through:

1. Valorizing their status as "diverse" learners (as opposed to erasing the Arab learners who are categorized similarly in the curriculum) through explicitly defining them as a target audience (through the kind of "explicit statement" discussed in Chapter 3) and through offering relevant guidelines for teachers and schools on the ministry's official website;
2. Distinguishing NS from NNS classes through the use of positive lexical selections (van Dijk, 2006) that highlight how NS classes offer "better" learning environments. It also becomes clear that they are granted special budgets as the following sample examples – all quoted from the curriculum (Ministry of Education, 2018) – show:

   - All class interaction, oral and written – teacher-student and student-student – is totally in English.
   - Because of the basic differences in approach between teaching English to native speakers and to other students, and considering the substantial gap between the two groups' skills levels, the native speaker students should, whenever possible, study separately.
   - The alternative framework in elementary and junior high schools for budgeting native speaker programs is *Talan* (*Tochnit Limudim Nosefet* [Hebrew for Additional Educational Program]).

3. Directly suggesting, while indirectly requiring, that only NS teachers are qualified to teach NS learners:

[I]t is most strongly recommended that only native speakers teach in these programs. *Experience* has shown that lack of total proficiency, both oral and written, on the part of the teacher inevitably leads to the undermining of his/her authority with both students and parents.

(Ministry of Education, 2018; my emphasis)

Note how assessing teacher's professionalism in the last quote is based on the individual "experience" of those setting these policies and not on a set of professional standards or theoretical frameworks according to which a teacher might (or might not) be professionally *fit* to teach a supposedly competent group of learners. NS learners are definitely highly proficient for the simple reason that English is their mother tongue, just as native speakers of Arabic are proficient in Arabic to speak it as their mother tongue. Being a NS of English by no means testifies to the linguistic competence of that specific learner, nor to that of the teacher capable of teaching them. As a native speaker of Arabic, I am not by default a potentially better Arabic teacher than someone who is not. Had the ministry wished to guarantee that NS learners receive an adequate level of teaching that caters to their special proficiency needs, they could have fairly required that highly professional English teachers should teach these classes, and to specify the professional standards that a teacher should meet for qualifying. However, constructing NS teachers as the most professional teachers contributes to reproducing and perpetuating hegemonic native speakerist ideologies, as well as enshrining false assumptions about English teaching professionalism. NNS English teachers in Israeli schools could just as easily teach NS learners, just as many NNS professors from various places in the world hold high teaching positions at prestigious universities in English-speaking countries, using English as their non-native medium of instruction.

The centrality of the native speaker plays an integral role in the whole architectural structure of English language education in Israel. This observation becomes even more prominent when analyzing the policy document "Teaching English in Israel" (Ministry of Education, 2016, hereinafter TEI) issued by the Inspectorate. The text begins as follows:

> English is without question a global language, used in international trade and tourism, in academia and research, and in the electronic media. Therefore, *professional* English teachers are in high demand in Israel and the Ministry of Education is interested in encouraging *new immigrants* to teach English. The purpose of this document is to provide *you* with information regarding how to become an English teacher in Israel.
>
> (TEI; my emphasis)

As I will now argue, analysis of the above documents reveals a systematic tendency toward (1) prioritizing NSs over NNSs as *the* professional English teachers; and (2) constructing the EFL teaching context as exclusively Jewish.

Prioritizing NS over NNS as Ideal English Teachers

The above-mentioned passage provides a clear definition of the audience to whom the text is addressed. It is intended for a "you" who must be a "new immigrant." In the Israeli context it is clear that "you" must be a Jew – currently living in an English-speaking society – and not just any "native speaker" of English, since the passage is explicitly directed at "new immigrants." Within the Jewish-Zionist context, encouraging Jewish immigration to Israel has always been a fundamental principle in constructing the national Jewish-Zionist collective, even before the establishment of the State of Israel in 1948. The use of the notion of Zionist immigration to Israel in the EFL context designates the new immigrants, who are native speakers of English, as ideal "professional" English teachers. Constructing the new immigrant as the ideal English teacher evidently excludes many other teachers from the "professional" category, and further contributes to situating NS teachers as superior to their new NNS compatriots.

As I noted earlier in the analysis of the document "Native Speakers," designating the new immigrant teachers as the "professional" teachers in the TEI document calls for further questioning of the notion of "professionalism" the Ministry of Education seems to ascribe. For one, those calling for professional English teachers to come and make *Aliya* and teach English in Israeli schools seem to be imbricated with hegemonic ideologies of native speakerism whereby the native speaker is perceived as the ultimate expert in teaching English. Note that the TEI document offers new immigrants names of teaching colleges and academic institutions where they may obtain a teaching certificate *following* their arrival in Israel, as the following excerpt shows: "*If you do not have a teacher's license*, there are retraining courses for academics in the Teacher Training Colleges. (See Appendix One for contact information for the Teacher Training Colleges.)" (Ministry of Education, 2016, p. 2; my emphasis).

Therefore, constructing new immigrants as *the* professional teachers – although they might not yet even have obtained a teaching certificate – contributes to an unjust and *chauvinistic* (Holliday, 2013) act of weakening the status of other NNS teachers who might be highly professional, academically qualified, and skilled. Constructing the native speaker as the ultimate English teacher and professional also explains to some extent why Palestinian Arab professionals (who are either locally based in Israel or tend not to grow up in an English-speaking diaspora with any hope of emigrating to Palestine) are not included in policy-making, textbook production, or national matriculation/test design, and the dominance of NS in filling teaching and other jobs requiring English.

It could be fair to conclude, then, that prioritizing NS teachers over NNS teachers contributes to the exclusion of other NNS professionals (who might be Palestinian Arabs or other NNS Jewish professionals) from decision-making bodies relevant to the EFL context in Israel. Such a practice perpetuates a status quo of unbalanced power in educational decision-making. This might directly, and negatively, affect the populations in need of special attention and planning in order for them to reach higher levels of achievement in English since those controlling the system prioritize interests not necessarily compatible with those of the above-mentioned groups.

Constructing the EFL Teaching Context as Exclusively Jewish

Analysis of the TEI document also reveals a systematic tendency to construct the educational system in general and the EFL context in particular as Jewish. This is done through an overt and direct use of terms and content that are exclusively

Jewish and Zionist. In introducing the Israeli educational system to "prospective" English teachers who are encouraged to immigrate to Israel, the text states, "Some high schools provide a general academic education while others may be vocationally oriented. *Yeshiva* High Schools combine general studies with *Torah* study" (Ministry of Education, 2016, p. 1; my emphasis). The description of the Israeli schooling system constructs it as exclusively Jewish, albeit secular or religious. Nonetheless, there is no mention of how the Israeli Ministry of Education maintains two schooling systems for the Hebrew- and Arabic-speaking populations, for whom the English curriculum is uniform.

Situating the Israeli schooling system in a Jewish framework is also evident in using expressions such as "if you taught in schools prior to making *Aliyah*" (Ministry of Education, 2016), for instance, to inform those interested in English teaching in Israel of the issue of teachers' salaries. The use of "prior to making *Aliya*" explicitly connects English language education in Israel to ideology and demonstrates how language is a political enterprise *par excellence*. Namely, other than the Jewish-Zionist role of making *Aliya*, encouraging native speakers to do so through the medium of English language teaching is meant to serve other implicit agendas for fortifying Western ideologies (i.e. the home ideologies of native speakers) as part of the Israeli-Jewish cultural arena and hence fix Israel's micro-site as a supporter and even partner in Western (and mainly American) hegemony.

Following the description of salaries, TEI gives an account of how school vacations are allotted in Israel: "Teachers receive approximately two months paid vacation in the summer, one week before and during *Passover*, a week during *Sukkot*, plus additional *Jewish* holidays and *Israeli national* days" (p. 1; my emphasis). This excerpt demonstrates the way Israel's general policies and more specifically its educational policies exclude the Palestinian Arab minority's culture, religions, and communities from Jewish-Israeli cultural and educational contexts. Aside from the overtly systematic marginalization, the implications of specifying how Israeli schools are on vacation only during the highlighted holidays and national events, also convey the message that new immigrant teachers are expected to teach only in Jewish schools, and not in Palestinian Arab schools, whose existence is not even mentioned. The last subsection in the TEI document entitled "Requirements for Teaching English in Israel" further confirms that NS teachers are constructed as Jews who will teach in Jewish schools, since "English teachers must be able to speak, read and write in Hebrew" (p. 2). Additionally, the TEI, as mentioned earlier, offers the new teachers names of teaching training colleges where they can obtain their teaching certificate. All 11 listed colleges are Jewish, while Arab teaching training colleges in Israel (e.g. the Academic Arab College for Education in Haifa, and Sakhnin College) are excluded from the list.

Even supposing we accept the notion of "professionalism" associated with NS teachers that the Ministry of Education nurtures, I would call into question the ministry's reluctance to provide Arabic-speaking schools with NS teachers who are "professional." If the NS is the ultimate English teacher, why would the Ministry of Education intentionally exclude Arabic-speaking schools from the NS scenario, so as not to offer them better chances of learning English? This is clearly deliberate and discriminatory, since the whole discourse presented in the TEI document explicitly defines who is to be considered "the superior" teacher and who is to be considered "the superior" student.

The Anglo-centric Nature of EFL Discourse

As an example of the inconsistencies between stated policies and actual practices in English language education, the description of the globalization of English from the introduction to the National English Curriculum is a good place to start:

> Perhaps the most dramatic development that has taken place in the field of English language teaching in the last generation has been the shift in its primacy: *from being the native language of nations, such as the UK or USA, to being mainly a global means of communication.* The speakers of English whose mother tongue is another language vastly outnumber the English native speakers, and their relative number continues to grow.
>
> *(Ministry of Education, 2018, p. 7; my emphasis)*

The curriculum further states:

> For most of its learners, English is therefore no longer a foreign language (i.e. one that is owned by a particular 'other' nation or ethnic group) but first and foremost an international language (one that has no particular national owner).

These well-meaning gestures to the fact that English is no longer under the ownership of American or British nations and cultures seem to be overlooked when implementing curricular policy in textbook design. Although the curriculum postulates that English should be approached from a global rather than an Anglocentric perspective, the textbook analysis presented in Chapter 3 indicates that almost 70 percent of characters' names and place names in English textbooks are Western (American or British) and the other 30 percent are Jewish. Thus, most of the texts and narratives present stories and details that are relevant to Western characters and issues (see Awayed-Bishara, 2015). Furthermore, discourse analysis of English matriculation exams in Israel has revealed an almost exclusive coverage of Western – chiefly American – related topics (Zaher, 2015).

Analysis of textbooks also suggests that despite including culture as a significant component in presenting a language to learners (as required in EFL textbook design and teaching by the English curriculum), this practice is problematic. While other non-Western cultures are mentioned in the six studied English textbooks, these cultures are mostly represented negatively or as lacking agency to advance themselves, and are therefore dependent on Western, mainly white, support. As shown earlier, these textbooks offer no fair and accurate description of the 20 percent of EFL learners who are Palestinian Arabs, as the only two examples offered in the textbooks deal with Bedouins (without referring to them as Arabs) (Awayed-Bishara, 2015). The general tendency is to present non-Western cultures as inferior to Western cultures.

To what extent a Western bias or Anglocentrism was manifested in EFL textbook writing was what my interviews with textbook writers set out to examine. Through a close analysis of how textbook writers describe the way they perceive the process of textbook production, the final analytical section seeks to deepen understandings of how policy and language practices are interrelated.

The Textbook Writer: Other-Oriented or Self-Centered?

Analysis of the interviews with EFL textbook writers indicates a link between the way these writers perceive their role and the way the aforementioned EFL policy documents describe teaching/learning standards. This link could be established on the premise that in both cases "good intentions" get lost somewhere in the practice. Analysis of the way the four participants freely described the process (i.e. without being requested to respond to a specific question on my part) indicates that the central focus of textbook writing is language teaching processes and methodologies. All participants seemed mainly to be concerned with authoring a textbook that offered new and nuanced teaching methods which might take EFL teaching and learning to a different level. Descriptions also pertained to advancing learners' social interaction skills, as well as digital and linguistic competences, so that they might competently navigate the world of the twenty-first century. Yet when asked about the way they selected the cultural themes for their teaching units and reading/writing/speaking/listening tasks, most of them reported that they were trying to write about universal topics. One participant clarified this point as follows:

> We [she and her co-authors] were trying to write something that is universal, which might be considered both generic and global contents. With 'generic' I mean something that can be suitable or adaptable by anybody regardless of who they are or where they have come from. 'Global' content would probably deal with different cultures or what is acceptable by different cultures.
>
> *(M., email correspondence)*

Despite the blurring definitions M. provides for what she perceives as "global" and "generic" themes, she supposedly acknowledges the role English plays in relation to other different cultures who need to find the cultural themes of textbooks suitable or adaptable. When asked how the naming selections were made in order to guarantee "global" or "generic" content, M. reported that names were selected either based on the names of the real people in the stories/articles they adopted for use in the textbooks, or based on the writers' random selections, specifically in uncontextualized sentences. The other participants shared similar naming practices, and yet when asked about the inclusion of Arabic names, responses varied. The two participants corresponding by mail chose simply not to respond to this question; one writer stated only that they had made sure their textbooks included Arabic glossaries (i.e. Arabic translation of key words usually appearing at the bottom of a page or end of a section). A significant response to this same question in one interview, however, adds another dimension:

> I admit that it didn't occur to us to include neither Arabic names nor anything else relevant to Arabic speakers because we only had the Jewish population in mind.
>
> *(S., personal interview)*

S. accompanied this statement with sincere apologies, and an assurance that disregarding Arab learners was by no means intentional. Being an Arab researcher has apparently situated me in a representative position, to which S. felt compelled to apologize. To my query on whether writers receive any guidelines or instructions of what these textbooks need to include and to whom they must cater, S. explained:

> No guidelines are given since once the textbook proposal is accepted for publishing, the Ministry assumes that the authors catered their textbook proposal to curricular requirements. I believe that if texts about speakers of Arabic had been included, the ministry would have still approved the textbook.
>
> *(S., personal interview)*

This excerpt gestures to how diffuse the problem of cultural representation in EFL textbooks is. Who is responsible for the marginalization of the Arabic-speaking community? Is it the Ministry of Education which authorizes a textbook, even though 20 percent of its target population is not addressed in it? Or is it the EFL textbook writers who might be more self-centered than Other-oriented in their choice of materials? To further understand how the ministry deals with the issue of cultural representation in its authorization process, S. recalls one incident when the ministry required changes, as the following excerpt shows:

> It was the textbook we wrote almost ten years ago. Before authorizing the book, the ministry commented that the book discriminated against women and students in religious schools. Regarding women, the claim was that there were more pictures of men than that of women and they asked us to provide more photos. They also claimed that some of the themes discussed in the book are not suitable for the religious schools. We of course added more photos of women but didn't change anything regarding the unsuitable content since we agreed that the religious schools use their own textbooks anyway. And, that is about it, this is the only time I recall the process of authorization was interrupted due to an issue of content suitability or equal representation.
>
> *(S., personal interview)*

One thing that the above excerpt shows is that the Ministry of Education is indeed aware of and responds to issues of misrepresentation and cultural unsuitability. Interviewing only four textbook writers limits the conclusions that can be drawn from this, and suggests the value of further research into this state of affairs. Yet considering the analyses of EFL textbooks and how the Arab learners report feeling excluded from the cultural context of these textbooks, as reported in earlier chapters, the comments by S. are suggestive of a thoroughgoing practice producing congruence between these texts. Granting equal opportunities to, and adequately representing all of the diverse populations who comprise the EFL target learners, might appear to some not among the ministry's priorities when it comes to planning EFL policy, and authorizing its implementation practices. The fact that these four textbook writers say they only had the Jewish population in mind while writing is a point that stakeholders and educational scholars in Israel and elsewhere must seriously consider. How could stakeholders and practitioners be so expressly mindless to the needs of the largest minority in their country? Is it perhaps either an intentional policy to keep the status quo of dissonance, conflict, and Jewish supremacy, or a tangible manifestation of an unwitting state of ignorance and self-centeredness *par excellence*?

Conclusion

This chapter presented a critical discourse analysis of policy documents in order to examine the level of compatibility between the stated aim of these policies, and their actual implementation by the Israel Ministry of Education. Analysis shows a high level of inconsistency between what the policies state, and the ways in which they are implemented. For one, stating that the English curriculum is uniform for both Hebrew and Arabic speakers contradicts the practices of consistent marginalization and absence of the Arabic speakers, prevalent in EFL discourse. Furthermore, despite acknowledging the new globalized status of English and the need to situate the teaching of English in a global rather than an Anglocentric framework, analysis shows a systematic tendency towards constructing the Anglocentric native speaker of English as superior, and as the ultimate professional English teacher, thus reinforcing hegemonic ideologies of native speakerism. By the same token, through a systematic use of Jewish-Zionist vocabulary, national symbols, and the centering of *Aliyah* as a typical NS teacher experience, such policies construct the EFL context in Israel as exclusively Jewish, thus reinforcing the exclusion of the Palestinian Arab minority and its collective practices from the EFL educational context. Textbook writers, meanwhile, seem to be mainly writing from their own personal and communal position, without being seriously guided on what must govern the process of producing an equally representative schoolbook in a multicultural educational setting. In short, EFL discourse fails to address the issue of learner diversity as it prioritizes native speaker learners/teachers over non-native – particularly Palestinian Arab – learners/teachers, whose existence is basically erased. These tendencies are ideologically encoded, perhaps perpetuating the status quo of an unequal educational system that functions as a gatekeeper holding Palestinian Arab learners from reaching higher levels of performance in English.

One crucial observation that arises from the analysis is the way in which EFL discourse in Israel has ignored the shift in the field of foreign language education over the past two decades. I opened this book by referring to this shift, and emphasizing the transformative goals any foreign language pedagogy, let alone that of English as the global language, must set for its learners and educational systems (Byram, 2008; 2011; Kumaravadivelu, 2008; Risager, 2007). The core of these transformative goals is that foreign language education ought to result in learners who are locally minded, globally aware citizens, who are trained to become critically reflective (Kumaravadivelu, 2008), politically conscious, engaged (Byram, 2011), and cosmopolitan citizens (Rizvi, 2005). In a conflict-ridden place such as Israel, EFL pedagogy could become part of a transformative project toward peace and social justice. In fact, the Ministry of Education has recently launched a new project for English language education entitled "Diplomacy and International Communication in English" that aims at teaching students about conflicts and resolutions. This initiative is supposedly aligned with the United Nations 2012 initiative calling for "global citizenship education" worldwide. It is too early to gauge how successful this project is, since in its current form it is essentially elitist and directed at students learning English at the highest level only. It is not targeted at all EFL learners, but only at a group of already highly competent learners. Its scope of influence is limited, and it is still at an early stage of implementation. A future study might critically analyze this new direction, and examine whether the program offers new ideological challenges for constructing critical EFL learners who might become agents of social change, or whether it simply reproduces and perpetuates the same discourse of Western-Jewish hegemony and Palestinian Arab marginalization. I will partially relate to this program while trying to underpin EFL discourse as cultural practice within the framework of global citizenship education in Chapter 6.

The insights we gain from this chapter are closely related to my previous analyses of EFL textbooks (in Chapter 3) and of EFL learners' responses (in Chapter 4) as they shape and reshape each other in a synergistic relationship, offering a link between EFL policy documents, local ideological state practices, and global notions of native speakerism and professionalism in various English teaching frameworks. EFL policy discourse in Israel is hence clearly imbued with power, and an ideology that exerts a direct impact on specific social actors, interpellating subjects into positions that reproduce a particular hegemonic ideology perpetuating the status of English as an Anglocentric and American-biased dominant force. This tendency calls into question the global perception of English as the language of the world, and situates EFL policy discourse in a self-contradictory position owing to the significant gaps between the stated policies and the implemented practices. The fact that EFL discourse also fails to engage both in policy and in practice with the diversity of the learning population poses a serious dilemma in the field of English teaching to speakers of other languages – who numerically are becoming a dominant force, but practically still are being marginalized. The tangible manifestation of this failure is the superior role granted to native speaker learners, and the relegation to subaltern status of other groups of diverse learners, such as speakers of Arabic in the Israeli context, whose linguistic repertoire compels a solid and well-planned pedagogical policy. We may, in this regard, understand EFL discourse as a cultural practice that serves to enshrine hegemonic ideologies of native speakerism, and situates EFL in Israel within wider international frameworks of native speakerist dominance.

One critical point that I have not yet tackled is related to the roles and responsibilities of Palestinian Arab scholars, teachers, parents, students, and other social actors against the backdrop of these discriminatory state policies. Should we remain passive receivers reproducing victimization narratives about state discrimination and inequality? Or, should we act as subversive agents who take responsibility to alter the practices that impede the progress of the Palestinian Arab minority, educationally speaking or otherwise? I devote the final chapter of this book to elaborate on how moving from a discourse of rights to a discourse of responsibilities is an essential step that Palestinian Arab pedagogues, teachers, parents, and learners *must* take in order to construct a transformative EFL pedagogy aimed at effecting social change.

Note

1 See http://cms.education.gov.il/educationcms/units/mazkirut_pedagogit/english/inspectoratesdesk/whatsnew.htm

References

Policy Documents

Ministry of Education. (2016). Teaching English in Israel. Jerusalem: Ministry of Education, State of Israel. August. Retrieved from http://meyda.education.gov.il/files/Mazkirut_Pedagogit/English/TeachingEnglishinIsrael5.doc

Ministry of Education. (2018). Revised English curriculum including Band III lexis: Principles and standards for learning English as an international language for all grades. January. Jerusalem: Ministry of Education, State of Israel. Available at: http://meyda.education.gov.il/files/Mazkirut_Pedagogit/English/Curriculum2018July.pdf (accessed February 24, 2019).

Ministry of Education. (n.d.). Inspectorate's desk: Stay up-to-date! Department of Languages – English. Israeli Government. Available at: http://cms.education.gov.il/educationcms/units/mazkirut_pedagogit/english/inspectoratesdesk/whatsnew.htm (accessed May 7, 2019).

Works Cited

Akere, F. (2006). The English language in Nigeria: The sociolinguistic dynamics of decolonization (pp. 2–16). Paper presented at the Conference of the Nigerian English Studies Association, University of Ilorin.

Alptekin, C. (1993). Target-language culture in EFL materials. *ELT Journal*, 47(2), 136–143. doi:10.1093/elt/47.2.136.

Althusser, L. (1971). Ideology and ideological state apparatuses (Notes towards an investigation). In L. Althusser, *Lenin and philosophy, and other essays* (pp. 121–173). London: New Left Books.

Awayed-Bishara, M. (2015). Analyzing the cultural content of materials used for teaching English to high school speakers of Arabic in Israel. *Discourse & Society*, 26(5), 517–542. doi:10.1177/0957926515581154.

Baumel, S. D. (2003). Teaching English in Israeli Haredi schools. *Language Policy*, 2, 47–67.

Bhabha, H. K. (1994). *The location of culture*. New York: Routledge.

Byram, M. S. (2008). *From foreign language education to education for intercultural citizenship: Essays and reflections*. Clevedon: Multilingual Matters.

Byram, M. S. (2011). Intercultural citizenship from an international perspective. *Journal of the NUS Teaching Academy*, 1(1), 10–20.

Canagarajah, A. S. (1999). *Resisting linguistic imperialism in English teaching*. Oxford: Oxford University Press.

Davies, A. (2003). *The native speaker: Myth and reality*. Clevedon: Multilingual Matters.

Ferguson, C. A. (1959). Diglossia. *WORD*, 15(2), 325–340. doi:10.1080/00437956.1959.11659702.

Graddol, D. (2006). English next: Why global English may mean the end of "English as a Foreign Language." London: British Council. Available at: http://englishagenda.britishcouncil.org/sites/default/files/attachments/books-english-next.pdf (accessed February 18, 2019).

Gray, J., O'Regan, J. P., & Wallace, C. (2018). Education and the discourse of global neoliberalism. *Language and Intercultural Communication*, 18(5), 471–477. doi:10.1080/14708477.2018.1501842.

Hinkel, E. (1999). *Culture in second language teaching and learning*. Cambridge: Cambridge University Press.

Holliday, A. (2013). "Native speaker" teachers and cultural belief. In S. A. Houghton & D. J. Rivers (Eds.), *Native-speakerism in Japan: Intergroup dynamics in foreign language education* (pp. 17–28). Bristol: Multilingual Matters.

Jenkins, J. (2000). *The phonology of English as an international language: New models, new norms, new goals*. Oxford: Oxford University Press.

Jiang, W. (2000). The relationship between culture and language. *ELT Journal*, 54(4), 328–334. doi:10.1093/elt/54.4.328.

Karayanni, M. (2018). Multiculturalism as covering: On the accommodation of minority religions in Israel. *The American Journal of Comparative Law*, 66(4), 831–875. doi:10.1093/ajcl/avy039.

Kramsch, C. (1998). *Language and culture*. Oxford: Oxford University Press.

Kramsch, C. (2015). Applied linguistics: A theory of the practice. *Applied Linguistics*, 36(4), 454–465. doi:10.1093/applin/amv039.

Kramsch, C., & Sullivan, P. (1996). Appropriate pedagogy. *ELT Journal*, 50(3), 199–212. doi:10.1093/elt/50.3.199.

Krzyżanowski, M., & Wodak, R. (2011). Political strategies and language policies: The European Union Lisbon strategy and its implications for the EU's language and multilingualism policy. *Language Policy*, 10(2), 115–136. doi:10.1007/s10993-011-9196-5.

Kumaravadivelu, B. (2008). *Cultural globalization and language education*. New Haven, CT: Yale University Press.

Kymlicka, W., & Grin, F. (2003). Assessing the politics of diversity in transition countries. In F. Daftary & F. Grin (Eds.), *Nation-building, ethnicity and language politics in transition countries* (pp. 3–27). Budapest: LGI Books.

Luk, J. (2004). Voicing the 'Self' through an 'Other' language: Exploring communicative language teaching for global communication. In A. S. Canagarajah (Ed.), *Reclaiming the local in language policy and practice* (pp. 247–268). Mahwah, NJ: Lawrence Erlbaum Associates.

Milani, T. M. (2008). Language testing and citizenship: A language ideological debate in Sweden. *Language in Society*, 37(1), 27–59. doi:10.1017/S0047404508080020.

Nault, D. (2006). Going global: Rethinking culture teaching in ELT contexts. *Language, Culture and Curriculum*, 19(3), 314–328. doi:10.1080/07908310608668770.

Onyemelukwe, N. H., & Alo, M. A. (2015). Making Nigerian English pedagogy a reality. *American Journal of Linguistics*, 4(1), 11–17.

Pinar, W. F., Reynolds, W. M., Slattery, P., & Taubman, P. M. (1995). *Understanding curriculum: An introduction to the study of historical and contemporary curriculum discourses*. New York: Peter Lang.

Risager, K. (2007). *Language and culture pedagogy: From a national to a transnational paradigm*. Clevedon: Multilingual Matters.

Rizvi, F. (2005). Identity, culture and cosmopolitan futures. *Higher Education Policy*, 18(4), 331–339. doi:10.1057/palgrave.hep.8300095.

Sharifian, F. (2013). Globalisation and developing metacultural competence in learning English as an international language. *Multilingual Education*, 3(1), 7. doi:10.1186/2191-5059-3-7.

Spolsky, B., & Shohamy, E. (1999). *The languages of Israel policy, ideology and practice: Bilingualism education and bilingualism*. Clevedon: Multilingual Matters.

van Dijk, T. A. (2006). Discourse and manipulation. *Discourse & Society*, 17(3), 359–383. doi:10.1177/0957926506060250.

Witherspoon, G. (1980). Language in culture and culture in language. *International Journal of American Linguistics*, 46(1), 1–13.

Wodak, R., & Meyer, M. (2009). Critical discourse analysis: History, agenda, theory and methodology. In R. Wodak & M. Meyer (Eds.), *Methods of critical discourse analysis: Introducing qualitative methods* (2nd ed., pp. 1–33). London: SAGE.

Yiftachel, O. (2006). *Ethnocracy: Land and identity politics in Israel/Palestine*. Philadelphia, PA: University of Pennsylvania Press.

Yoshino, K. (2002). Covering. *Yale Law Journal*, 111, 769–940.

Zaher, R. (2015). The Israeli National English Curriculum, de jure and de facto: The implementation of the English curriculum principles in high-school English books. In *The Arab Education Curricula in Israel: Critical Studies* (vol. 2, pp. 81–110). Nazareth: The Follow-up Committee of Arab Education.

6

EFL AS A CULTURAL DISCOURSE

Toward a Transformative EFL Pedagogy

This chapter reconstructs EFL discourse in the service of a cultural politics of peace, social justice, and human prosperity. Toward this end, it will situate methodologies from Cultural Discourse Studies (CDS) within the frameworks of foreign language education and critical pedagogies so as to offer a holistic and transformative EFL pedagogy, understood as a cultural discourse. Reclaiming non-Western voices in producing EFL cultural discourses, fostering dialogicity in EFL classrooms, and increasing students' and teachers' agency and reflexivity in EFL educational programs, might strategically promote the discursive role of English as an instrumental tool for implementing global understanding and social justice. This aim is linked to the "Global Citizenship Education" initiative laid out in 2012 by former UN Secretary-General Ban Ki-moon.

Introduction

My main claim in this volume is that EFL discourse shapes, and is shaped by, ideological agendas that serve the interests of dominant groups in Israel. As the previous analytical chapters have shown, the ideological role of English as a foreign language seems to exceed its pedagogical and educational makeup. Instead of facilitating learning processes about mutual understanding and enabling the growth of a multicultural learning community, in Israel, EFL discourse perpetuates ideologies of dominance, native speakerism, Anglo-centric superiority, and Western hegemony. Building on the insight that EFL pedagogy is a cultural discourse reproducing difference and inequality, this chapter initiates a critical discussion of possible alternative ways to reconstruct EFL pedagogy as a transformative cultural discourse of harmony and social justice. I shall start by briefly rearticulating the central findings of the previous three analytical chapters, which investigated EFL discourse from three different angles: textbooks, practice, and policy. I will then show how these findings constitute the basis for *reconstructing* EFL discourse as an arena for effecting social change.

Summary of the Analysis

Chapter 3 showed how English textbooks in Israel use discursive devices that reproduce and perpetuate a discourse of inequality, a lack of fair multicultural representations, and discriminatory values. Findings indicate that through the reoccurrence of Western, largely American, and Jewish cultural themes, EFL textbooks interpellate learners as Western-oriented Jewish-Zionist subjects, thus contributing to the reproduction and perpetuation of Western and Jewish hegemony. Concomitantly, English textbooks in Israel reinforce the marginalization of the Palestinian Arab minority. To counter the oppressive work done by the discourse of EFL textbooks, I will advocate in this chapter an application of Fairclough's (1992, 2003) *discourse-as-discursive-practice* approach (see Chapter 2), which foregrounds the power of texts in effecting social change, and interpellating critically conscious learners who are able to form positive attitudes, beliefs, and practices about other people, the world, and diverse cultures.

Analysis in Chapter 4 confirmed Chapter 3's conclusions about the problematic reproduction of harmful social differences in EFL textbooks. EFL discourse seems to complicate identity construction processes, and hamper learning about and acceptance of the Other. Most Hebrew speakers' responses in the focus groups and interviews indicated how superior they felt toward the Other, how uninformed they are about who the Other is, and how fully they accept the legitimacy of the Jewish-Zionist values promoted in the texts. Conversely, most Arabic speakers demonstrated an understanding of how marginalized they are in the Israeli educational system and other spheres, how cultural and religious narratives may be contradictory to national narratives within their Palestinian Arab community, and how they seem to accept their role as victims of discrimination. This chapter also pointed out an emerging agency among some EFL learners (both Jews and Arabs) who subversively criticized the presentation of negative values about the Other. I will argue in this chapter that the way these learners have critically challenged the predominant ideologies presented in the EFL texts they read should form the basis of a productive method for teachers in developing their students' critical thinking and agentive faculties when engaging in topical discussions about the world and other cultures.

The final analytical chapter of EFL policy discourse (Chapter 5) pointed out numerous inconsistencies between the stated EFL policies, and the ways in which they are implemented. For one, the assumption that equal treatment is an effect of the fact that the English curriculum is uniform for both Hebrew and Arabic speakers – the contextual observation with which I started this volume – is undermined by the actual practices of consistent marginalization or even erasure of Arabic speakers prevalent in EFL discourses. Furthermore, despite acknowledging the globalized status of English and the need to situate the teaching of English in a global rather than an Anglo-centric framework, analysis shows a systematic tendency toward constructing the Anglo-centric native speaker of English as superior and as the ultimate professional English teacher, thus reinforcing hegemonic ideologies of native speakers' supremacy. By the same token, such policies also construct the EFL context in Israel as exclusively Jewish, thus reinforcing the exclusion of the Palestinian Arab minority from the EFL educational context. To contest such native speakerist, and Jewish/Anglo-centric dominance in the EFL context, policy conversations must be launched from a *local* point of departure through the lenses of professional scholars and experts who are capable of articulating the barriers that *all* diverse populations face while tackling their EFL teaching/learning experience.

Making the Connection: From Deconstruction to Transformation

In light of the current emphasis on developing critical intercultural competences (Byram, 2008, 2011), and the role of English as *the* global language, the above findings point to an alarming condition: the ideological orientation of EFL discourse stifles the voices of marginalized populations. Mainly operating as a top-down and majority-controlled state apparatus, EFL policy discourse in Israel imposes dominant ideologies through curricular policies and authorized textbooks aimed at the institutionalization of difference. The National English Curriculum (Ministry of Education, 2018) ostensibly encourages teachers to discuss culturally related topics as part of promoting their students' linguistic and intercultural competence. However, teachers generally conduct EFL lessons with their students in ways that merely reproduce the *preferred* ideas about other people, other cultures, and the world offered in authorized textbooks, whose content is ideological (Awayed-Bishara, 2015). As shown in Chapter 4, analysis of students' responses to the cultural content of EFL texts indicates that such educational materials fail to foster in students the ability to effectively construct critical stances about other cultures on both the local and the global scales. Against this non-dialogical backdrop, students act as passive receptacles. This chapter focuses, then, on the need to construct a transformative EFL pedagogical discourse that might promote students' agency and advance a cultural politics of peace, social justice, and human prosperity. The question is: How could EFL discourse be reconstructed and transformed toward a more promising – educational or otherwise – reality, when minority learners are excluded from the dominant educational discourse?

To tackle this question, I propose reconstructing a transformative EFL discourse that is connected to the same three central frameworks examined in this study: textbooks, practice, and policy. For this task, I will discuss the following:

1. How EFL textbooks could be designed so as to offer egalitarian, democratic, and genuine multicultural representations of the Self and the Other.

2. How the discursive patterns of teachers and students inside the EFL classroom could be fostered toward becoming more dialogical and critical during culturally-oriented topical discussions and activities.
3. How EFL policy and planning could be locally grounded, egalitarian, inclusive, and representative of all the learning populations, so that it genuinely serves globally common values.

This task might be enabled with the aid of a theoretical framework that captures the link between the cultural orientation of EFL discourse and its potential function as a transformative discourse for effecting social change and promoting a cultural politics of peace and human prosperity. Let me first shortly revisit some of the theoretical terms from Cultural Discourse Studies (CDS) I presented in Chapter 2, which I will apply in this chapter. I will then situate the reconstruction of EFL pedagogy as a culturally transformative discourse within the general theoretical frameworks of foreign language education and critical pedagogies, so as to underpin how it may serve transformative goals.

Methodological Reflections: A CDS Approach to EFL Discourse

Analysis of EFL discourse in Israel shows the constitutive role language plays in constructing individual identities and attitudes. Language is after all itself a *discourse* that is socially constituted and shaped. Just as discourse contributes to the reproduction and perpetuation of hegemonic and dominant ideologies, so too is it the medium of their transformation. The findings so far potentially open up possibilities for contesting the reproduction of power and inequality, and effecting educational and social change.

Approaches to analyzing EFL discourse as a cultural practice were set out in the theoretical chapter within the two overarching analytical strategies of political ethnography (Shi-xu, 2005): deconstructive (i.e. deconstructing repressive discourses) and transformational (i.e. formulating new, transformative discourses). Inspired by Paulo Freire's *The Pedagogy of the Oppressed* ([1970] 2005), I understand my vocation as being the construction of a transformative EFL pedagogy

> as a humanist and libertarian pedagogy, [which] has two distinct stages. In the first, the oppressed unveil the world of oppression and through the praxis commit themselves to its transformation. In the second stage, in which the reality of oppression has already been transformed, this pedagogy ceases to belong to the oppressed and becomes a pedagogy of all people in the process of permanent liberation. In both stages, it is always through action in depth that the culture of domination is culturally confronted.
>
> (p. 52)

The analytical tools of CDA enabled the deconstruction of EFL discourse as an ideological discourse working to fortify cultural differences and discrimination. Complementing my analysis of EFL discourse within the framework of political ethnography, this chapter undertakes a transformational strategy to "suggest ways of initiating and advocating discourses of cultural harmony and prosperity" (Shi-xu, 2005, p. 73).

Similar to Critical Discourse Analysis (CDA) and its focus on pressing social problems, critique serves as a central constituent and objective of the CDS program. Yet, rather than merely criticizing power and dominance, Jan Blommaert (2005) urges CDA scholars taking a cultural approach to focus on the role of discourse in the production and effects of power in addition to their consequences for individuals, groups, and societies in the globalized world. Shi-xu (2005) focuses on problems of cultural repression and domination while critiquing those in power by exposing and undermining culturally repressive discourses and offering *new* transformative discourses that integrate Western and non-Western views. Proposing new discourses is what CDS can offer, in addition to the critique and critical analysis associated with both CDA and CDS (Scollo, 2011). In this sense, both CDA and CDS are "explicitly critical in their desire to aid in solving pressing social problems in the globalized world, critiquing power relations and effects in their research, offering solutions and new discourses to aid in the process" (p. 25).

To offer alternative cultural discourses that may contest current hegemonic EFL discourses, we need to use a locally grounded paradigm. A locally grounded paradigm not only identifies different cultural values and norms that a non-Western group of learners have as part of their socio-linguistic repertoire, it also uses the cultural particularities of non-Western groups for devising alternative forms and practices for constructing a holistic, socially inclusive, and egalitarian EFL discourse. In the field of foreign language education, particularly English as a global/foreign language, there is a need to shift the goal "away from its focus on the development of native-speaker competence towards more realistic competencies to facilitate communication between speakers from a wide range of cultural backgrounds" (Sharifian, 2013, p. 2). As discussed in detail in Chapter 5, the rapid rise in the number of non-native speakers of English and the dominant role English currently plays in communicative contexts worldwide (Graddol, 2006) call for examining new forms for teaching English that capture the dynamic link between the cultural multiplicity of its speakers and its globalizing, albeit often still Anglo-centric, nature.

That said, research paradigms for studying the linguistic, cultural, or socio-political practices of users of English globally must by no means continue to be dominated by native speaker models of American or British English. Rather, research in EFL education must be launched from a *local* point of departure, so that nuanced practices for promoting true intercultural competence are formed. It is to these non-Western academic endeavors that CDS directs itself. In contrast to understanding West, non-West, or East as essential cultural-political entities, I consider my use of the terms as what Spivak calls *strategic essentialism* (see Spivak, 1995), which serves to underscore existing power inequality and "the globalization of Western capitalism, and to reclaim the cultural identity and diversity for the underdeveloped and developing cultures" (Shi-xu, 2012, p. 487). My aim, then, in utilizing CDS to reconstruct EFL pedagogy as a cultural discourse is to enable different communities of practice to transform their discourses from inequality and dominance to discourses of coexistence and collaboration. To this end, I rely on Shi-xu's common principles for the construction and practice of CDS models:

1. Be locally grounded with regard to culture-specific needs and perspectives.
2. Be globally minded with regard to culturally diverse perspectives and human concerns (especially coexistence, common prosperity, knowledge innovation).
3. Be susceptible to communicating with relevant international scholarly traditions in terms of concepts, theory, methods, terminology, etc. (p. 485).

From a CDS perspective, I take an interventionist approach in which English serves as a tool through which learners and teachers negotiate their subjectivities in compassionate and critical dialogues acting "as speaking agent[s], to be questioned, listened to and understood" (p. 495). In this spirit, I now present how reconstructing EFL discourse could serve the goals of a transformative pedagogy within the larger frameworks of foreign language education and critical pedagogies. I hope that this is the beginning of a productive, multi-voiced conversation, with other dominant approaches for analyzing the cultural aspects of foreign language education, with a specific emphasis on English in its global context.

EFL Cultural Discourse as a Critical Pedagogy

Exploring the ways in which EFL discourse might become transformative largely amounts to constructing students not as passive receptacles of knowledge, but as creative agents of social change. Many scholars in the field of foreign language education maintain that language pedagogy must play a transformative role resulting in *global cultural consciousness* and *intercultural citizenship* (Byram, 2008; 2011; Kumaravadivelu, 2008; Risager, 2007). According to Byram, intercultural citizenship is achieved when teachers demonstrate to students "how they can and should engage with the international globalized world in which they participate" (2008, p. 229). To Byram, the term "citizenship" entails, therefore, "the need for self-aware judgment, the willingness to become engaged, [and] the skills and the knowledge which facilitate engagement." However, students in classroom settings are often not treated as having full agency in the learning process, and the case of minority students, who deal with arduous realities on a daily basis, is even more complex. The feelings of alienation that minority students experience when tackling their local positionality for the sake of constructing their knowledge of global or Western issues might further contribute to their lack of agency, as was argued in the case of the Palestinian students in Chapter 4. To remedy this, students need to become active co-partners with their teachers in the creation of knowledge as they "are both Subjects, not only in the task of unveiling that [arduous] reality, and thereby coming to know it critically, but in the task of re-creating that knowledge" (Freire, [1970] 2005, p. 67). The assumption is that by centering students' perspectives on multicultural issues and encouraging teachers to use dialogical and problem-posing, according to Freire's principles, discursive methods in their classrooms might bring about a transformative English pedagogy, whereby students use English – the global language – to become global citizens (Rizvi, 2005), who are critically reflective (Kumaravadivelu, 2008), politically conscious and engaged (Byram, 2011).

Reconstructing EFL Textbooks

From Ideological Reproduction to Social Change

The discursive orientation of EFL textbooks potentially allows particular discourses of inequality and discrimination to prevail through interpellating learners as subjects of the dominant ideology. In contrast to this reproductive tendency, the constitutive nature of discourse allows for the possibility that EFL discourse might work in the other direction, contributing to effecting social change and equality. Based on this premise, I argue that students should be given textual exposure that interpellates them as motivated *agents* who are able to question and eventually contest discourses of inequality and Anglo-/West-centrism.

As a first step, moving from a hegemonic to a conciliatory EFL discourse is essential to frame the globalizing facet of English, and situate it in relation to other world cultures and languages. Neither *Anglo-centrism* nor *domestication* should be used as approaches to the teaching of English as a foreign language in Israel. Rather, a balanced approach should be adopted that is inherently pluralistic. My understanding of a pluralistic pedagogy indicates the use of values and themes that are locally grounded, while at the same time globally minded. Such an approach would entail a replacement of the current biased EFL discourses that fortify Self-Other distinctions, and Western and American hegemonies, while reproducing dominant groups' ideologies (such as native speakerism), and marginalizing specific groups of learners, with what Gavriely-Nuri (2016, p. 35) terms an "ecological discourse" that

> promotes *positive universal values* and cultural codes … [and aims at promoting] peace and reconciliation, as well as freedom, equality, justice and other values that are included in a 'culture of peace', as it is officially defined by the UN.
>
> (p. 35; emphasis in original)

To put this into practice, I would like to demonstrate the implementation of such an approach through the use of an example text about the late Israeli astronaut Ilan Ramon from one of the authorized EFL textbooks I analyzed in Chapter 3. The text presents an interview with Ilan Ramon, in which Ramon's Zionist and Jewish identity is highlighted through presenting facts about his army service, being born to Holocaust survivors, and his Jewish-Israeli patriotism. In order to construct EFL as a pluralistic cultural discourse, such a text needs to highlight what constitutes Ilan

Ramon as a normative human being with ambitions to excel and make a difference in this world. This, it could be argued, is a locally grounded yet globally minded educational objective. Instead of highlighting political, national, ethnic, or religious distinctions – which alienate Other learners and perpetuate divisions, in this case, between Jews and Palestinian Arabs – the text could emphasize the elements that may enable every learner to "look up to Ilan Ramon" and judge his achievements based on his unique resourcefulness as a human being. This could be done through underscoring the role Ramon plays in his career (as an engineer), his family (as a spouse and parent of four), as well as his social skills (as a member of the crew on the space shuttle Columbia), his willingness to risk his life for scientific advancement, and as an otherwise exceptional man with a charismatic personality.

Applying pluralistic values in the texts used for teaching English situates EFL in its global framework and may, according to Holliday (2013), enable a shift from a *cultural disbelief* to a *cultural belief* in EFL pedagogy. On the one hand, a paradigm of cultural disbelief

1. views the cultural background of non-native speaker learners/teachers as problematic or deficient;
2. frames non-native speakers as somehow restricted by their collectivist cultures;
3. defines and pins down the foreign culture.

On the other hand, a paradigm of cultural belief

1. considers the cultural difference of any teacher or learner as *the* source;
2. makes a special effort to centralize the cultural experience that people (of all backgrounds) bring with them;
3. initiates the opening up of possibilities within a cosmopolitan climate in which all cultural practices are open to contestation (see also Delanty, 2008).

Language educational policies in Israel should seek the construction of a representative cultural common ground for all those affected by their implementation. Namely, instead of considering the cultural milieu of each population (e.g., the religious Jewish groups discussed in Chapter 5) – which leads not only to maintaining but also to increasing the distance between populations in conflict – there is an urgent need to reconstruct a pluralistic cultural milieu that accepts, includes, and valorizes difference. Constructing the *local* in Israel entails, then, a policy of inclusion and empowerment of people with different cultural and linguistic repertoires.

Within the EFL context, the local can be discursively constructed in EFL textbooks through highlighting commonalities, rather than differences. Generally speaking, the citizens of Israel are divided by their multifaceted identities because of different religions, ethnicities, nationalities, histories, narratives, gender identities, political preferences, and collective memories. Such divisions are, unfortunately, augmented in educational discourses even though most citizens share similar daily realities, characterized by shared difficulties with financial, social, health, and other basic needs. Many Israeli citizens, including Jews and Palestinian Arabs, share intimate and friendly relationships that extend to inter-group home visiting, and sharing each other's celebrations and sorrows. These relationships are often formed through working together (as nurses, doctors, university professors, factory workers, business people, etc.), studying together, living next door to each other (as in mixed cities such as Haifa, Jaffa, Acre, etc.), or meeting while on vacation abroad, among many other circumstances. While sharing these everyday "normal" activities, most people do not seem to be intimidated by the differences and in fact, enjoy the benefits of having "friends" with a different cultural repertoire. The teaching of English as a foreign language may, therefore, use these commonalities as a point of departure in a pedagogy that empowers the local, while enabling EFL learners to situate English as a language of global communication. In other words, it is when every learner is able to find his/her place in EFL narratives that they will be able to accept the role of English as a global language and consequently learn that English is a tool through which their voice can be heard in the world. This idea is inspired by the general critique by Mark Warschauer (2000) of the TESOL (Teaching English to Speakers of Other Languages) enterprise in imposing hegemonic ideologies in English language education. According to Warschauer, "If English is imposing the world on our students, we as TESOL professionals can enable them, through English, to impose their voices on the world" (p. 530).

Constructing the local is, then, a construction of a new discourse that Canagarajah (2005) sees as a process

> of negotiating dominant discourses and engaging in an ongoing construction of relevant knowledge in the context of our history and social practice. What is important is the *angle* from which we conduct this practice – that is, from the locality that shapes our social and intellectual practice.
>
> *(p. 13)*

Although this notion may risk the regeneration of *We* versus *Them*, *global* versus *local*, or *Western* versus *non-Western* binaries, Canagarajah explains that

> the difference is that although we previously adopted a positionality based on Western or modernist paradigms that were imposed on everybody, we are now going to think from the alternate position of *our* own locality, which is more relevant to our community life and speaks to our interests.
>
> *(my emphasis)*

Within such an educational discourse "We" includes practitioners that, despite having diverse backgrounds, are equal human beings entitled to equal educational opportunities and who are encouraged to use their cultural idiosyncrasies to construct new realities – educational or otherwise.

From Division to Unification in EFL Textbooks

In this section, I present "positive" discursive strategies that might promote an ecological EFL discourse oriented toward peace and reconciliation. In her discussion of how such a discourse could function as a *peace-normalizing discourse* in Israeli public discourses, Gavriely-Nuri (2016) attempts to put her approach into practice through a reconstruction of a Jewish collective memory. She offers an alternative lexicon that is inherently universalist, and enables the construction of what Levy and Sznaider (2005) term a *cosmopolitan collective memory*. In her analysis of the use of *unifying discursive strategies* in writing obituaries in the Israeli leftist newspaper *Ha'aretz*, she identifies the use of three such strategies that could, in her view, bring about, an *ecological* collective memory.

The first strategy is *selectivity*, which involves the way writers select individuals and events embodying cosmopolitan values rather than social exclusion (e.g. selecting environmental activists instead of political or military figures). The second strategy is *conciliation*, through which writers highlight commonalities rather than differences with the Other (e.g. focusing on the human traits of a political or military figure). The last and third strategy is the avoidance of oppositional terminology including the avoidance of judgmental tones or any form of delegitimization, diminishing, or dehumanization (e.g. avoiding the use of terms such as "terror," "enemy," "victim," "atrocity," etc.). In the case of Israel, the internal Jewish-Arab conflict not only involves determining legitimate ownership of the contested territories, but also a cognitive conflict over ownership of national narratives and collective memories. In other words, accepting one narrative potentially invalidates that of the Other, as is the case with constructing the memory of 1948. For Israeli Jews, 1948 is the year of their independence, whereas for Palestinian Arabs it is the year of their *Nakba* (catastrophe in Arabic). As Hammack (2006, p. 6) explains, "The acceptance of one group's identity and aspiration for national self-determination is often interpreted as necessarily invalidating the identity of the other – given the extent to which each group desires a monopoly on political and territorial control."

Gavriely-Nuri (2016) suggests that reconstructing a collective memory might be achieved without invalidating the Other's narrative through using the above three positively oriented and *unifying* rather than *oppositional* discursive strategies. However, using the above discursive paradigm to construct an EFL ecological discourse constitutes a one-sided reconstruction of conflictual narratives. The act of positively reconstructing national or culturally based narratives without concurrently acknowledging the existence of other – equally legitimate – narratives could not possibly get any further than its own good intentions. Constructing an EFL ecological discourse entails not only the use of positive and humanistic values but also, first and foremost, an *explicit acknowledgment* of the Other as equally capable of contesting hegemonic paradigms, and constructing his/her own local cultural discourse.

In conflict-ridden educational settings dominated by power differences, education ought to focus on raising the critical consciousness of *all* learners: those associated with either "side." To this end, we "must never provide the people with programs which have little or nothing to do with their own preoccupations, doubts, hopes, and fears" (Freire, [1970] 2005, p. 96). In alignment with my Freire-inspired commitment to a pluralistic EFL discourse, I will now question whether applying Gavriely-Nuri's unifying discursive strategies may in fact fall short of promoting peace and reconciliation. To demonstrate this, I reintroduce an example I discussed very briefly in Chapter 3 about the manner in which Jerusalem – specifically, Yossi Banai's childhood neighborhood – is presented in one EFL textbook.

Applying Gavriely-Nuri's unifying discursive strategies to the text about the Israeli singer Yossi Banai reveals the shortcomings of this approach in attaining the status of an "ecological" pedagogical discourse. First, regarding the selectivity principle, as a musical performer and singer (not a political or military figure), we can fairly argue that Banai embodies a cosmopolitan value. Second, the text uses conciliatory strategies, as it depicts Banai's longing for his childhood neighborhood, which might also be perceived as an emotional experience shared by people across lines of difference. Third, the text uses positive terms and offers a romantic description of Banai's childhood neighborhood in Jerusalem, while avoiding the use of oppositional terms such as "occupation," "annexation," or any other term that might be negatively associated with a discussion of Jerusalem. However, despite the use of the three above strategies, omitting elements from the text (such as the fact that Banai was born before the establishment of Israel) and the absence of any mention of the existence of the Palestinian Other do constitute contextual gaps that prevent us from considering such a text as an example of an ecological EFL discourse.

As a unifying discursive strategy, the notion of "selectivity" must be expanded. Individuals who embody "cosmopolitan values" should clearly include people from diverse social locations within the conflict setting. Otherwise, selectivity could function as a deliberate act of silencing that erases the existence of specific groups. In Freire's words,

> Human existence cannot be Silent, nor can it be nourished by false words, but only by true words, with which men and women transform the world. To exist, humanly, is to name the world, to change it. Once named, the world in its turn reappears to the namers as a problem and requires of them a new naming. Human beings are not built in silence, but in word, in work, in action-reflection.
>
> *([1970] 2005, p. 86)*

Therefore, I offer the use of *Self and Other* – as opposed to the dichotomous *Self/Other* – as a discursive device for both embodying cosmopolitan values *and* avoiding social exclusion in texts. Thus, when presenting a controversial text about Jerusalem, for example, more characters could be included, namely, Arabic-speaking characters of different religious/cultural orientations, who also embody cosmopolitan values. These could be artists, musicians, professionals, or lay individuals who adequately and positively represent local Palestinian Arab culture. In fact, such a practice might promote the process of learning about and accepting the very existence of the Palestinian Arab Other, who lives in the same country and holds the same citizenship. Negotiating the existence of the Other or any other tangible manifestation of that Other's culture in the EFL classroom opens up possibilities for true learning. Specifically, knowledge about the world emerges only when teachers and students argue, contest, challenge, and even doubt the new/old input presented to them. Only then might learners and teachers bring themselves to a position where they begin to question what they perceived as "common" knowledge.

Some would argue against my proposition to discuss sensitive issues in classroom settings, claiming that it is best for classrooms to remain apolitical. In fact, some scholars who study second/foreign language acquisition processes view the classroom as detached from larger historical, political, and social conditions (Lantolf, 2000). In this approach, the classroom is a self-contained bubble isolated from the outer world. Clearly, from this vantage point, it is hard to capture the complex interplay between language socialization, socio-cultural aspects of learning, and learners' multiple identities. In theorizing the failure of such approaches to the classroom to capture the socio-cultural aspects of learning a language, Canagarajah argues:

> Methods are not value-free instruments, but cultural and ideological constructs with politico-economic consequences. There is no "apolitical neutrality of English", therefore it is unwise to overlook the issues of power and social inequality that lie behind English teaching and are manifested frequently in the forms of sexism, classism, and racism in classrooms.
>
> *(2002, p. 134)*

Along similar lines, Kumaravadivelu (2001) warns that ignoring local exigencies entails ignoring the lived experience of language learners. The practice of facilitating the construction of knowledge in the classroom, then, should be undertaken through "invention and re-invention, through the restless, impatient, continuing, hopeful inquiry human beings pursue in the world, with the world, and with each other" (Freire, [1970] 2005, p. 70). Complementing the selection of socially inclusive themes requires teachers to use problem-posing methods (which I will elaborate on next in this chapter) through which they can help students to see issues in critical ways, and promote their participation as well as sensitivity to issues they rarely tackle in the classroom (Morgan, 1998).

As for the second and third discursive strategies of conciliation and avoidance of oppositional terms, unless they are complemented by crucial details regarding the discussed topic (normally erased in school textbooks), these two strategies might unwittingly function as discursive tools for socio-political manipulation. In order to avoid such negative discursive practices, texts could possibly offer more details about the actual reality that constructs Jerusalem, in our example, as a holy city in the minds of diversified groups. In such highly controversial issues, we could alternatively use the positive cultural and religious values associated with Jerusalem in order to teach learners universal principles stemming from the three monotheistic religions that form the fundamentals of the notion of The Holy Land. The Christian notion of the victory of good over evil, the Jewish Kabbalistic idea of *Tikkun ha-Olam* (restoration of the world), and the Islamic notion of Tawhid (the doctrine of Oneness) (Shi-xu, 2015) are all examples of what may construct an ideational basis for an EFL pedagogy targeted at learners who are born into conflictual, multifaceted cultural, religious, or national realities. Through applying these principles and offering problem-posing methods, learners might render the role of English as the global language a possible arena for a cooperative human effort aimed at making the world a better place for all.

EFL pedagogies should offer new discourses that could benefit EFL learners in Israel, and elsewhere. Alongside the importance of recognizing the realities of Eastern or Arabic-speaking discourses, Shi-xu (2009) emphasizes that "Eastern wisdoms in understanding the universe can be mobilized for the paradigmatic reconstruction, for identity, creativity and authenticity" (p. 38). Instead of presenting non-Western cultures as inferior to Western cultures, EFL textbooks could use the wisdom of Other cultures to understand the world and reconstruct egalitarian and prosperous EFL learning communities. In practice, such an appraisal of the Other could be done by replacing narratives that depict African or Asian cultures in contexts of poverty, neediness, inferiority, and/or underdevelopment with narratives that highlight the uniqueness of African and Asian holistic worldviews and interconnected humanness (Asante, 1998; Chen, 2001). Based on the work of African and Asian researchers (e.g. Asante, 1998; Ayisi, 1972; Chen, 2004; 2006), Shi-xu (2009) offers an account of how in many African and Asian cultures, "ontologically, the tendency is to see all things in the universe, from nature to man, as One, i.e. as interconnected and unified whole; in close connection with that, axiologically, they take everything to be in Harmony and Balance" (p. 38). The Eastern notion of harmony, oneness, and human interconnectedness might serve as a guiding principle in offering EFL pedagogies that cater to diversity and super-diversity, and modifying Western paradigms that highlight Self-Other distinctions and West-centric ideologies, which apparently – and unfortunately – are associated with global rifts and the distancing from each other of diverse cultures. EFL learners, wherever they are, should learn English through diversified texts involving different unique cultures in order to rightfully situate English in its new international framework.

To sum up my view on reconstructing EFL textbooks to promote transformative goals, a *holistic* EFL ecological discourse ought to be offered. Within this holistic model, textbook writing in multicultural settings could not possibly be the product of individual writers who are mostly Anglo-Saxon, nor could it be monopolized by one or two publishers whose agenda is ideologically skewed. Rather, textbook writing must be perceived as a collaborative pedagogical mission that involves recruiting diverse groups of professionals who: come from various cultural and linguistic backgrounds; are knowledgeable of issues of structural inequalities, cultural representation, and socio-political issues of language (education); and are highly competent English users, though not necessarily native speakers. Joining the boards of textbook writing might be open to all those who could qualify as EFL professionals, regardless of national, religious, linguistic, gender, or any other distinctive affiliation. Together, these guidelines could increase the chances of producing a more inclusive and pluralistic EFL discourse that offers equal representations of all those to whom these textbooks are directed. The use of various positive and cosmopolitan values would entail granting the Other a voice, since

> saying that word is not the privilege of some few persons, but the right of everyone. Consequently, no one can say a true word alone – nor can she say it for another, in a prescriptive act which robs others of their words.
> *(Freire, [1970] 2005, p. 86)*

Transforming Practice in EFL Classroom Discourse: Dialogical and Problem-Posing Methods

Through shifting the focus of EFL education from aiming to inculcate "native speaker" competence to promoting a critical intercultural education oriented toward democracy and peace, I contend that the EFL classroom in Israel might be a unique setting for initiating bottom-up grassroots democracy and localized multi-ethnic/cultural dialogues. The question of how EFL classroom discourse in Israel might transform how students are constructed from passive receptacles to creative agents of change is under-researched. To address this question, I propose an action-based, dialogic approach enabling teachers to become more knowledgeable about the socio-political structures associated with language teaching.

The term "pedagogy" has its roots in the Ancient Greek roots *pais*, a child, and *ago*, to lead. Pedagogy is "to lead a child," and this core notion suggests that education is inherently directive, and must always be transformative (see Macedo, 2000, p. 25). To become transformative pedagogues, teachers need to seriously consider their vocation as social agents and mediators of knowledge construction. My aim, then, is to discuss possible *dialogical* approaches that English teachers might use in their classroom to transform students from passive receptacles of knowledge to committed agents of change. Fostering dialogicity could potentially enable teachers to depend less on the authorized textbook, with its fixed notions. In dialogical settings, students become more frequently engaged in routines of reflection and action spanning local and global topics. Drawing upon Freire's notion of the dialogical theory of action, whereby "one cannot expect positive results from an educational or political action program which fails to respect the particular view of the world held by the people" ([1970] 2005, p. 95), I argue that employing EFL pedagogy in multicultural educational settings to achieve peace and social justice should be based on the learners' critical perception of the future, as well as their knowledge of history.

Enabling Israeli students (both Arabs and Jews) to critically examine who the Other is, in what way *We* and *They* differ, what *We* and *They* share, and how *all of us* should take responsibility to effect social change, might offer new ways of representing the Self and the Other. Instead of treating the Other as a "problem," students learn to accept the Other as "different" but also and mainly as equal. The idea is to teach students how to challenge what Foucault (1989) calls acts of "problemization" prevalent in school textbooks and other official policy documents. Problemization refers to discursive practices aimed at making difference a problem, rather than simply a feature of diversity. Young students who learn to see the Other as different and yet equal and equally worthy might become agents of change capable of bringing about peace and reconciliation.

In their study of the interactional patterns teachers use in Israeli classrooms, Peled-Elhanan and Blum-Kulka (2006) identify three sub-genres of classroom discourse. The first is *pseudo-dialogue*, where students believe they are engaged in a topical discussion, which is in fact being assessed by the teacher on the basis of interpersonal relationships and mode (i.e. addressing the formal features of the child's speech). The second is *monologue in the guise of a dialogue*, where the teacher asks topical questions while seeking the reproduction of her own text. This final is *Socratic dialogue*, which produces a final text that is created by students and teacher in concert. Peled-Elhanan and Blum-Kulka's findings suggest that Israeli classroom instruction is primarily based on the first two sub-genres, creating a classroom environment that reproduces the teacher's dominance, "emphasize[s] inequality, and act[s] against the possibility of maintaining conversation" (p. 113). In many classes, lessons are still teacher-led, as opposed to emerging from a collaborative student-centered approach where learners are encouraged to consider a variety of creative responses to suggested topical inquiries. If teachers construct their lessons only to promote predetermined questions and answers, there is not much room for a learner to offer any original thought. Classroom interactions in the form of pseudo-dialogue or monologue in the guise of dialogue often train students to please the instructor, deliberately or otherwise, inviting the question of who is truly doing the student's speaking. To tackle this question, Peled-Elhanan and Blum-Kulka explain that "the child needs on one hand to respond to a teacher's question in a specific kind of discourse, and on the other hand to anticipate her evaluation, his utterance may be but a ventriloquation of the teacher's (guessed) voice" (p. 116). Students might feel threatened by the teacher's authority, and thus feel hesitant to present any original thought or question for the fear of disrupting the course of the lesson. Such practices that the authors critique fall within the prevalent "banking" concept of education, where the scope of action allowed to the students extends only as far as receiving, filling, and storing deposits. Contrary to these "anti-dialogical and non-communicative 'deposits' of the banking method of education" (Freire, [1970] 2005, p. 109), teachers and students could create meaning through questioning each other on more equal grounds, reducing thus the prevalence of teacher-dominance. This might be achieved through the use of a Socratic-type of dialogue that uses problem-posing methods where the final text is determined through a joint effort by the teacher and students "in a way that would inherently convince the students and have them reach the desired conclusion apparently by themselves" (Peled-Elhanan & Blum-Kulka, 2006, p. 120). Encouraging learners to critically examine the topic they are introduced to in class and construct their own knowledge of it presents a different model to the pseudo-dialogue or monologue in the guise of dialogue, where the learner is only expected to accept what the teacher has in advance prepared for him/her to accept and fill in the deposit. A problem-posing approach to education recognizes that knowledge should not be deposited from the teacher to the student. Rather, knowledge is discursively constructed through dialogue between the two, solving to some extent thus the student-teacher contradiction.

Bringing the perspectives of students more powerfully into classroom conversations may suggest new theories of action for implementing a transformative EFL pedagogy, and offer problem-posing methods which in contrast to anti-dialogic banking methods "[are] constituted and organized by the students' view of the world, where their own generative themes are found" (Freire, [1970] 2005, p. 109). Within this dialogical framework, such values are thought to be able to transform students from passive receivers to creative agents of social change. Conversely, a transformative EFL pedagogy offers a dialogical method for engaging with local and global cultural formations that allows students to engage in active, democratic, and multicultural dialogues motivated by their own understanding of these matters. In these settings, students negotiate pressing issues related to their national, religious, cultural, gender, ethnic, or any other distinctive aspect of their identity.

Language acquisition processes are shot through with relations of power and inequality, which require the need to study how learners of English position themselves within a specific community, along with how this same community positions them (De Costa, 2011; 2016; 2018). In her study of some of the complexities of EFL teaching in the Bandar Abass urban area in southern Iran, Sadeghi (2008) focuses on the partnership between critical pedagogy and an indigenous way of thinking in which both teacher and learners are aware and proud of their traditions, beliefs, and priorities, and work collaboratively to create a richer pedagogical context. Sadeghi reports using a menu approach, which allows students to negotiate the content of the course, as they are given the opportunity to choose between topics, and are also invited to bring their own texts, pictures, or other personal belongings to be discussed in class. The overall goal of her study is to investigate how the problem-posing process of learning helps students maintain discussion, dialogue, and raise critical consciousness. As part of developing their EFL writing skills, students are also asked to keep a dialogue journal. Topics were locally and globally situated and ranged from discussing the prohibition of traditional dress, to the Holocaust, and discrimination between religious groups. Her findings indicate that discussing issues that are derived from the learners' own lived experiences, as opposed to decontextualized exercises, raises the critical consciousness of students, who resist and challenge common-sense knowledge. Being both the researcher and the teacher, Sadeghi reports that her position as "a transformative intellectual, has a crucial role in the problem-posing process: to learn from learners, to welcome and appreciate their perspectives and engage in the dialogical process" (p. 16). The language acquisition processes that might take place inside this type of EFL classroom could include dialogue journals, which have also been shown to significantly increase literacy and writing proficiency.

As Socratic types of dialogue are rare in Israeli classrooms, the critical EFL pedagogy I am suggesting clearly necessitates radical changes to the teacher's role, as it constructs the classroom as a learning community (Crookes & Lehner, 1998), in which the teacher and the students negotiate, construct, and contest their understanding of the world. In critical frameworks of pedagogy that tend to be fortified by localized and particularized politics, students and teachers strive toward a redistribution of power at all levels as part of their "Great Refusal" (Marcuse, 1964) of ideological state agendas. Centering students' definition of knowledge promotes bottom-up, inductive conceptions of the world, promoting grassroots social change that would require decentralized, non-hierarchical, and disseminated forms of action. Specifically, the grassroots themes would be derived from the students' current problematic reality, rather than what textbook writers perceive as general-interest cultural content. While negotiating such themes, teachers of minority students (such as Palestinians in Israel) would encourage students not merely to blame the state for the current realities of unequal educational opportunities, oppression, marginalization, and indifference. Rather, students might act to change this situation through a discourse of self-empowerment, or of structural critique, and also through critical examinations of their own local community. In order to realize this potential, students need to engage in dialogue with other people (students and teachers) about their views of the world and their reflections on the problems they encounter.

Such critical pedagogies have often been attacked as idealistic and utopian paradigms offering few practical methods that might aid in the actual building of a more just and unprejudiced society. It is against such a skeptical backdrop that I propose to reconstruct EFL pedagogy with regard to textbooks, practice, and policy. More specifically, proponents of dialogical pedagogies might consider the use of textbooks as a major impediment to centering the role of students in constructing their own knowledge and shaping the learning processes and outcomes. On that basis, my suggestion in the previous subsection to reconstruct the cultural content of EFL textbooks, so that English is adequately situated within its global context, might be critiqued as contradicting the dialogical, problem-posing approach I call for here. Having approached EFL guided by the discourse-as-discursive-practice approach (Fairclough, 1992; 2003), which captures the constitutive role of discourse in effecting social change, I am compelled to offer a practical critical pedagogy that would encourage teachers and educators to take action in that direction. In idealistic, deinstitutionalized schooling systems, I would encourage teachers to engage in dialogue with their students about the themes and the content of the learning, and to minimize the use of textbooks altogether. And yet, it is important to recognize that heavy curricular burdens and institutional instructions are imposed on teachers and school communities, limiting the scope of action we might fairly expect from them. In order for critical pedagogies to become more practical, we need to offer "true-to-life" tools so that teachers working in all schools can take action to liberate themselves from institutional constraints. Working as a critical applied linguist and teacher educator exploring ethical issues in applied linguistics, Peter De Costa (2018) invites scholars committed to criticality to accept that despite being aware of social injustices:

> [W]e need to be cognizant of how they [individuals] respond to such injustices because a one-size-fits-all approach is not the solution. What works in one country may not necessarily work in another because we need to be acutely aware that speaking up can have real imperiled consequences, including the palpable threat of long-term internment, and in some cases, even punishment by death.
>
> (p. 2)

In conflict-ridden educational settings such as Israel, change depends on opening the eyes of teachers and pedagogues to the essence of dialogue, not merely as a teaching method, but as a philosophy of life (Freire, [1970] 2005). Subsequently, the use of textbooks should not necessarily be perceived as contradicting the construction of a dialogical EFL classroom, since both learners and teachers are invited to learn how to critically interpret and negotiate discourses that are ideologically laden. Critical reading of texts is a crucial skill learners must develop in a high-risk era, where the spread of hateful and racist discourses is enabled by digital technology. It becomes essential, then, that we "stay cautious about our complicity with the knowledge, gaze, power, and language that have perpetuated oppression and seek instead to reframe, appropriate, or replace the existing systems" (Kubota & Miller, 2017, p. 145). A critical language pedagogy – whether first, second, or foreign – must aim through dialogical and problem-posing methods at making teachers and learners aware of the socio-political nature of language as a system of signs in order to become critical and conscious readers of life's *world-textbooks* (i.e., not only school textbooks). Fostering dialogicity in EFL classroom discourses is the *raison d'être* for a transformative pedagogy that could situate English in its truly inclusive global position, and encourage its non-native users to appropriate English to find a voice for themselves in the world.

Transforming EFL Policy Discourse: Towards Global Citizenship Education

The spread of English is a global enterprise in which teaching programs, parents, policy makers, and educational institutes valorize English as instrumental for "real" economic and academic success. English is part and parcel of neoliberalism as a political enterprise, and as a linguistic and intercultural phenomenon (Gray,

O'Regan, & Wallace, 2018). Against the backdrop of attempts to commodify English to enable the expansion of global markets and industries, there is the need to evaluate the alternative role that English could play in shaping global education programs in terms of teaching values and promoting global understanding. In this sense, English teaching might impact adult learning processes, and the role learners play as citizens of the world.

The notion of global citizenship education (GCE) has been prevalent in international educational discourses since the United Nations' Global Education First Initiative in 2012, when then-UN Secretary-General Ban Ki-moon stated that education is about more than only literacy and numeracy, and must "fully assume its essential role in helping people to forge more just, peaceful and tolerant societies" (quoted in Torres, 2017, p. 4). The initiative heralded a shift in focus within the world education community, which has since paid increasing attention to the global community, and the well-being of humanity as a whole. For education theorist Carlos Torres, global citizenship is "a form of intervention searching for a theory and an agency of implementation because the world is becoming increasingly interdependent and diverse, and its borders more porous" (p. 14). Following Oxfam (2015), I view the *global citizen* as someone who is "outraged by social injustice" and "willing to act in order to make the world a more equitable and sustainable place" (p. 3). In this sense, GCE is identified as a main component in social transformation, where notions of equality and planetary sustainability are central concerns.

Along similar lines, we have seen that EFL pedagogies have shifted their emphasis from focusing on linguistic competence, to developing a broader intercultural competence and critical global consciousness. Hence, EFL educational ideologies are inevitably intertwined with the promotion of GCE worldwide, whether through textbooks, curricula, or other pedagogical practices. In his Introduction as the editor to the second issue of the *Global Common Reviews*, Carlos Torres reports that the work of the UNESCO Chair at UCLA on implementing GCE has reached countries on all continents, including Israel (Torres, 2018, p. 7). Joining this global educational effort could be linked to EFL in Israel, as the Ministry of Education initiated a program entitled "Diplomacy and International Communication in English" in 2014 that is meant to promote intercultural understanding and conflict management skills. The program is currently implemented in 39 schools in Israel (as reported in the program's official website, Ministry of Education, n.d.) of which three are Arabic-speaking schools (in Baqa Algarbia, Nazareth, and Sacknin). The website states that the program will be offered to more schools in the future, specifically to those who could comply with the program's requirements. The program is, however, only currently available to students learning English at the highest level, and not all teachers could qualify to take the in-service training to become certified to teach it. A thorough analysis of the program and its potential transformational role in Israel would be the work of future research, as this task is beyond the scope of this study. For now, I will only comment that a preliminary analysis of the program's documents suggests that it situates conflict resolution and international communication skills as primarily needed for participating in the global market and politics. In all of the documents, there is no mention or use of terms such as "Arab-Israeli conflict," "social justice," or "inequality." When it comes to describing the types of conflicts to be discussed in the program, the units of teaching are listed as:

- Conflict within Myself
- Conflict within My Family and Friends
- Conflicts within and between Groups
- Conflicts in Global and International Contexts.

The fact that Israel is a conflict-ridden place seems to be overlooked in this program and a more global, locally detached, and general framework of conflict management is offered instead. Emphasis is put on "management" instead of "resolution," transforming these conflicts into axiomatic situations people need to learn how to cope with instead of resolving. Nevertheless, the initiative might at some point offer new transformative directions in EFL pedagogy toward peace and social justice in Israel if more populations and adequate locally designed materials were incorporated. Future research might determine whether these ends could be attainable and, thus, induce transformative outcomes.

For now, the elitist nature of the program, and the way local ideological state practices, global notions of native speakerism, and professionalism heavily shape the current EFL policy discourse in Israel (as discussed in Chapter 5) call into question whether EFL pedagogies could serve GCE values. From a non-Western, subaltern position, I argue that the globalization of English must be employed to promote genuine multicultural democratic discourses in the service of world peace and social justice. Otherwise, the "globalization of English" ethos is no more than a reproduction of Anglo-centric and Western neo-colonial attempts to maintain dominion over other cultures and the world.

In the ambitions for GCE that the UN lays out, English – the global language – is said to function as a possible means for exploring students' deeper involvement in global matters, while emphasizing everyday practices of renewal and responsibility in other local/global communities with which they co-exist on the planet. To realize this, EFL policy conversations in Israel must become more inclusive and representative, so that scholars and professional pedagogues are able to make their voices heard in matters as pivotal as the role young adults of the state could play as future citizens. Granting other professional voices the right to interpret and apply locally grounded, and at the same time globally minded, forms of practices might promote true intercultural competence and develop a prosperous EFL cultural pedagogy. That would require the Chief Inspector of English and other official stakeholders to invite professionals from various groups to take an active part in planning the teaching of English to speakers of other languages, bearing in mind that a transformative EFL pedagogy *must* result in learners who are critically reflexive, locally minded, global citizens. In a conflict-ridden place like Israel, such pedagogy might even advance peace and social justice.

Conclusion

This chapter set out to initiate a culturally critical discussion of possible practical ways to reconstruct EFL discourse within the transformative frameworks of CDS, foreign language education, and critical pedagogy. Armed with ontological assumptions about the constitutive aspect of discourse in bringing about social change, I proposed a dialogical, problem-posing EFL discourse that could guide teachers in transforming students from passive receivers of knowledge to active agents of change. A transformative EFL discourse encourages educators and policy-makers to design their materials and curricula based on the cultural conceptions and philosophies of students, teachers, and other local actors. In non-Western educational settings, students' knowledge and cultural perceptions could enrich and re-invigorate existing Western attitudes toward values related to implementing the values of global citizenship education, such as sustainability and connection to the land and its natural resources. In the next and final chapter, I discuss what roles minority students, teachers, parents, and other civil society actors may take in order to effect social and educational change. Based on a 15-year experience as an EFL teacher in Arabic-speaking high schools, I offer some personal and professional insights on how Palestinians in Israel could pragmatically construct a "culture of action" by contesting a "culture of silence."

References

Asante, M. K. (1998). *The Afrocentric idea* (rev. ed.). Philadelphia, PA: Temple University Press.

Awayed-Bishara, M. (2015). Analyzing the cultural content of materials used for teaching English to high school speakers of Arabic in Israel. *Discourse & Society*, 26(5), 517–542. doi:26376399.

Ayisi, E. O. (1972). *An introduction to the study of African culture*. London: Heinemann.

Blommaert, J. (2005). *Discourse: A critical introduction*. Cambridge: Cambridge University Press.

Byram, M. S. (2008). *From foreign language education to education for intercultural citizenship: Essays and reflections*. Clevedon: Multilingual Matters.

Byram, M. S. (2011). Intercultural citizenship from an international perspective. *Journal of the NUS Teaching Academy*, 1(1), 10–20.

Canagarajah, A. S. (2002). Globalization, methods and practice in periphery classrooms. In D. Block & D. Cameron (Eds.), *Globalization and Language Teaching* (pp. 134–150). London: Routledge.

Canagarajah, A. S. (2005). Reconstructing local knowledge, reconfiguring language studies. In A. S. Canagarajah (Ed.), *Reclaiming the local in language policy and practice*. Mahwah, NJ: Lawrence Erlbaum Associates.

Chen, G.-M. (2001). Towards transcultural understanding: A harmony theory of Chinese communication. In V. H. Milhouse, M. K. Asante, & P. O. Nwosu (Eds.), *Transcultural realities: Interdisciplinary perspectives on cross-cultural relations* (pp. 55–70). Thousand Oaks, CA: Sage.

Chen, G.-M. (2004). The two faces of Chinese communication. *Human Communication*, 7, 25–36.
Chen, G.-M. (2006). Asian communication studies: What and where to now? *Review of Communication*, 6(4), 295–311.
Crookes, G., & Lehner, A. (1998). Aspects of process in an ESL critical pedagogy teacher education course. *TESOL Quarterly*, 32(2), 319–328. doi:10.2307/3587586.
De Costa, P. I. (2011). Cosmopolitan and learning English: Perspectives from Hye Lan Alias Joanne. *The Arizona Working Papers in Second Language Acquisition and Teaching*, 18, 55–76.
De Costa, P. I. (Ed.). (2016). *Ethics in applied linguistics research: Language researcher narratives*. New York: Routledge.
De Costa, P. I. (2018). Toward greater diversity and social equality in language education research. *Critical Inquiry in Language Studies*, 15(4), 302–307. doi:10.1080/15427587.2018.1443267.
Delanty, G. (2008). Dilemmas of secularism: Europe, religion and the problem of pluralism. In G. Delanty, R. Wodak, & P. Jones (Eds.), *Identity, belonging and migration* (pp. 78–97). Liverpool: Liverpool University Press.
Fairclough, N. (1992). *Discourse and social change*. Cambridge: Polity Press.
Fairclough, N. (2003). *Analysing discourse: Textual analysis for social research*. London: Routledge.
Foucault, M. (1989). *The archeology of knowledge*. (A. M. Sheridan Smith, Trans.). London: Routledge.
Freire, P. ([1970] 2005). *Pedagogy of the oppressed*. (M. B. Ramos, Trans.). (30th Anniversary). New York: Continuum.
Gavriely-Nuri, D. (2016). *Israeli peace discourse: A cultural approach to CDA*. Amsterdam: John Benjamins.
Graddol, D. (2006). English next: Why global English may mean the end of "English as a Foreign Language." London: British Council. Available at: http://englishagenda.britishcouncil.org/sites/default/files/attachments/books-english-next.pdf (accessed February 18, 2019).
Gray, J., O'Regan, J. P., & Wallace, C. (2018). Education and the discourse of global neoliberalism. *Language and Intercultural Communication*, 18(5), 471–477. doi:10.1080/14708477.2018.1501842.
Hammack, P. L. (2006). Identity, conflict, and coexistence: Life stories of Israeli and Palestinian adolescents. *Journal of Adolescent Research*, 21(4), 323–369. doi:10.1177/0743558406289745.
Holliday, A. (2013). "Native speaker" teachers and cultural belief. In S. A. Houghton & D. J. Rivers (Eds.), *Native-speakerism in Japan: Intergroup dynamics in foreign language education* (pp. 17–28). Bristol: Multilingual Matters.
Kubota, R., & Miller, E. R. (2017). Re-examining and re-envisioning criticality in language studies: Theories and praxis. *Critical Inquiry in Language Studies*, 14(2–3),129–157. doi:10.1080/15427587.2017.1290500.
Kumaravadivelu, B. (2001). Toward a postmethod pedagogy. *TESOL Quarterly*, 35(4), 537–560. doi:10.2307/3588427.
Kumaravadivelu, B. (2008). *Cultural globalization and language education*. New Haven, CT: Yale University Press.
Lantolf, J. P. (2000). *Sociocultural theory and second language learning*. Oxford: Oxford University Press.
Levy, D., & Sznaider, N. (2005). Memory without limits: The Holocaust and shaping cosmopolitan memory. In G. Margalit & Y. Weiss (Eds.), *Memory and amnesia: The Holocaust

in Germany (זיכרון ושכחה: גרמניה והשואה) (pp. 398–418). Tel Aviv: ha-Ḳibuts ha-me'uḥad (הקיבוץ המאוחד).

Macedo, D. (2000). Introduction. In P. Freire, *Pedagogy of the oppressed*. New York: Continuum.

Marcuse, H. (1964). *One-dimensional man: Studies in the ideology of advanced industrial society*. Boston, MA: Beacon Press.

Ministry of Education. (2018). Revised English curriculum including Band III lexis: Principles and standards for learning English as an international language for all grades. Jerusalem: Ministry of Education, State of Israel. Available at: http://meyda.education.gov.il/files/Mazkirut_Pedagogit/English/Curriculum2018July.pdf (accessed February 24, 2019).

Ministry of Education. (n.d.). *Conflict management and resolution*. Jerusalem: Ministry of Education, State of Israel. Available at: http://edu.gov.il/mazhap/IntlComm/description-elective/Conflict-management-resolution/Pages/Conflict-Management-Resolution.aspx (accessed May 18, 2019).

Morgan, B. D. (1998). *The ESL classroom: Teaching, critical practice, and community development*. Toronto, ON: University of Toronto Press.

Oxfam. (2015). *Education for global citizenship: A guide for schools*. Oxford: Oxfam Education, Oxfam GB. Available at: www.oxfam.org.uk/education/resources/education-for-global-citizenship-a-guide-for-schools (accessed May 18, 2019).

Peled-Elhanan, N., & Blum-Kulka, S. (2006). Dialogue in the Israeli classroom: Types of teacher–student talk. *Language and Education*, 20(2), 110–127. doi:10.1080/09500780608668716.

Risager, K. (2007). *Language and culture pedagogy: From a national to a transnational paradigm*. Clevedon: Multilingual Matters.

Rizvi, F. (2005). Identity, culture and cosmopolitan futures. *Higher Education Policy*, 18(4), 331–339. doi:10.1057/palgrave.hep.8300095.

Sadeghi, S. (2008). Critical pedagogy in an EFL teaching context: An ignis fatuus or an alternative approach? *Journal for Critical Education Policy*, 6(1).

Scollo, M. (2011). Cultural approaches to discourse analysis: A theoretical and methodological conversation with special focus on Donal Carbaugh's Cultural Discourse Theory. *Journal of Multicultural Discourses*, 6(1), 1–32. doi:10.1080/17447143.2010.536550.

Sharifian, F. (2013). Globalisation and developing metacultural competence in learning English as an international language. *Multilingual Education*, 3(1), 7. doi:10.1186/2191-5059-3-7.

Shi-xu. (2005). *A cultural approach to discourse*. New York: Palgrave Macmillan.

Shi-xu. (2009). Reconstructing Eastern paradigms of discourse studies. *Journal of Multicultural Discourses*, 4(1), 29–48. doi:10.1080/17447140802651637.

Shi-xu. (2012). Why do cultural discourse studies? Towards a culturally conscious and critical approach to human discourses. *Critical Arts*, 26(4), 484–503. doi:10.1080/02560046.2012.723814.

Shi-xu. (2015). Cultural discourse studies. In K. Tracy (Ed.), *The international encyclopedia of language and social interaction*. Malden, MA: Wiley-Blackwell.

Spivak, G. C. (1995). *The Spivak reader*. (D. Landry & G. MacLean, Eds.). London: Routledge.

Torres, C. A. (2017). *Theoretical and empirical foundations of critical global citizenship education*. New York: Routledge.

Torres, C. A. (2018). Letter to the reader. *Global Commons Review*, 2, 6–10.

Warschauer, M. (2000). The changing global economy and the future of English teaching. *TESOL Quarterly*, 34(3), 511–535. doi:10.2307/3587741.

7
CONCLUSION
EFL as a Cultural Discourse of Action

This chapter discusses the constitutive role of EFL as a cultural discourse of action and empowerment through which subordinated people act as agents of social and educational change. Toward this end, it will situate the role that Palestinian Arab EFL practitioners could play in effecting a more equal educational reality within the larger Arab educational system in Israel. Drawing upon Christopher Stroud's (2018) notion of *linguistic citizenship*, the dynamics are examined, surrounding the way Palestinian Arabs respond to imposed Israeli linguistic and educational policies through the mobilization of rights discourse, and their political agency in contesting unequal educational policies. A critique is presented of the shortcomings of this rights discourse as a basis for transformative processes, and it is argued that Palestinian Arab school communities and practitioners should move toward positioning themselves agentively. The aim of this transition is to construct a bottom-up, grassroots culture of action in which marginalized populations build faith in their power to build a more equal educational reality.

Introduction

My first-hand experience with EFL discourse has served as the point of departure for this book from the outset, and guided me in underpinning EFL pedagogy as a cultural discourse. This experience, which has sparked within me the desire to unravel the dialectic between English as a dominant world force and majority-controlled pedagogical discourses in Israel, will also guide me in winding up my argument. In these closing remarks I will address Palestinian Arab school communities – whether situated within the EFL context or otherwise – in order to encourage a critical examination of their possibilities for taking an agentive role within the Israeli educational system. By using the notion of *linguistic citizenship* (Stroud, 2018) to capture the way people agentively come out against discriminatory language and other educational policies, this chapter advocates the need to construct a cultural discourse of action within the Palestinian Arab educational system. As a theoretical concept that was first introduced as part of a critique of rights discourse, linguistic citizenship "refers to what people *do* with and around language(s) in order to position themselves agentively, and to craft new emergent subjectivities of political speakerhood, often outside of those prescribed or legitimated in institutional frameworks of the state" (p. 4; my emphasis). I hope that the arguments I present to conclude this book will inspire other marginalized groups, wherever they are, to oppose unjust and discriminatory educational policies.

Empowering the Subaltern as a Precondition for Effecting Change

Consistent with my enduring commitment to utilize EFL for promoting justice-sensitive education (Awayed-Bishara, 2015a; 2017), and despite the exclusionary ideologies prevalent in EFL discourses (Awayed-Bishara, 2015b; 2018), I argue that English education as a cultural discourse worldwide, and more particularly in conflict-ridden places such as Israel, could constitute a potentially unique educational platform for bringing populations in conflict closer together and constructing a prosperous global community. In Chapter 6, I demonstrated how reconstructing EFL discourse in textbooks, practice, and policy might render EFL a transformative pedagogy in alignment with global educational goals that advance critical intercultural consciousness and global citizenship. Considering how EFL education is still largely constrained by state-controlled institutions with a delineated hierarchy of power, I examine the power that subordinate groups could mobilize socially, culturally, and educationally. Following Cummins' (2001) views on empowering minority students, I argue that, irrespective of how oppressive their working conditions are, individual educators must never envision themselves nor their students as powerless.

While my analysis of EFL discourse has been conducted with an eye critical of what might be achieved through a *uniform* curriculum for two populations in conflict (i.e. Jewish Israeli and Palestinian Arabs), the power that EFL discourse in Israel exerts seems to be centrifugal rather than centripetal: in other words, instead of working to bring both sides closer together, not only does EFL discourse fail to fulfill its integrative potential but it also tends, sadly, to pull people further apart. To increase the centripetal forces of English as a global language, those involved with EFL teaching must be empowered, specifically those whose voices are often stifled. I mean to address EFL practitioners on the other side of the spectrum who are supposedly the receivers of policy and curricular *communiqués* and who are often excluded from *communicating* back to the core of these policies. From this position, I encourage teachers, schools, learners, parents, and other actors in civil society who are marginalized and socially excluded to critically examine the conditions under which they can contest unjust state-controlled educational practices. In the case of Israel, and considering the distinctive status of English education, I ask: What responsibilities lie on the shoulders of Palestinian Arab EFL communities when it comes to contesting imposed educational subjectivities so they are able to sculpt alternative educational realities?

In order to address this question, I examine the intersection between a top-down *discourse of rights* related to educational equality, and a bottom-up social struggle constituted within a culture of action that feeds on *notions of agency and responsibility*. My understanding of the notion of responsibility when it comes to initiating social or educational change could be perceived within the overarching principles of linguistic citizenship, which "refers to cases when speakers exercise agency and participation through the use of language or other multimodal means in circumstances that may be orthogonal, alongside, embedded in, or outside of, institutionalized democratic frameworks for transformative processes" (Stroud, 2018, p. 4). The difficulties marginalized groups may encounter, then, while extending a rights framework to contesting institutionalized subjectivities are inherent within the paradoxical constituents of a rights discourse; namely,

> The paradox of rights is that, although they are universal, appeals to them are situated in local space and time and filtered through contingent local political, social and economic structures by which the specifics of each nation-state polity constrain the choice of rights and to what extent that choice is actually provided for.
>
> (p. 6)

In the case of Palestinian Arab citizens of Israel, the provision of equal educational rights is contingent on appeals to the nation-state, which clearly aims at maintaining Jewish Israeli supremacy, and a Palestinian Arab subaltern state. Against this backdrop, there is a need to critically foster people's consciousness about issues of structural inequality and social injustices so they are stirred to take action to change them. Within this discursive framework, change is envisioned as an outcome of constructing a bottom-up initiative of teachers, school communities, and other civil actors who not only demand equal rights and struggle against discriminatory state practices, but also take responsibility for critical pedagogical action to advance their classrooms and schools. Finding ways to reconceive the management of their educational system would encourage Palestinian Arabs in Israel to realize how consistently "the framing of rights as political/legal entitlements has deemphasized the cultural responsibilities and relationships that indigenous peoples have with their families" (Corntassel, 2008, p. 107), as well as their identities and socio-historical heritage.

Constructing a critical basis for educational action entails a challenge to prevalent reform discourses that call for a top-down "salvation." My critique of such discourses is that they have often overlooked the heavy price marginalized populations must pay while walking this line. Specifically, I would argue that top-down initiatives to reform the Arab educational system should be reconsidered for two main reasons. First, it is unrealistic to expect a Ministry of Education constellated around the idea of Israel as a Jewish nation-state to grant equal educational rights, as I shall explore in more detail below. Second, and more importantly, waiting for top-down educational reforms from a government that has long disregarded the needs of its largest minority weakens the Palestinian Arab minority's sense of its own self-worth. In the context of this systematic marginalization, an educational policy discourse that reinforces Jewish Israeli hegemony "dulls the national consciousness of [Arab] students, erodes their attachment to each other and their sense of mutual responsibility and weakens their desire to work together to achieve common goals" (Jabareen & Agbaria, 2010, p. 9). Rights discourses are "neither ethnically unambiguous nor neutral" (Cowan, Dembour, & Wilson, 2001, p. 11) and in practice "carry widely divergent implications and produce very unequal subjects with different opportunities for agency" (Stroud, 2018, p. 9). It would be naïve for oppressed groups "to expect the oppressor elites to carry out a liberating education" (Freire, [1970] 2005, p. 136). It is precisely because the educational system is used instrumentally to submerge marginal groups in a *culture of silence* that it needs to be discursively contested through a *culture of action*.

Advancing notions of agency and responsibility could help to constitute a culture of action in which marginalized populations break their silence, and activate their agentive capabilities to act creatively within their schools, classrooms, communities, families, and other socio-cultural arenas. Under these conditions, people might strive to re-establish their place as equal and critical practitioners who are proud of their own cultural identity, knowledgeable about their past, conscious of their present, and ambitious about their future. The act of (re)establishing the bond that minority members have with their own socio-cultural identity and community is a crucial step toward activating agency. Before delving into the practices needed to reinforce cultural belonging and the actions required from social actors to achieve such a mission, let me first tackle the importance of redefining the scope of action enabled by a discourse of rights in transforming educational realities.

Linguistic Citizenship and the Paradox of Rights Discourses

Throughout the world, minority or otherwise marginalized groups have powerfully reframed rights discourse, fueled by rhetoric that captures the tension between the rights supposedly guaranteed by the citizenship they hold, and the substantive equality that they lack. In many cases, the pressing needs of minority members are manifested in the demands they make against the state's policies and procedures in impeding the strategic growth of their community at the educational, economic, and socio-political levels. For Palestinian Arab citizens in Israel, the educational institutions and working conditions of their educational system have long been seen as deteriorating and vulnerable, and in genuine need of an intervention (Jabareen & Agbaria, 2010). The proposed changes to the Arab educational system in Israel include:

- equal budgetary allocations;
- participation of the Arab community in policy-making and design of curricula;
- acceptance of Palestinian Arab students' cultural and linguistic needs.

The rights discourse, specifically following the success of the anti-apartheid movement in South Africa and the civil rights movement in the United States, "has come to be seen by many minorities or oppressed groups as a basic, even primary, tool in their struggle for justice" (Zreik, 2004, p. 77). Notwithstanding its status as a liberating tool that marginalized groups use for transforming unjust realities, "the rights discourse runs the risk of overemphasizing the legal aspects of rights" (Robeyns, 2006, p. 70) specifically when the *de facto* granting of rights is in the hands of stakeholders whose ideologies are often not in alignment with those demanding these rights. It is to these contingent situations where rights may not be recognized that the notion of linguistic citizenship might help "comprise an empowering politics of language for agency and change" (Stroud, 2018, p. 6). Linguistic citizenship critiques the contingencies of rights discourses as they "disadvantage significant factions of speakers who, for lack of symbolic and human capital, or for contingent material reasons, subsequently lack agency and voice" (p. 1). Alternatively, the notion of linguistic citizenship "engages with the contradictions and tensions arising from the historical imposition of vulnerable subjectivities and the manufacture of multilingual spaces as sites of contention and competition for scarce resources" (Stroud, 2018). The lack of provision of rights in nation-state contexts is directly related to the tensions between notions of citizenship as contingent, historical, and political, and those of rights, which are depoliticized, ahistorical, and universal (Yeatman, 2001).

Struggling against structural inequalities in education should not only be pursued as a demand on the government to implement top-down change in educational policy and the provision of equal rights. Change must also be understood as a bottom-up effort that generates the power necessary to achieve the goal that gives substance to the right. If not, as Stroud (2018) postulates, "rights become a technique of social discipline that orders and regulates citizens into state-accepted social taxonomies, or that strategically disadvantages some groups" (p. 8). To demonstrate the difficulties in attempting to extend a rights framework to transform educational realities, let me survey some of the calls for intervention in the Palestinian Arab educational system that have been made in the past few decades in terms of budgets, policy-making, and cultural and linguistic needs.

Equal Allocation of Resources in Education

Perhaps the most powerful and insidious form of discrimination is that exercised against the educational opportunities of marginal groups who are often also socioeconomically stigmatized as lacking economic resources and power (Stroud, 2001). In the case of Israel, official data from the Ministry of Education consistently reveal a substantial gap in achievement between Jewish and Arab students. Jabareen and Agbaria (2010) report that the proportion of students eligible for the matriculation certificate required to access tertiary education in 2009 was highly unequal: for Jewish students it was 59.74 percent but for Arab students it was 31.94 percent, i.e. just over half. Comparison with figures published in the following years suggests a gap that is, if not widening, not closing either. Poor achievement is directly related to poor funding and discriminatory policies, rendering the allocation of resources as the most tangible form of discrimination mainly targeting the education of the Palestinian Arab minority (Zreik, 2004).

For the past few decades, the Israeli government has used different legislative strategies to control the allocation of resources to towns and cities in different regions of the country. One prevailing strategy is to classify Israel's towns and cities based on national security criteria, by designating localities under categories such as "National Priority A" areas, "National Priority B" areas, and towns without national priority. Cataloging schools in terms of national priorities is geared toward allowing the government to grant benefits and incentives in the field of education to certain towns and exclude others. Upon first introducing the three national priority categories, out of the 535 towns included in the first two categories, only four were Arab towns which are small in size and almost insignificant in population (Jabareen & Agbaria, 2010, p. 19). In reaction to this decision, the Follow-Up Committee on Arab Education in Israel[1] filed a petition in the Supreme Court (sitting as the High Court of Justice) calling for the decision to be overruled on the basis that it discriminates against the Arab community. Initially, the Supreme Court accepted the Committee's claims, holding that the government's decision was illegal and calling for it to put greater effort into developing just and more equitable criteria. Despite the government's release of a more egalitarian map for resource allocations for Jewish and Arab schools in 2009, implementation of these policies has been blocked. Apparently, a gap in the law allows the relevant ministries to have the final say about the distribution of monies in accordance with the specific criteria they determine for budgetary allocations (Jabareen & Agbaria, 2010). More equitable resource allocation in terms of the new map has yet to achieve fruition.

So despite the fact that the highest court in Israel ordered the *de jure* cancelation of discriminatory allocations and incentives to schools, these continue unabated. The indecisive *de facto* role the Supreme Court respectively plays in either preventing or determining the implementation of discriminatory or equal educational policies demonstrates how the Israeli government could easily overlook its highest court's decisions, constituting a major impediment for the Arab minority to pursue their struggle for equal budgetary allocation through a discourse of rights.

Equal Participation in Policy-making and Curricular Design

The analysis of official documents regarding the planning and implementation of EFL educational policies in Israel in Chapter 5 demonstrated how Israel's Ministry of Education and the English Inspectorate exclude Palestinian Arab practitioners from policy discourses, stifling their voices. In Chapter 6, and while mobilizing a discourse of rights, I explicitly called on the ministry and the general Inspectorate to conduct more inclusive policy conversations in which the professional voice of the Palestinian Arab minority is not only heard, but also taken into practical consideration in implementation. It is far from self-contradictory to state both that struggling for justice-oriented educational policies through rights discourse is not to be abandoned or dismissed, and that change must also come from the bottom up. Calling for equal educational rights must go hand in hand with local, grassroots action to advance the Arab educational system so as to safeguard against a situation in which, according to Jabareen and Agbaria (2010), Arab education is kept on hold. To demonstrate the challenges and shortcomings of pursuing the struggle for equal rights in policy-making and curriculum design using the tools of a rights discourse, I will now discuss instances of this difficulty even in cases where Israeli policy discourse is oriented toward the values of multiculturalism and of equal rights, leaving to one side for now consideration of instances where it is explicitly oriented toward discrimination.

Despite its failings in using multiculturalism as an instrument for securing equal democratic citizenship for all (as we have seen throughout the chapters of this volume), Israeli discourse has not been one-sided when it comes to determining educational policies concerning the Palestinian Arab minority. Perhaps the most forceful, positively-oriented wording in this matter could be traced in Israel's Declaration of Independence stating that the State of Israel "would ensure complete equality of social and political rights to all its inhabitants irrespective of religion, race or sex and guarantees freedom of religion, conscience, language, education and culture" (Ministry of Foreign Affairs, n.d.). Within the spirit of these words, the Knesset also passed a law regarding curriculum development, whose objective was to ensure that the syllabus and learning materials issued by the Ministry of Education addressed all the populations in Israel, including majority and minority groups. The law stipulates

> the objectives of state education with regard to teaching universal values; the values of the State of Israel as both Jewish and democratic; the history and heritage of the land of Israel and the Jewish people; the remembrance of the Holocaust and heroism; the development of child's personality, creativity, talents and intellectual competences; and *acquaintance with the culture and heritage of the Arabs and other minorities in Israel.*
> (Council of Religious Institutions of the Holy Land, 2013, p. 5; my emphasis)

These documents allow for a pluralistic view of educational equality that includes the Palestinian Arab minority, and correspond to universal principles of human rights and dignity. However, these pluralistic inclinations do not tangibly manifest themselves in practical implementation. First, the Knesset maintains that the Declaration of Independence is neither a law nor an ordinary legal document, and thus should be considered as no more than a non-obligatory guiding principle (Dorner, 1999). As a result, the Supreme Court occasionally accepts nullification of a particular ordinance even if it is inconsistent with the declaration's principles. For Palestinian citizens, the centralized nation-state "has rarely been a benign protector of citizenship – it has rather been a vehicle for assimilation or exclusion" (Kymlicka, 2012, p. 115). To the state of Israel, as the Nation State Law has recently reiterated, the ultimate goal of the policy toward the Palestinian Arab minority is that of non-assimilation (Karayanni, 2018) rendering exclusion as the only possible outcome.

As for the official policies regarding curriculum design and foreign language teaching, I have described in earlier chapters how other studies of Israeli textbooks and curricula have shown how an inegalitarian picture is achieved, whatever the rhetoric of policy. Yiftachel (2006), Yonah (2005), Peled-Elhanan (2012), Nasser and Nasser (2008), Podeh (2000; 2002), Awayed-Bishara (2015b; 2018), and others have concluded that Arabs are substantially marginalized in Israeli schoolbooks in the same way that they are excluded from Israeli cultural discourse and social life. The fact that ideological nation-state considerations surpass the universal principles of human rights and equality curtails the possibilities that Palestinian Arabs have for correcting some of their grievances within the framework of a discourse of rights.

Acceptance of Palestinian Arab Students' Cultural and Linguistic Needs

Joint initiatives between Jewish and Arab citizens of Israel constitute a major force in the plethora of appeals made to the Ministry of Education to reform educational policies so that they cater to Palestinian Arab students' cultural and linguistic needs. Efforts to reform the educational reality of linguistic minorities are often connected to the notion that they "have different histories and hold different positions in networks of political discourses" (Stroud, 2018, p. 9). Intergroup initiatives have aimed at an inclusive educational policy that both addresses the problems of the Palestinian Arab minority, and devises curricula for "Education Toward Shared Life" (i.e. that of both Jews and Arabs in Israel). One of the most remarkable attempts was when Professor Yuli Tamir of the Labor Party (commonly viewed as a moderate Zionist-socialist party), served as Minister of Education. As Jabareen and Agbaria (2010) report, in August 2007, Tamir, in agreement with representatives of the Committee of the Heads of Local Arab Councils and the Follow-Up Committee on Arab Education, decided to establish *four* committees on Arab education. While they were under the joint supervision of the Ministry and the Follow-Up Committee, the final authority was still vested in the Ministry of Education. Their central task was to assess the needs of the Arab education system, and provide recommendations to the Ministry. Although the minister supposedly accepted the recommendations the committees provided, the actual implementation of these recommendations is to this day still on hold. This initiative was, however, the first joint effort by Jews and Arabs to effect change within the Arab educational system.

The recommendations that are on hold include:

- improvement in the instruction of core subjects so as to narrow the gap between the two populations;
- improvement in the way Arab schools deal with students with learning disabilities that the committees have identified as worrying;

- improvement in the classroom deficiencies that the committee required to resolve by building more classes in Arab schools.

Ironically, the collaboration between the ministry and Arab committees came to an end over a dispute between members of the fourth committee over who was in charge of curriculum design. The committee was unable to formulate a joint articulation of recommendations about how to set the goals and values upon which Palestinian Arab education should be based (Jabareen & Agbaria, 2010).

Regardless of the fourth committee's failure, continued attempts were made to convince the next Minister of Education, Gideon Saar, of the right-wing Likud Party, to adopt the committees' recommendations. In response to these calls, the minister initiated a counterplan entitled "The Government of Israel Believes in Education" (Jabareen & Agbaria, 2010). Not only did the new plan ignore insights stemming from the joint Jewish-Arab committees' work, it completely overlooked the deteriorating performance of Arab students, and disregarded the need for intervention to strengthen achievement levels. Contrary to the "shared life" ethos of the former joint committees, the overall spirit of the new plan centralizes the role education in Israel must play in: "the area of Zionist, democratic and civic values, including reinforcing students' connection to Jewish heritage through academic studies, visits to historical sites, promoting enlistment in the Israeli army and bolstering the overall connection between society and the education system" (p. 9). The plan sets no explicit goals whatsoever for the Arab education system, completely overlooking any possible rights of Palestinian Arabs to education shaped by the values, histories, language, or socio-cultural realities of their communities.

The total failure of successive Israeli ministries of education and their joint committees to give any substance to Palestinian Arab minority rights to co-design (let alone design) their curricula has serious implications in the struggle for equal educational rights. For one, the general educational policy in Israel is situated within the larger Jewish-Zionist political discourse, which is ideologically oriented toward reproducing and maintaining Jewish supremacy in the state of Israel, even at the expense of granting minorities equal educational rights, in line with the universal declaration of human rights. What is more concerning, and irrespective of how sincere both parties are, is the ideological barrier that seems to block attempts at collaborative work between Jewish and Palestinian Arab citizens. Despite the progressive and pluralistic nature of these joint efforts, we must seriously consider the failure of people on both sides to reach an agreement on how to effect a more egalitarian reality, educational or otherwise.

My proposal is that the uniform EFL curriculum in Israel has the discursive potential to advance a cultural politics of joint understanding and collaboration that is needed to resolve conflicts. This suggestion aligns with the statement released by the co-directors of the joint committees in 2009, that "education toward a shared life should employ diverse methods and multiple means, should be *multi-disciplinary*, open to new ideas, relevant, experiential, and have a community orientation" (Solomon & Essawi, 2009, p. 45; my emphasis). Addressing the agentive role

Palestinian Arab EFL pedagogues could play in this matter in the next section, I situate EFL pedagogy as a cultural discourse of action within the framework of linguistic citizenship so as to gain a nuanced understanding of the practices the Palestinian Arab minority in Israel has been developing to effect educational change.

Toward a Culture of Action: From Notions of Rights to Notions of Agency and Responsibility

Over the past two decades, the voices of intellectuals, academics, and activists calling for the empowerment of Palestinian Arab schools have been amplified through various grassroots academic, legal, and civic organizations in Israel. The Follow-Up Committee on Arab Education, the Arab Center for Applied Social Research (Mada al-Carmel), the Legal Center for Arab Minority Rights in Israel (Adalah), and the Association for Civil Rights in Israel, among other grassroots organizations, have advanced a bottom-up strategy for cultural-educational action targeted at bolstering the Arab educational system through addressing some of its most pressing needs. Irrespective of their different orientations, what these organizations share is their use of responsibility- and action-based discourses that capture the subtle links between the role of collective action, and the possibility of effecting change. Perhaps the most notable attempt in this vein is "The Haifa Declaration" (2007) of Mada al-Carmel. Through utilizing the unifying first-person-plural "we," the declaration documents the outcome of an extensive effort undertaken over a number of years by a group of Palestinian Arab intellectuals, academics, and activists aimed at "making possible a free and open public debate, both amongst ourselves as a community, and between us and the state and the Jewish citizens, on our vision for our place and status in our homeland" (The Arab Center for Applied Social Research (Mada al-Carmel), 2007, pp. 4–5).

The goals of the Haifa Declaration focus on internal social issues, the relationship between the Palestinian citizens of Israel and the State of Israel, the relationship between the Palestinian people and the Arab nation, and Palestinian Arab national identity. Two related documents have recently been published: the "Future Vision," which was developed under the sponsorship of the Committee of the Heads of Local Arab Councils in Israel, and the "Democratic Constitution," which was developed by Adalah. The publications of all three complementary documents strongly indicate that the Palestinian Arab community is *ready* to articulate its collective vision and make its voice heard.

Fueled by the aspirations of these documents, my contention is that Arab school communities in Israel should also be ready to take part in sparking "a democratic, open, and constructive dialogue within our society and with the Israeli-Jewish society, one that might enable us to work together towards building a better future between our peoples" (p. 5). The importance of working out and developing these positions is an aspect of linguistic citizenship that frames such practices as "an empowering tactic in the sense that the voice of the community stakeholders is being put into text and made legitimate" (Stroud, 2018, p. 8). To demonstrate how the spirit of the documents enables bottom-up improvement within the Arab educational system, I will present three areas of agentive action:

- tailoring the content of materials used in Arab schools to their cultural and linguistic contexts;
- consolidating teachers within forums of action and support;
- training teachers to become critical and politically aware pedagogues inside their classrooms.

Tailoring the Content of Materials in Arab Schools

The overriding concern of activist and pro-equality initiatives is to transform teachers in Palestinian Arab schools from passive receptacles of unjust educational policy into critical and politically aware agents who might creatively and responsibly act. The assumption is that, despite being largely restrictive, the democratic sphere in Israel still enables teachers to choose, to some extent, what and how to teach inside their classrooms. To demonstrate the plausibility of this argument, it is important to examine what teachers are up against. The government's educational policy towards the Palestinian Arab minority reached a turning point in 2009, under Gideon Saar. Following the educational plan he introduced, the chairman of the pedagogical secretariat of the Ministry of Education required the re-writing of the commonly used civics textbook, *To Be a Citizen in Israel*, arguing that it "is too critical of the state" (cited in Jabareen & Agbaria, 2010, p. 10). The chairman expressed his annoyance that the book states that "since its establishment, the State of Israel has engaged in a policy of discrimination against its Arab citizens" (Jabareen & Agbaria, 2010). As a result, a new mandated civics textbook was authorized to be used in all Israeli schools. The textbook reflects the dominant ideologies of most right-wing parties, and reproduces Jewish-Zionist hegemony while at the same time marginalizing the Palestinian Arab minority and its communal practices.

This move heralded a shift in the way Palestinian Arab teachers and other grassroots organizations responded to discrimination in the education system. In an unprecedented gesture of resistance, Palestinian Arab civics teachers decided that it was time for them to act against these unjust educational trends, by going further than mere condemnation. Under the auspices of the Follow-Up Committee on Arab Education, they established the first forum for Palestinian Arab civics teachers, whose extensive effort resulted in a textbook and other educational materials that offer complementary and alternative materials to those issued by the ministry. By offering methods and dilemmas for critically examining the content of official curricular materials, the forum seeks to give civics teachers and students a more nuanced understanding of ideologically laden materials (Hassan, 2018). These teachers exercised control over the content of the materials to resist acts of othering by the state through curricular imposition. The materials they developed demonstrate the refusal of Palestinian Arab teachers to adopt the subjectivities imposed on them by the official civics textbook, and reinforce instead their voice as a community acting, according to Stroud (2018), as linguistic citizens.

Two years later, and along similar lines, Mada al-Carmel released a booklet in Arabic entitled: "The Project of the Haifa Declaration as a Pedagogical Approach."[2] Working within the spirit of the Haifa Declaration, the booklet addresses the aspirations of younger Palestinian Arabs in high school and university, encouraging a reflexive examination of their reality against the background of Israeli dominant (educational) and systematic policies. Executing the lesson plans offered in the booklet requires that students and teachers go beyond the boundaries of educational politics and the limitations imposed on them and their school communities by state-controlled curricula to freely discuss their perception of their past, present, and future. In the Introduction to the booklet, the authors valorize the role younger generations could potentially play not only as active co-partners in constructing the future perception of their community, but also as agents who have the legitimate right to speak their truth. Fostering the consciousness of high school and university students becomes, then, a central task that the center sets for itself. To this end, the center offers training workshops for teachers so they are guided to help students appreciate the saliency of their narrative and history, and understand the socio-political aspects that constitute their status as citizens of Israel. Considered as a whole, the project offers school communities a future vision that might stimulate them to teach their students to critically examine the intersection between the political nature of the state of Israel, and their future as Palestinian Arab citizens, so that they take action toward constructing a better future for both peoples.

Within a similarly agentive perspective, the Association for Civil Rights in Israel published a report in August 2010 describing the request to mandate the civics textbook as disturbing. The report cautions against the dominance of militaristic values within school cultures, arguing it is a major infringement on teachers' rights to freedom of expression inside their classroom (Jabareen & Agbaria, 2010). A few years later, and in tandem with its non-partisan and justice-oriented inclination, the Association released a book entitled: *Lesson for Life: Anti-Racist Education from K-12* (The Association of Civil Rights in Israel, 2015). The book is the product of a partnership between Jewish and Palestinian Arab academics, schoolteachers, and activists who came together through their sincere belief that it is only through joint efforts that people could fortify and deepen the commitment of *all* members of Israeli society to equal human rights and dignity. Based on a theoretical framework constellated around definitions of racism surveyed by Yehuda Shinhav, the book offers a number of pedagogical tools that combat stereotypical and unjust practices, and advance anti-racism (e.g. in history, Arabic for Hebrew speakers, math, science, and English, among other topics).

As the author of the English-related chapter, "Integrating the Teaching of English as a Foreign Language (EFL) and Anti-Racist Instruction" (Awayed-Bishara, 2015a), I aimed to promote and facilitate anti-racism education through the teaching of English in Israeli schools. Insofar as the National English Curriculum is uniform in Israel, my ultimate goal was to ensure that the methods offered for teachers would enable every student, whether Jewish Israeli or Palestinian Arab, to acquire the appropriate and effective skills to address and deal with their own or others' experiences of racism. To this end, and through offering practical lesson plans that teachers might use in their instruction, I called upon English teachers of all backgrounds to commit themselves sincerely and responsibly to exploring the texts and materials they use in class with a more critical eye, and greater sensitivity in order to help advance a cultural politics of peace and social justice within the Israeli educational system. Since its publication in 2015, I have been deeply moved by feedback from both Jewish and Palestinian Arab EFL teachers on the book as a whole, and the EFL toolkit in particular. While working as a teacher educator observing pre-/in-service teachers, I have witnessed how opening the eyes of EFL teachers to issues of racism, structural inequalities, cultural misrepresentation, and other discriminatory practices pertaining to EFL educational discourses could (even if at times only slightly) activate their and their students' critical faculties. Indeed, I will discuss later some initial findings of ethnographic work I am currently conducting to critically examine the sustainability of this capacity among Palestinian Arab EFL teachers.

What progressive people, organizations, and activists have been doing to address discriminatory practices constitute an agency we can understand as linguistic citizenship. In this sense,

> [linguistic] citizenship works to change or shift – however minimally … the rules of engagement: it shifts the chain of command of a program or institution, away from those tasked with authoring or participating in terms of other, more included actors; it works in subtle ways to alter or create a tributary while the program unfolds, creating a crease in the unfolding, a perturbation, an interruption.
>
> *(Stroud, 2018, p. 10)*

Suffice it to say here that such agentive, grassroots endeavors for taking responsibility over the content of materials used in Israeli classrooms in general, and in Palestinian Arab ones in particular, demonstrate the very simple, yet extremely powerful message: it is possible!

Consolidating Palestinian Arab Teachers in Organized Forums

The Palestinian Arab educational community has recently consolidated teachers into organized forums aimed at fostering them professionally and as critical pedagogues. The new mandated civics textbook and, more recently, the legislation of the Nation State Law that calls for canceling the official status of Arabic, along with the general systematic policy of educational discrimination, have functioned as spurs to constructing a progressive, responsibility-driven culture of action among Palestinian Arab educators. Although formed as a framework for Palestinian Arab educational action, and as a direct outcome of Israel's separated education system, Arab teachers' forums have articulated a comprehensive vision for effecting change.

At the core of this vision is the need for a joint Jewish-Arab struggle to change curricular policies and educational inequality in both schooling systems (Hassan, 2018). In this respect, joint Jewish-Arab endeavors constitute a prerequisite for effecting a fundamental and genuine change requiring, thus, both populations to recognize the existence of other legitimate narratives, histories, and traumas.

Today, the Follow-Up Committee on Arab Education ("the Committee") stands as the major entity in terms of consolidating Palestinian Arab teachers in organized forums based on the subject matter they teach. To further understand the scope of action of the Committee in this direction (and since there is no research yet on this topic), I interviewed the head of the Committee, Dr. Sharaf Hassan,[3] who is also the Director of the Human Rights Education Department in the Association for Civil Rights in Israel. The interview brought out a number of crucial points that intertwine with my general vocation regarding the salient role teachers and other civic actors could potentially play in fortifying notions of agency and responsibility when it comes to transformational processes.

As an independent and professional entity, which was founded under the auspices of the High Follow-Up Committee for Arab Affairs in Israel, the Committee sees the possibility of building politically aware Arab teachers who could function as critical pedagogues in their classrooms as a crucial mission toward bringing about social and educational justice. For this reason, the Committee has set the consolidation of Palestinian Arab teachers in organized forums as a top priority, which has resulted so far in two forums: one for civics teachers, and one for teachers of Arabic. The most tangible manifestation of the action-based nature of both forums could be traced as: (1) releasing new teaching materials for the teaching of civics (as discussed earlier); and (2) organizing school activities in many Arab schools aimed at contesting the antagonism the Nation State Law has created toward Arabic and its native Palestinian speakers, fortifying its status as their native mother tongue. Dr. Hassan asserts that establishing these two forums are indeed only the beginning, since the Committee aims to reach more teachers and establish forums for teachers of other subject matters, including EFL teachers whose role he also valorizes in consideration of the distinctive status of English education in Israel.

To enable a more efficient and organized partnership between the Committee, Arab schools, and the Ministry of Education, Hassan accentuates the role that the Committee of the Heads of Local Arab Councils must play in this matter. Hassan points out that so far local Arab councils in Israel have mainly played a bureaucratic role when it comes to educational affairs and policies, when in practice they could and are compelled to take a more pioneering role. Moved by this consideration, the Committee has established a forum for the directors of education divisions at local Arab councils, aimed at aiding these divisions to identify pressing problems and challenges pertaining to schools in their localities, so they could offer attainable solutions.

In summary, all of these endeavors point to an emerging agentive culture of action that is growing among Palestinian Arab civic and educational communities, whose sincere goal is to bring about a more just and equitable educational reality. Alongside this growing bottom-up action stands the Committee's determination to continue its struggle against the discriminatory educational policies the government is still perpetuating. It continues to aspire to establish a pedagogical secretariat for Arab schools in Israel, a move the Ministry of Education has rejected since Israel's establishment.

Training Teachers in Criticality and Political Awareness

In terms of my interest in opening up alternative ways of thinking about the possibilities that marginalized teachers in institutionalized educational systems have for effecting change, there is a need to first present a pressing question: How can we expect teachers who have been trained to work under oppressive conditions to become politically aware, critical pedagogues? To understand the core of this conflict, it is essential to understand that the liberation of an ethnic minority from the bonds of oppression under a high-handed majority involves – beyond the obvious resistance to the oppressor – a carefully and respectfully conducted critical process of interrogating some aspects of its classroom culture. In Palestinian Arab school communities, one may find authoritarian models of student-teacher relationships, along with overly formal teaching approaches, still practiced within a number of classrooms (Abu-Nimer, 1999; Bekerman, 2005). Teachers' assertion of themselves as authorities demanding respect, however, needs to be understood in the context of their "sense of conflict regarding their loyalty both toward their employer, the Ministry of Education, and their loyalty toward their Palestinian community" (Bekerman, 2005, p. 4). In such oppressive settings, the oppressor's model becomes, in many cases, the only familiar type of dominant-subordinate relationship available (Freire, [1970] 2005) causing some teachers to adopt oppressive methods in the classroom.

Against this backdrop, and based on first-hand experience, the Committee sets out to offer teacher training that combats teachers' "fear of freedom" (p. 46), and helps them to become more knowledgeable about the features of the educational system in Israel. Teacher training, according to Hassan, includes:

- training teachers about the values of human rights;
- releasing teacher guidebooks contextualized in Palestinian Arab socio-cultural and linguistic needs;
- publishing materials that acquaint teachers with updated and existent literature on educational policy and curriculum design;
- organizing conferences, study days, and workshops, among other pedagogical activities.

The overriding concern of the Committee and Mada al-Carmal (which, as mentioned earlier, also organizes teacher training workshops), in our examples, is to directly address Palestinian Arab teachers' needs so they can understand the importance of the role they can play to disrupt vicious cycles of oppression, and realize not only that they *should* take responsibility in their classrooms but also that they *can*.

It is worthwhile noting, as a closing remark, that the Association for Civil Rights in Israel has also taken on an essential role in teacher training, for both Jewish and Palestinian Arab teachers, aimed at fostering their critical consciousness and prompting them to take positive steps toward constructing a prosperous, just, and equal Israeli society. The Association has also been working with educational colleges and academic institutions, through organizing workshops or giving lectures, all of which are meant to draw teachers' attention to the urgency of reconsidering syllabi, and changing teacher training programs (see www.english.acri.org.il). Regardless of how skeptical some people might be about the outcomes of such initiatives, Stroud (2018) argues that alternative voices inserted into educational structures, that could otherwise be alienating, capture the way people agentively exercise their linguistic citizenship to push forward transformative processes. Specifically, the building-up of a new normative regime involves the use of everyday practices of classroom interactions alongside communicating with officials from the ministry as a process that will, however slowly, ultimately effect social change.

Constructing a solid culture of action within the educational sphere in Israel entails, then, true partnerships between pedagogical and civic organizations and societies who are brought together through a belief that dialogue and collaboration are our best human resources. We would do well to bear in mind the words of Paulo Freire: "To surmount the situation of oppression, people must first critically recognize its causes, so that through transforming action they can create a new situation, one which makes possible the pursuit of a fuller humanity" ([1970] 2005, p. 47).

Conclusion: EFL Discourse as a Cultural Discourse of Human Responsibility

To conclude this book, from a subaltern, non-Western, scholarly, and personal position, I recommend a new pedagogical trajectory that might lead both EFL learners and teachers toward a more promising future. A more promising future entails being able to live in dignity and pride, without having to justify your existence, without having constantly to correct the negative stereotypes perpetuated in EFL discourses about ethnicity, culture, nation, race, gender, ability, and religion. A more promising future would be one in which policy-makers take your equal rights as a person into account when determining (language) educational policy. It is also a future where people across the educational system are exposed to positive valorization of the Other, where discursive practices involving negative representations are replaced with positive ones.

I also call upon marginalized educational communities, and specifically upon Palestinian Arab learners and teachers, to focus more on their agentive capabilities and powers in advancing themselves and their communities. Palestinian Arab teachers must be more aware of their students' specific needs in light of the complexity of their linguistic and socio-cultural repertoires, which might constitute a major obstacle to their learning English as a foreign language. As such, they should consider alternative methods and strategies that might facilitate language acquisition. This entails acquiring up-to-date expert insights on how to teach English to speakers of Arabic; expanding their capabilities of educating for values of human responsibility and collaboration; and empowering their students through making them proud of themselves, their history, their culture, and their abilities to take part in the co-building of a better world for themselves and others.

This volume has underpinned EFL pedagogy as a cultural discourse that reproduces Anglo-/West-centric and native-speakerist hegemonic ideologies in a way that defeats, as I have shown, the purpose it might serve as a global discourse for facilitating intercultural understanding and common global partnerships. As I have argued, despite its hegemonic forces, English could potentially and *possibly* function as a unifying tool, enabling people who use it to promote an intercultural politics of human collaboration, of peace, and even of planetary sustainability. Mutual respect between human beings from all backgrounds must be our shared and most urgent pedagogical goal.

Notes

1 The Follow-Up Committee on Arab Education in Israel is an independent, professional entity that operates under the auspices of the Committee of the Heads of Local Arab Councils and the Supreme Committee for Arab Affairs in Israel, established in the 1980s as the highest collective leadership of the Palestinian minority.
2 Translations from Arabic by the author.
3 Dr. Hassan's position is voluntary and unpaid.

References

Abu-Nimer, M. (1999). *Dialogue, conflict resolution, and change: Arab-Jewish encounters in Israel*. Albany, NY: State University of New York Press.

Awayed-Bishara, M. (2015a). Integrating the teaching of English as a foreign language (TEFL) and anti-racist instruction. In *A lesson for life: Anti-racist education from K-12* (pp. III–XXV). Tel Aviv: The Association for Civil Rights in Israel.

Awayed-Bishara, M. (2015b). Analyzing the cultural content of materials used for teaching English to high school speakers of Arabic in Israel. *Discourse & Society*, 26(5), 517–542. doi:26376399.

Awayed-Bishara, M. (2017). EFL materials: A means of reproduction or change?, PhD thesis. University of Haifa, Haifa.

Awayed-Bishara, M. (2018). EFL discourse as cultural practice. *Journal of Multicultural Discourses*, 13(3), 243–258. doi:10.1080/17447143.2017.1379528.

Bekerman, Z. (2005). Complex contexts and ideologies: Bilingual education in conflict-ridden areas. *Journal of Language, Identity & Education*, 4(1), 1–20. doi:10.1207/s15327701jlie0401_1.

Corntassel, J. (2008). Toward sustainable self-determination: Rethinking the contemporary indigenous-rights discourse. *Alternatives*, 33(1), 105–132. doi:10.1177/030437540803300106.

Council of Religious Institutions of the Holy Land. (2013). "Victims of our own narratives?" Portrayal of the "other" in Israeli and Palestinian school books. Council of Religious Institutions of the Holy Land. Available at: https://d7hj1xx5r7f3h.cloudfront.net/Israeli-Palestinian_School_Book_Study_Report-English.pdf (accessed May 30, 2019).

Cowan, J. K., Dembour, M.-B. & Wilson, R. A. (2001). Introduction. In J. K. Cowan, M.-B. Dembour, & R. A. Wilson (Eds.), *Culture and rights: Anthropological perspectives* (pp. 1–16). Cambridge: Cambridge University Press.

Cummins, J. (2001). *Negotiating identities: Education for empowerment in a diverse society* (2nd ed.). Walnut, CA: California Association for Bilingual Education.

Dorner, D. (1999). Does Israel have a constitution? *Saint Louis University Law Journal*, 43, 1325–1336.

Freire, P. ([1970] 2005). *Pedagogy of the oppressed*. (M. B. Ramos, Trans.) (30th Anniversary). New York: Continuum.

Hassan, S. (2018). فضاء تربوي للديمقراطية وحقوق الإنسان | منتدى معلمي ومعلمات المدنيات العرب كمثال [The forum for Arab civics teachers as an example]. The Association of Civil Rights in Israel. Available at: https://education.acri.org.il/ar/2018/09/25/-منتدى-معلمي-ومعلمات-المدنيات-العرب-كم/ (accessed May 30, 2019).

Jabareen, Y. T., & Agbaria, A. (2010). Education on hold: Israeli government policy and civil society initiatives to improve Arab education in Israel (executive summary) (p. 23). Haifa: DIRASAT: The Arab Center for Law and Policy and The Arab Minority Rights Clinic at the Faculty of Law, University of Haifa. Available at: www.iataskforce.org/sites/default/files/resource/resource-223.pdf (accessed May 30, 2019).

Karayanni, M. (2018). Multiculturalism as covering: On the accommodation of minority Religions in Israel. *The American Journal of Comparative Law*, 66(4), 831–875. doi:10.1093/ajcl/avy039.

Kymlicka, W. (2012). Neoliberal multiculturalism? In P. A. Hall & M. Lamont (Eds.), *Social resilience in the neo-liberal era* (pp. 99–126). Cambridge: Cambridge University Press.

Ministry of Foreign Affairs. (n.d.). Homepage. Israel Ministry of Foreign Affairs. State of Israel. Available at: https://mfa.gov.il/MFA/Pages/default.aspx (accessed May 30, 2019).

Nasser, R., & Nasser, I. (2008). Textbooks as a vehicle for segregation and domination: State efforts to shape Palestinian Israelis' identities as citizens. *Journal of Curriculum Studies*, 40(5), 627–650. doi:10.1080/00220270802072804.

Peled-Elhanan, N. (2012). *Palestine in Israeli school books: Ideology and propaganda in education*. London: I.B. Tauris.

Podeh, E. (2000). History and memory in the Israeli educational system: The portrayal of the Arab-Israeli conflict in history textbooks (1948–2000). *History and Memory*, 12(1), 65–100. doi:10.1353/ham.2000.0005.

Podeh, E. (2002). *The Arab-Israeli conflict in Israeli history textbooks, 1948–2000*. Westport, CT: Bergin and Garvey.

Robeyns, I. (2006). Three models of education: Rights, capabilities and human capital. *Theory and Research in Education*, 4(1), 69–84. doi:10.1177/1477878506060683.

Solomon, G., & Essawi, M. (2009). A report of the committee to define the state policy in the field of education for a shared life for Arabs and Jews (Executive Summary). Israeli Ministry of Education, State of Israel. Available at: http://commonground.cet.ac.il/ShowItem.aspx?itemId=706&itemState=VIEW&language=HEB&itemType=1 (accessed May 30, 2019).

Stroud, C. (2001). African mother-tongue programmes and the politics of language: Linguistic citizenship versus linguistic human rights. *Journal of Multilingual and Multicultural Development*, 22(4), 339–355. doi:10.1080/01434630108666440.

Stroud, C. (2018). Linguistic citizenship. In L. Lim, C. Stroud, & L. Wee (Eds.), *The multilingual citizen: Towards a politics of language for agency and change* (pp. 17–39). Bristol: Multilingual Matters.

The Arab Center for Applied Social Research (Mada al-Carmel). (2007). *The Haifa Declaration*. Jerusalem: The Arab Center for Applied Social Research (Mada al-Carmel).

The Association of Civil Rights in Israel. (2015). Lesson for life: Anti-racist education from K-12. Tel Aviv: The Association for Civil Rights in Israel. Available at: https://education.acri.org.il/wp-content/uploads/2015/08/book-full-version.pdf

Yeatman, A. (2001). Who is the subject of human rights? In D. Meredyth & J. Minson (Eds.), *Citizenship and cultural policy* (pp. 104–119). Thousand Oaks, CA: Sage.

Yiftachel, O. (2006). *Ethnocracy: Land and identity politics in Israel/Palestine*. Philadelphia, PA: University of Pennsylvania Press.

Yonah, Y. (2005). *In virtue of difference: The multicultural project in Israel*. Tel Aviv: Hakibbutz Hameuchad and Van Leer Jerusalem Institute.

Zreik, R. (2004). Palestine, apartheid, and the rights discourse. *Journal of Palestine Studies, 34* (1), 68–80. doi:10.1525/jps.2004.34.1.68.

INDEX

Abu-Nimer, M. 169
Abu-Raki'eh, M.: learners' cultural representations, analysis of 88, 92, 93, 95–6, 97, 98, 99, 102, 103; textbooks as ideological vehicles 66, 72, 73, 75, 77
Abu-Saad, I. 4, 5, 7
academic identities, shaping of 50
academic literature on culture teaching in foreign language classrooms 17–18
action, EFL as cultural discourse of 155–71; active role Palestinian Arab minority, call for 164–70; Arab schools, tailoring content of materials in 165–7; challenge of pursuit of equal rights in policy-making 161; *To Be a Citizen in Israel* (civics textbook) 165; Council of Religious Institutions of the Holy Land 161; criticality, training teachers in 169–70; cultural and linguistic needs of Palestinian Arab students, acceptance of 162–4; cultural discourse in action (Education Ministry) 157, 159, 160, 161, 162, 165, 168, 169; education, equal allocation of resources in 159–60; equal participation in policy-making and curricular design 160–62; Foreign Affairs Ministry 161; Haifa Declaration, 2007 (Mada al-Carmel) 164; human responsibility, EFL discourse as cultural discourse of 170–71; "Integrating the Teaching of English as a Foreign Language (EFL) and Anti-Racist Instruction" (Awayed-Bishara, M) 166–7; *Lesson for Life: Anti-Racist Education from K-12* (The Association of Civil Rights in Israel) 166; linguistic citizenship, paradox of rights discourses and 158–9; linguistic citizenship, Stroud's notion of 155–6; Mada al-Carmel (Arab Center for Applied Social Research) 164, 166, 169; organized forums, consolidation of Palestinian Arab teachers in 167–9; Palestinian Arab school communities, address to 155–6; policy-making, linguistic citizenship and 158–9; political awareness, training teachers in 169–70; responsibility and agency, from notions of rights to notions of 164–70; subaltern as precondition for change, empowerment of 156–8
Adalah (Legal Center for Arab Minority Rights in Israel) 6, 7, 164
agent creation, global cultural consciousness and 90–92; black people, discrimination against 91–2
Akere, F. 63, 113
Al-Haj, M. 4, 5, 7
Alptekin, C. 14–15, 18, 115
Althusser, L. 2, 13, 33, 38, 40, 86, 111, 112
Anglo/West-centrism: contest against discourses of 38; hegemonies of, perpetuation of 1–2; nature of EFL discourse and 124–5
Arab schools, tailoring content of materials in 165–7

Arabic language: criticism of writing practices in EFL textbooks by speakers of 103; Jewish feelings towards 5; speakers of, examples of national identity discourse construction among 94
Asante, M.K. 144
Asiyi, E.O. 144
Association of Composers, Authors, and Publishers awards' ceremony in Tel Aviv (2017) 7
attitudes, foreign language learning and 19
Austin, J.L. 39
Awayed-Bishara, M. 2, 3, 7, 16, 20, 82n1, 134; cultural discourse in action 156, 162, 166–7; discourse beyond language education 27, 37, 42, 45; global and local perceptions of policy discourse 115, 124, 125; learners' cultural representations, analysis of 85, 86, 88, 89, 92, 97, 101

Bakhtin, M.M. 31, 32, 37
Banai, Y. 80, 142
Barker, C. & Galasiński, D. 44, 50–51
Baumel, S.D. 117–18
Bekerman, Z. 169
Bernstein, B. 9, 79
Bhabha, H.K. 49, 114
Bishara, A. 93
Blommaert, J. 29, 50, 87, 136
Blommaert, J. & Bulcaen, C. 30, 33, 38
Bloor, M. 50
Boaz, F. 47
Bourdieu, P. 29, 39
Bourdieu, P. & Wacquant, L.J.D. 45
Briscoe, F., Arriaza, G., & Henze, R.C. 45
Brown, P. and Levinson, S.C. 90, 100
Bucholtz, M. & Hall, K. 58, 59, 64, 87
Building Blocks 77
Butler, J. 39, 46, 87
Byram, M.S. 1, 5–6, 11–12, 14, 17–18, 19, 51, 85; global and local perceptions of policy discourse 112, 128; transformative pedagogy, working towards 134, 137, 138

Canagarajah, A.S. 37, 57, 116, 140, 143
Cappella, J.N. 50
Carey, J.W. 45
Carrell, P.L. 63
Chan, J.J. 37
Cheater, A.P. 102
Chen, G.-M. 45, 144
Chiu, S. & Chiang, W. 59–60

To Be a Citizen in Israel (civics textbook) 165
Cohen, J., Loney, N., & Kerman, S. 64, 65, 66, 71, 80, 82; learners' cultural representations, analysis of 87, 98
collective memories 58, 59, 79–81; construction and maintenance of 64; cosmopolitan collective memory 141; divisions caused by 139–40; ecological collective memory 141; Holocaust and 80–81; ideological symbolism and construction of 80; national identity and construction of 7–8; peace-normalizing discourse and reconstruction of 141
Collier, M.J. 45
comprehension, knowledge and 63
Corntassel, J. 157
Council of Europe 5–6
Council of Religious Institutions of the Holy Land 161
Cowan, J.K., Dembour, M.-B. & Wilson, R.A. 158
critical cultural awareness, education students towards 19
Critical Discourse Analysis (CDA) 2, 58, 116, 136; discourse beyond language education 27, 29, 30–31, 32–3, 45–6, 48, 49, 51; EFL discourse in Israel 29–31; learners' cultural representations, analysis of 84, 86, 89, 105; native-speakerism and 15–16
criticality: critical pedagogy, critical agency and 20; educational policies, learners' criticism of 101–5; EFL cultural discourse as critical pedagogy 137–8; social injustice, criticality and awareness for 149; training teachers in 169–70
Crookes, G. & Lehner, A. 148
Cultural Discourse Studies (CDS) 2, 3; discourse beyond language education 26, 27, 48, 49, 51; EFL discourse in Israel 45–6; Shi-xu's perspective on 48–9, 51; transformative pedagogy, working towards 132, 135, 136–7, 152
culturally specific prior knowledge 63; data collection and analysis on 78–9
culture: academic literature on culture teaching in foreign language classrooms 17–18; cultural and linguistic needs of Palestinian Arab students, acceptance of 162–4; cultural bias, analysis of 58; cultural suitability of EFL textbooks 57, 81; EFL pedagogy, shift from cultural disbelief to cultural belief in 139; instructional materials as cultural mediators 36–7; intracultural

understanding, EFL textbooks and enabling of 92–8; situating within critical study of EFL discourse 47–51; teaching of, problematic notion of 17
Cummins, J. 156

Darwish, M. 7, 86–7, 107n1
data collection, analysis and findings: investigatory methodology and data 116–17; learner interviewees, distribution of 89; learners' cultural representations 90–105; textbooks as ideological vehicles 64–81
Davies, A. 14, 112
Dayan, M. 80
De Certeau, M. 44
De Costa, P.I. 147, 149
De Saussure, F. 32, 34
Delanty, G. 139
Derrida, J. 28
dialogical and problem-posing methods 145–9; banking method of education 146; dialogical theory of action, Freire's notion of 145–6; EFL education, shifting focus of 145; fostering dialogicity 145–6; interactional patterns in Israeli classrooms, study of 146; knowledge, centering students' definition of 148; language acquisition processes 147; monologue in guise of dialogue 146; Other and Self, critical examination of 146; pedagogy, roots of 145; problem-posing approach to education 147–8; pseudo-dialogue 146; self-empowerment, discourse of 148; social change, role of discourse in effecting 148–9; social injustice, criticality and awareness for 149; Socratic dialogue 146, 148; teacher-dominance, prevalence of 147; topic situatedness 147–8; utopian paradigms, critical pedagogies as 148
"Diplomacy and International Communication in English" project (Israel, Ministry of Education) 128
Discourse & Society 82n1
discourse-as-discursive-practice approach (Fairclough) 133
discourse-as-text approach 34–6
discovery skills, foreign language learning and 19
discursive practice, discourse as 36–7
discursive strategies, positivity in 141–5; conciliation, strategy of 141, 143–4; cosmopolitan collective memory 141; critical consciousness of learners, raising of 142; "Eastern wisdoms,"

understanding and 144; ecological collective memory 141; harmony and balance. Eastern notion of 144; holistic worldviews, interconnected humanness and 144–5; knowledge, facilitation of construction of 143; learning, complexity of interplay in 143; Other, explicit acknowledgement of 141; peace-normalizing discourse 141; selectivity, strategy of 141, 142; Self and Other and 142–3; unifying discursive strategies 141–2
diversity and cultural difference, issues of 106
Dobkins, J. 65, 66, 68, 74, 77, 82
documents, analysis of: Anglo-centric nature of EFL discourse 124–5; construction of EFL teaching context as exclusively Jewish 122–4; inconsistency and incompatibility between documents 117; National English Curriculum in Israel 117–20, 124; native speaker superiority 120–24; prioritizing of native speakers over non-native speakers as ideal English teachers 121–2
dominant ideologies 9, 27, 32, 57–8, 165; critical challenges against 133; imposition of 134; interpellation of learners and 39, 90, 138; learners' cultural representations and 105–6; mainstream groups and 38; policy-makers and 79; reproduction of 36–7, 38–40, 58, 70, 135; subversive stances against 42; textbook writers and 79; transmission of 57–8, 81
Dominant/Subordinate binary 1–2
Dorner, D. 161
Duff, P.A. & Uchida, Y. 36
Dwairy, M. 4

education: banking method of 146; conflict-ridden settings dominated by power differences 142; discourse of global neoliberalism, education and 114; educational politics, boundaries of 166; EFL education, shifting focus of 145; equal allocation of resources in 159–60; identity politics in educational system 86–7; language-culture link in issues of 114–15; policies in, learners' criticism of 101–5; political educational objectives 18; problem-posing approach to 147
Education Ministry in Israel 6, 12, 15, 20, 36, 64, 101, 134, 150; cultural discourse in action 157, 159, 160, 161, 162, 165, 168, 169; global and local perspectives on

policy discourse 111, 116, 117, 119–20, 121, 122, 123, 124, 126, 127, 129

EFL (English as a Foreign Language): cultural and ideological aspects of EFL discourse, investigation of 2; discursive pedagogization of 2; evaluation of EFL discourse as cultural practice 2, 3; Israel, separate schooling systems in 4–5; planning EFL teaching, discursive trajectories for 3; reconstruction of EFL discourse towards cultural transformation 2; teaching to Palestinian Arab learners, distinctive educational experience in 4–5

EFL as cultural discourse 132–52; action, EFL as cultural discourse of 155–71; alienation of minority students 137; alternative cultural discourses, offer of 136; authorized textbooks, ideological content of 134; critical intercultural competences, emphasis on development of 134; Cultural Discourse Analysis (CDA), focus of 136; Cultural Discourse Studies (CDS) approach to EFL discourse 135–7; Cultural Discourse Studies (CDS) models, Shi-xu's principles for construction of 137; discourse-as-discursive-practice approach (Fairclough) 133; EFL cultural discourse as critical pedagogy 137–8; EFL pedagogy, shift from cultural disbelief to cultural belief in 139; global cultural consciousness 137; harmony and social justice, reconstruction of EFL pedagogy as discourse of 132–3; intercultural citizenship 137; Israel, ideological agendas of dominant groups in 132; language educational policies in Israel 139; majority-controlled state apparatus and 134; making connections, deconstruction to transformation 134–5; methodological reflections, CDS approach to EFL discourse 135–7; multicultural issues, centering students' perspectives on 137–8; *The Pedagogy of the Oppressed* (Freire, P.) 135; policies stated and implementation of, inconsistencies between 133–4; positive universal values, promotion of 138; reconstruction of EFL textbooks 138–52; strategic essentialism, Spivak's notion of 136–7; Teaching English to Speakers of Other Languages (TESOL) 140; textbooks as ideological vehicles, summary of analysis of 133–5; transformative cultural discourse, reconstruction of EFL pedagogy as 132–3, 134–5; transformative EFL discourse, effects of 152; transformative pedagogy, working towards 132–52; working together, relationship formation and 140

EFL as discourse: construction of 27–8; context of 33, 37, 41

EFL as ideological discourse, theory underpinning 111–16; Anglo-centrism *versus* domestication in EFL ideologies 113–16; discourse of global neoliberalism, education and 114; global and local perceptions of policy discourse 115, 124, 125; global communications and 113; language-culture link in education issues 114–15; multilingual ideologies, globalization and 113–14; native speakerism, construction of notion of 112–13

EFL discourse in Israel 26–51; academic identities, shaping of 50; Anglo/West-centrism, contest against discourses of 38; construction of EFL as discourse 27–8; context 33, 37, 41; Critical Discourse Analysis (CDA) 29–31; Cultural Discourse Studies (CDS) 45–6; Cultural Discourse Studies (CDS), Shi-xu's perspective on 48–9, 51; culture, situating within critical study of EFL discourse 47–51; discourse-as-text approach 34–6; discursive practice, discourse as 36–7; elements of 32–3; ethnolinguistic minorities, discriminatory realities for 44; Fairclough's three-dimensional approach 33–8; ideological function of discursive devices, examination of 35; "ideological product," discourse as 32; "Ideological square," application of 35–6; in-between cultural stance, pragmatism in 50–51; inequality, contest against discourses of 38; instructional materials as cultural mediators 36–7; interpellation of subjects, discourse and 38–45; interpretation, dependence of meaning on 34; intertextuality, discursive change and 38; language, reality and 32; language as semiotic tool 30–31; legitimacy of voice of Other, acceptance of 28–9; linguistic forms, imposition of socio-cultural meanings by 31; "linguistic relativity," notion of 46; "living discourses," context of 41; manipulation, subjectivity and 42–3; methodological framework 26–7; non-white (or non-western) discourses, disregard for 46, 47–8; "orientation towards difference," power struggle within text and 34–5; performativity as discourse analytical framework 39; reconstruction of EFL pedagogy as cultural discourse 49–50; reproduction of existing power inequalities 39–40; Sapir-Whorf hypothesis 47; Self-Other binary 38, 41, 44–5; social inequality, focused approach to dealing with 29–30; social practice, CDA and language as 30; social semiotics 32; socio-cultural practice, discourse as 37–8; subconscious aspects of subjects, awareness of 40; subjectivity as form of discursive manipulation 42; systematic discourse analysis, optimization of 32; text-oriented discourse analysis 31–3; theoretical framework 28–9; Us/Them binary 41, 43; Zionist self-image and 40

English language: as Anglocentric and American-biased force 128–9; compulsion to use 1; globalization of 1–2; interconnectedness between role as global language and 17–18; non-native speakers of 2; ownership of 1

English language, employment of 1–20; culture in 21st-century EFL education 16–20; National English Curriculum in Israel 12–13; "native speakerism," construction in EFL discourse 14–16; Palestine and Israel 4–9; status of English in Israel 9–12

Eric Cohen Books 58, 65

ethnolinguistic minorities, discriminatory realities for 44

Ezra, E. 65, 66, 70, 72–3, 75, 82, 88

face-threatening acts (FTA) 90, 100

Fairclough, N. 29, 31, 32, 42; learners' cultural representations, analysis of 87, 89, 101; textbooks as ideological vehicles 58, 59, 61; three-dimensional approach 33–8; transformative pedagogy, working towards 133, 148

Fairclough, N. and Wodak, R. 30, 33

Fairclough, N., Mulderrig, J., & Wodak, R. 3, 33

Ferguson, C.A. 10, 112

Filardo-Llamas, L. 89, 90

Foreign Affairs Ministry 161

foreign language education, shift in field of 128; epistemological shift in way language and ideology are linked 29; status of English, shift to global language of communication 85, 111, 124

foreign language learning: elements defining aims of 19; facilitation of 18–19

Foucault, M. 29, 31, 33, 45, 104, 146

Fowler, R., Hedge, B., Kress, G., & Trew, T. 31, 33

Freud, S. 40

Friends (NBC TV) 78

Freire, P.: cultural discourse in action 158, 169, 170; transformative pedagogy, working towards 135, 137, 142, 143, 145, 146, 147, 149

Frogner, T. 64

Gagel, A. 19

Gavriely-Nuri, D. 45; transformative pedagogy, working towards 138, 141, 142

Gee, J.P. 86

Geertz, C. 16

global awareness in learners, encouragement of 98–101

global citizenship education: working towards 149–52; worldwide United Nations initiative (2012) 128

Global Common Reviews 150

global cultural consciousness 137; EFL and 90–92

globalization 3, 36, 50, 124, 136–7, 151; era of 1, 20, 29; foreign language programs in era of 16–17; multilingual ideologies, globalization and 113–14

Goffman, E. 90

Grace, G.W. 31

Graddol, D. 1, 48, 113, 136

Gramsci, A. 33, 38

Gray, J. 85

Gray, J., O'Regan, J.P., & Wallace, C. 114, 149–50

Grimm Brothers 76

Guilherme, M. 2, 20

Gulliver, T. 35

Gumperz, J.J. & Levinson, S.C. 45

Ha'aretz (leftist newspaper) 141

Habermas, J. 29

Haifa Declaration, 2007 (Mada al-Carmel) 164

Hall, S. 16, 17, 87

Halliday, M.A.K. 31–2

Hamada, B.I. 77

Hammack, P.L. 87, 100, 141

Hassan, S. 165, 168, 169, 171n3

Hawking, S. 78

Heisey, D.R. 45

Herder, J. 47

Hinkel, E. 114
Holliday, A. 15, 16, 48, 111, 122, 139
Houghton, S. & Rivers, D.J. 15
human responsibility, EFL discourse as cultural discourse of 170–71
Human Rights Watch 5

identities: academic identities, shaping of 50; Althusserian perspective on 86–7; construction of 64, 105–6; data collection and analysis on 79–81; relational aspects of 87; self-invention, identity and 87; socially-situated identity 86; Zionist identity 67, 79, 81, 88, 138–9
identity politics in educational system 86–7
ideological content of EFL texts, influence on learners of 84–5
ideological function of discursive devices, examination of 35
"ideological product," discourse as 32
ideological reproduction, working towards social change 138–40
"Ideological square," application of 35–6
ideological state apparatuses, Althusser's notion of 111
in-between cultural stance, pragmatism in 50–51
Inbar-Lourie, O. 13
indexical pronouns 60–61; data collection and analysis on 67–70
inequalities: contest against discourses of 38; reproduction of existing power inequalities 39–40; social inequality, focused approach to dealing with 29–30
instructional materials as cultural mediators 36–7
"Integrating the Teaching of English as a Foreign Language (EFL) and Anti-Racist Instruction" (Awayed-Bishara, M) 166–7
interactivity skills, foreign language learning and 19
intercultural citizenship 137
intercultural communicative competence (ICC) 17–18
International Teen Magazine 74
internationalization, foreign language programs in era of 16–17
interpellation of subjects, discourse and 38–45
interpretation: dependence of meaning on 34; skills in, foreign language learning and 19
intertextuality, discursive change and 38
intracultural understanding, EFL textbooks and enabling of 92–8

Israel: curricular agendas in 7; diverse learning populations in 111; EFL language policies in 111, 127–8; ethnic diversity in 5; ideological agendas of dominant groups in 132; Israeli-Palestinian conflict 3, 4, 80, 87; language policies (LPs) and language educational policies (LEPs) in 11–12, 13; language teaching in, ideological aspects of 6–7; majority-controlled schooling system in 7–8; marginalization of Palestinian Arab community in 5; Palestinian Arab minority in population of 4; schoolbooks in, studies of 8–9; state-controlled apparatus in 9, 12–13; Zionist immigration to, notion of 122; *see also* Education Ministry in Israel; EFL discourse in Israel

Jabareen, Y.T. & Agbaria, A. 158, 159, 160, 161, 162–3, 165, 166
Jäger, S. 41
Jenkins, J. 14, 112
Jiang, W. 114

Kachru, B.B. 17
Kalnberzina, V. 20
Karayanni, M. 68, 118, 162
Ki-moon, B. 132, 150
Kincaid, D.L. 45
King, S. 78
knowledge: centering students' definition of 148; culturally specific prior knowledge 63, 78–9; facilitation of construction of 143; foreign language learning and 19
Koda, K. 10
Komet, C. & Partouche, D. 64, 65, 69, 75, 80, 82
Kramsch, C. 14, 17, 45, 47, 112, 113, 114
Kramsch, C. & Sullivan, P. 115–16
Kress, G. 31, 32
Kress, G. & Hodge, R. 33
Krzyz.anowski, M. & Wodak, R. 110
Kubota, R. & Miller, E.R. 149
Kumaravadivelu, B. 1, 17, 19, 51, 85, 101, 128; transformative pedagogy, working towards 137, 138, 143
Kuzar, R. 40, 43, 44; textbooks as ideological vehicles 69, 70
Kymlicka, W. 161
Kymlicka, W. & Grin, F. 110

Labov, W. 32
language: acquisition processes 147; educational policies in Israel 139;

language educational policies (LEPs) 11, 13, 111, 116, 117, 118, 139, 170; learning language, policies and process of 110–11; reality and 32; as semiotic tool 30–31
Language and Intercultural Communication 114
Lantolf, J.P. 143
learners' cultural representations, analysis of 84–106, 128–9; Adam (Arab interviewee), story of 89, 94, 99, 103; agent creation or subject interpellation 90–92; Ahlam (Arab interviewee), story of 89, 94; Ahmad (Arab interviewee), story of 89, 103; Ali (Arab interviewee), story of 89, 99, 103; Althusserian perspective on identities 86–7; Arabic speakers, examples of national identity discourse construction among 94; Arabic speakers' criticism of writing practices in EFL textbooks 103; Avishag (Jewish interviewee), story of 89, 99, 100, 105; criticism of educational policies 101–5; data analysis and findings 90–105; diversity and cultural difference, issues of 106; dominant ideologies 105–6; Edo (Jewish interviewee), story of 89, 99, 103, 104, 105; educational policies, Jewish and Palestinian Arab learners' criticism of 101–5; Eman (Arab interviewee), story of 89, 94, 103; Etai (Jewish interviewee), story of 89, 92–3; face-threatening acts (FTA) 90, 100; Fadi (Arab interviewee), story of 89, 94; findings and data analysis 90–105; global awareness in learners, encouragement of 98–101; global cultural consciousness, EFL and 90–92; Hebrew speakers' criticism of writing practices in EFL textbooks 103; identity construction 105–6; identity politics in educational system 86–7; ideological content of EFL texts, influence on learners of 84–5; Ilan Ramon "Israeli astronaut," story of 64, 69, 80, 88, 100, 138–9; interviewees, distribution of 89; intracultural understanding, EFL textbooks and enabling of 92–8; Jew-Christian-Muslim distinction 93–4; Layana (Arab interviewee), story of 89, 94–6, 98, 99, 103; learning processes, EFL discourse and 85–6; Liz "white homeless teenager," story of 71, 88, 104; Miriam "Bedouin entrepreneur," story of 66, 72–3, 75, 77, 88, 92–3, 95–9, 102, 103; multicultural understanding, EFL textbooks and enabling of 92–8; Omer (Jewish interviewee), story of 89, 92, 93, 98, 99, 100; Rami (Arab interviewee), story of 89, 91, 94–5, 99, 103; Ranya (Arab/Bedouin interviewee), story of 89, 94, 99, 102, 103; Rawad (Arab interviewee), story of 89, 94; relational aspects of identity 87; research design 88–90; research questions 90; resentment, examples of responses of 99; Rula (Arab interviewee), story of 89, 94, 99, 100–101, 103; Ryan "black teenage dropout," story of 71–3, 88, 90–92, 98, 103–4; self-invention, identity and 87; socially-situated identity 86; "storied selves" 84–5; "storied selves," identity politics in educational system and 86–7; superiority, examples of responses of 99; Tasnim (Arab/Bedouin interviewee), story of 89, 94, 103; text presentations 87–8, 106; Uriah (Jewish interviewee), story of 89, 96–7, 99, 103, 104, 105; Wajdi (Arab interviewee), story of 89, 94, 99, 103; writing practices in EFL textbooks, criticism of 103; Yael (Jewish interviewee), story of 89, 97, 103, 104, 105; Yara (Arab interviewee), story of 89, 90–92, 94–5
learning, complexity of interplay in 143
learning processes, EFL discourse and 85–6
Lee, D.B. 37
Lee, K.-Y. 85
legitimacy of voice of Other, acceptance of 28–9
Lesson for Life: Anti-Racist Education from K-12 (The Association of Civil Rights in Israel) 166
Lev-Ari, S. 5
Levy, D. & Sznaider, N. 141
Liberman, A. 7
Lin, L. 58, 59, 63
Lincoln, A. 78
linguistic citizenship: paradox of rights discourses and 158–9; Stroud's notion of 155–6
linguistic competence, focus on 1
linguistic forms, imposition of socio-cultural meanings by 31
"linguistic relativity," notion of 46
Liu, Y. 37
"living discourses," context of 41
Luk, J. 116
Luttrell, W. 86

Macedo, D. 145
Mada al-Carmel (Arab Center for Applied Social Research) 164, 166, 169
making connections, deconstruction to transformation 134–5
manipulation, subjectivity and 42–3
Maor, Z. & Ziv, M. 64, 65, 68, 74, 80, 82
Marcuse, H. 148
Mar'i, S.K. 5, 7
materials in Arab schools, tailoring content of 165–7
May, T. 45
methodologies: Critical Discourse Analysis (CDA) 2, 58, 116, 136; methodological framework, EFL discourse in Israel 26–7; methodological reflections, CDS approach to EFL discourse 135–7; research design for learners' cultural representations 88–90; text presentations of learners' cultural representations 87–8, 106; *see also* data collection, analysis and findings
Miike, Y. 45
Milani, T.M. 29, 39, 110
Mill, J.S. 76
Mingolo, W.D. 45
Morgan, B.D. 143
multicultural issues, centering students' perspectives on 137–8
multicultural understanding, EFL textbooks and enabling of 92–8
multilingualism: in Israel and Europe 5–6; positive connotations of 11
Murray, L. 71–2, 88, 104

naming practices 59–60; data collection and analysis on 64–7
narratives of dominant ethno-national group, reinforcement of 8
Nasser, R. & Nasser, I. 8, 57, 162
Nation State Law in Israel 5
National English Curriculum in Israel 2, 9, 17–20, 111; uniform or segregating? 117–20
Native/Non-Native binary 1–2
native speakers: native-speakerism 14–15; native-speakerism, CDA and 15–16; native-speakerism, construction of notion of 112–13; superiority of 120–24; teaching culture of 17
Nault, D. 114, 115
Ndura, E. 36, 37
non-white (or non-western) discourses, disregard for 46, 47–8

Onyemelukwe, N.H. & Alo, M.A. 113
Or, I.G. & Shohamy, E. 5
organized forums, consolidation of Palestinian Arab teachers in 167–9
"orientation towards difference," power struggle within text and 34–5
Other and Self, critical examination of 146
Oxfam 150

Palestinian Arab minority: English as third language for 10–11; as "foster citizens" in Israel 4; identity of, construction of 7; learning community, cultural milieu of 4; in population of Israel 4; students from, learning English as an international language for 3
Palestinian Arab minority, active role in cultural discourse for 129, 155–71; acceptance of Palestinian Arab students' cultural and linguistic needs 162–4; action, towards a culture of 164–70; Arab schools, tailoring content of materials in 165–7; *To Be a Citizen in Israel* (civics textbook) 165; consolidation of Palestinian Arab teachers in organized forums 167–9; criticality, training teachers in 169–70; empowering subaltern as precondition for effecting change 156–8; equal allocation of resources in education 159–60; equal participation in policy-making and curricular design 160–62; human responsibility, EFL discourse as cultural discourse of 170–71; "Integrating the Teaching of English as a Foreign Language (EFL) and Anti-Racist Instruction" (Awayed-Bishara, M) 166–7; *Lesson for Life: Anti-Racist Education from K-12* (The Association of Civil Rights in Israel) 166; linguistic citizenship, paradox of rights discourses and 158–9; linguistic citizenship, Stroud's notion of 155–6; Mada al-Carmel (Arab Center for Applied Social Research) 164, 166, 169; organized forums, consolidation of Palestinian Arab teachers in 167–9; Palestinian Arab school communities, address to 155–6; political awareness, training teachers in 169–70; responsibility and agency, from notions of rights to notions of 164–70; school communities, address to 155–6; tailoring content of materials in Arab schools 165–7; training teachers in criticality and political awareness 169–70
Pardo, L. 45

passive/active voice: data collection and analysis on 70–73; textbooks as ideological vehicles 61

Pêcheux, M. 32

pedagogy: difficulties in achievement of socially situated orientation to 9; pedagogical representation, role of ideology in 9; roots of 145; *see also* education

The Pedagogy of the Oppressed (Freire, P.) 135

Peled-Elhanan, N. 7, 8–9, 101, 162; textbooks as ideological vehicles 57, 80, 81

Peled-Elhanan, N. and Blum-Kulka, S. 146, 147

Pennycook, A. 39, 45

Peres, Y., Ehrlich, A., & Yuval-Davis, N. 5, 7

performativity as discourse analytical framework 39

Pinar, W.F., Reynolds, W.M., Slattery, P., & Taubman, P.M. 118

Podeh, E. 8, 57, 162

policy discourse, perspectives on 110–29; Anglo-centric nature of EFL discourse 124–5; "Diplomacy and International Communication in English" project (Israel, Ministry of Education) 128; documents, analysis of 117–25; EFL as ideological discourse, theory underpinning 111–16; "global citizenship education" worldwide United Nations initiative (2012) 128; ideological state apparatuses, Althusser's notion of 111; investigatory methodology and data 116–17; Israel, diverse learning populations in 111; Israel, EFL language policies in 111, 127–8; *Language and Intercultural Communication* 114; learning languages, policies and process of 110–11; National English Curriculum in Israel 111; National English Curriculum in Israel, uniform or segregating? 117–20; "Native Speakers" 120–24; politics, interplay between language policy and 110–11; shift in field of foreign language education 128; Teaching English in Israel (TEI) 121, 122, 123–4; textbook writers 125–7; transformative goals of foreign language pedagogy 128

policy-making 122, 158; challenge of pursuit of equal rights in 161; educational policy-making 32–3; equal participation in curricular design and 160–62; linguistic citizenship and 158–9

politics 30, 37, 43, 47, 115, 123, 128, 139, 148, 151, 159; cultural politics 50; cultural politics of coexistence and common prosperity 49; cultural politics of global/local coexistence 28; cultural politics of human prosperity 45; cultural politics of joint understanding and collaboration 163; cultural politics of peace and social justice 132, 134–5, 167; educational politics, boundaries of 166; identity politics, issues of 21; identity politics, "storied selves" in 86–7; intercultural politics of human collaboration 171; interplay between language policy and 110–11; language and, interplay between 110; linguistic form, socio-political interpretations of 31; misrepresentations and inequalities of 20; multiculturalism, failure as political project 3; political awareness, concept of 19; political awareness, training teachers in 169–70; political control, monopoly on 141; political discourse, Arabic language within 10; political educational objectives 18; political establishment 114; political ethnography 49, 135–6; political identity, construction of 20; political leadership in Israel 80; political thought relevant to discourse and language 33; politico-economic consequences 143; socio-political contexts, inequalities in 29; socio-political manipulation 143–4; socio-political practices of users of English 48; socio-political structures 145; world politics 85

politics, interplay between language policy and 110–11

Prah, K.K. 45

Prodromou, L. 17

Pulverness, A. 17

Rabin, Y. 80

Ramon, I. 64, 69, 80, 88, 138–9

reconstruction of EFL pedagogy as cultural discourse 49–50

reconstruction of EFL textbooks, EFL as cultural discourse and 138–52; dialogical and problem-posing methods 145–9; from division to unification in textbooks 141–5; global citizenship education, working towards 149–52; *Global Common Reviews* 150; ideological reproduction, working towards social change 138–40;

transforming EFL policy discourse 149–52; transforming practice in EFL classroom discourse 145–9
reflexive and globally aware learners, development of 18
Regev, M. 7
Reisigl, M. & Wodak, R. 32
relational skills, foreign language learning and 19
remote cultures: data collection and analysis on 75–8; representation of narratives of 62
resentment, examples of responses of 99
responsibility and agency, from notions of rights to notions of 164–70
Risager, K. 1, 17, 18, 51, 85, 128, 137
Rizvi, F. 85, 128, 138
Robeyns, I. 159
Rogers, R. and Elias, M. 86
Rorty, R. 28, 29

Saar, G. 163
Sadeghi, S. 147–8
Said, E.W. 15, 42, 93; textbooks as ideological vehicles 70, 73, 76
Saiegh-Haddad, E. 10
Saiegh-Haddad, E. & Henkin-Roitfarb, R. 10
Saiegh-Haddad, E., Levin, I., Hende, N., & Ziv, M. 10
Sapir, E. 46, 47
Sapir-Whorf hypothesis 47
Schneer, D., Ramanathan, V., & Morgan, B. 37
scholarship in language and culture pedagogies 1
Scollo, M. 45, 136
Searle, R.R. 39
Seidlhofer, B. 14
self-empowerment, discourse of 148
Self/Other binary 1–2, 7, 20, 28–9, 84–5, 142–3; EFL discourse in Israel and 38, 41, 44–5
Sharifian, F. 48, 112, 113, 136
Shen, X.L. 45
Shi-xu 2, 3; discourse beyond language education 27, 28, 38, 42, 43, 45, 46, 47–8, 49–50, 51; transformative pedagogy, working towards 135, 136–7, 144
Shin, J., Eslami, Z. R., & Chen, W.-C. 18, 65
Shinhav, Y. 166
Shohamy, E. 6, 10–11, 13

Shohamy, E. & Abu Ghazaleh-Mahajneh, M. 10
Shohamy, E. and Donitsa-Schmidt, S. 10
Sinclair, J.M. & Coulthard, R.M. 32
Skop, Y. 7
social change, role of discourse in effecting 148–9
social injustice, criticality and awareness for 149
social practice, CDA and language as 30
social semiotics 32
socio-cultural practice, discourse as 37–8
Socrates 77, 148
Solomon, G. & Essawi, M. 163
Spivak, G.C. 46, 136
Spolsky, B. and Shohamy, E. 9, 13, 14, 115
Spolsky, B., Ben Meir, D., Inbar, O., Orland, L., Steiner, J., & Vermel, J. 12
"storied selves," identity politics in educational system and 86–7
strategic essentialism, Spivak's notion of 136–7
Street, B.V. 17
Stroud, C. 155–6, 157, 158, 159, 162, 164, 166, 167, 170
Suaysuwan, N. and Kapitzke, C. 36, 37
subaltern as precondition for change, empowerment of 156–8
subconscious aspects of subjects, awareness of 40
subject interpellation, global cultural consciousness and 90–92
subjectivity as form of discursive manipulation 42
Suleiman, C. 86, 87
superiority, examples of responses of 99
Sweetser, E. 90
Swirski, S. 5, 6
systematic discourse analysis, optimization of 32

Tajfel, H. & Turner, J.C. 58, 59, 60
Tamir, Y. 162
target audiences: construction of 62; data collection and analysis on 74–5
Teaching English in Israel (TEI) 121, 122, 123–4
Teaching English to Speakers of Other Languages (TESOL) 140
Tel Aviv Municipality experimental project in English studies 13
text-oriented discourse analysis 31–3; systematic analysis, working towards 58–9
textbook writers 125–7; writing practices in EFL textbooks, criticism of 103

textbooks as ideological vehicles 57–81, 128–9; *Building Blocks* 77; characters in the context, pronoun use in depiction of 68–9; collective memories, construction of 64; collective memories, data collection and analysis on 79–61; comprehension, knowledge and 63; cultural bias, analysis of 58; cultural suitability of EFL textbooks 57, 81; culturally specific prior knowledge 63; culturally specific prior knowledge, data collection and analysis on 78–9; data collection, data analysis and 64–81; *Discourse & Society* 82n1; dominant ideologies, transmission of 57–8, 81; *Friends* (NBC TV) 78; identities, construction of 64; identities, data collection and analysis on 79–81; indexical pronouns 60–61; indexical pronouns, data collection and analysis on 67–70; *International Teen Magazine* 74; linguistic 'shifters' 60; naming people 65, 66; naming places 65–6, 66–7; naming practices 59–60; naming practices, data collection and analysis on 64–7; Other, analysis of discourse about 62; passive/active voice 61; passive/active voice, data collection and analysis on 70–73; remote cultures, data collection and analysis on 75–8; remote cultures, representation of narratives of 62; *Results for 4 Points* (EFL textbook) 71–2; Self and Other, presentation in discourse of 61, 70; summary of analysis of 133–5; systematic text-oriented discourse analysis, working towards 58–9; Taiwan, name rectification movement in 59–70; target audience, construction of 62; target audience, data collection and analysis on 74–5; textbook sampling 65; University Publishing Projects 65; West and East, pronoun use in depiction of 69–70

Tikkun ha-Olam (restoration of the world), Kabbalistic idea of 144

Times of Israel 7

Tirosh, R. 5, 6

Tomalin, B. & Stempleski, S. 17

Torres, C. 150

training teachers in criticality and political awareness 169–70

transformative cultural discourse of harmony and social justice, reconstruction of EFL pedagogy as 132–3

transformative EFL discourse, effects of 152

transformative goals of foreign language pedagogy 1, 128

transformative pedagogy, working towards 20, 132–52; EFL classroom discourse, transforming practice in 145–9; EFL policy discourse, transformation of 149–52; Freire's influence on 135, 137, 142, 143, 145, 146, 147, 149

Trilling, B. & Fadel, C. 85

Trump, D. 114

Turgeman, H. & Zaltzman-Kulick, R. 65, 68, 70, 74, 76, 82

Tyack, D.B. 8

unification in textbooks, working towards 141–5

University Publishing Projects 65

Us/Them binary 35, 60, 62, 140; EFL discourse in Israel and 41, 43

Van Dijk, T.A. 29–30, 33, 35, 36, 37, 42, 46, 120; learners' cultural representations, analysis of 87, 89, 91, 99; textbooks as ideological vehicles 59, 61, 62, 74, 78

Van Leeuwen, T. & Wodak, R. 32

Vološinov, V.N. 31, 32, 43

Von Humboldt, W. 46, 47

Warschauer, M. 140

Watts, R. 29

Weizmann, E. 80

Weninger, C. and Kiss, T. 17, 84

Wertsch, J.V. 8

Western/Non-Western binary 1–2, 3

Whorf, B.L. 32, 46, 47

Williams, R. 71–2, 73; learners' cultural representations, analysis of 88, 90, 91–2, 98, 103–4

Witherspoon, G. 114

Wodak, R. 30, 31, 33, 59, 89

Wodak, R. & Fairclough, N. 89

Wodak, R. & Meyer, M. 116

Wodak, R., de Cilla, R., Reisigl, M., & Liebhart, K. 87

Wortham, S.E.F. 58, 59, 60, 89

writing practices in EFL textbooks, criticism of 103

Yamanaka, N. 85

Yeatman, A. 159

Yiftachel, O. 8, 79, 101, 112, 162

Yonah, Y. 101, 162

Yoshino, K. 118

Yuen, K.-M. 85

Zaher, R. 124
Zerubavel, Y. 8, 79
Zionist agenda 85
Zionist hegemonic ideas 2, 165
Zionist identity 67, 79, 81, 88, 138–9
Zionist ideologies 7, 40, 80, 112, 118
Zionist immigration to Israel, notion of 122
Zionist movements in Israel 7–8, 65–6
Zionist neo-colonialism 4
Zionist self-image, EFL discourse in Israel and 40
Zionist values, promotion in EFL texts of 106, 133, 163
Zionist vocabulary, use of 123, 127
Zonszein, M. 98
Zreik, R. 159, 160